Hindsight – The Foresight Saga

BY

TERENCE P. O'HALLORAN
F.C.I.I., B.Sc.
Chartered Financial Planner

Hindsight – The Foresight Saga

Design and layout by Life Publications Ltd Lincoln
Front Cover artwork by Debbie Burke, Nottingham
Editing by Brenda Crouch
Graphics and layout by Jargonfree, Lincoln
All in conjunction with the author

Life Publications Limited
St James Terrace
88 Newland
Lincoln
Lincolnshire
LN1 1YA

www.lifepublications.co.uk   e-mail: tpo@ohal.org

Tel: +44 (0) 1522 522858   Fax: +44 (0) 1522 540442

ISBN 978-1-904980-05-6

CHAPTER SYNOPSES

PAGE

gold - The funding of government gilt edge securities - The Peston/Brown partnership - the demise of capitalism. The relevance to this book and the *classic market* theory. Academia versus vocational aspirations.

The Academonisation of Practitioners - A quango culture one of the important spin doctors - The siphoning of money from pension schemes - The relationship between equities and gilts - a stockbroking relationship - long term and short term saving strategy. The change in notional value over time - What is a billion? - The 'me too' attitude - The "it's different this time" philosophy - Timing in investment ignores political enterprise - Markets do what markets do.

The three pillar approach: Civil Service first - Inflation proofing benefits - An attempt at a two tier State Pension scheme. It worked. The abandoning of SERPS. An expensive exercise - The start of Superannuation Schemes government then major industries - Personal pensions. An international phenomenon - Pay as you go or funded?

A political dilemma - the need for state and commerce - investment strategies - a hard pill to swallow - the undeniable fact of the classic market. The experience of 'new' pension nations – a broadening market philosophy.

Commercial pensions - attractive funds - The need to understand the marketplace - the interaction of property and equities in particular - The role of the fund manager. The move to being out on a limb. Long, rather than short, termism - A solution to adopt.

The myth of gilt guarantees and the irony of fixed interest infatuation - The world as an international marketplace - is the world uniformly in synchronisation with the *classic market?* The consequences of disparities.

ACKNOWLEDGEMENTS

The Author is heavily indebted to the co-operation and support of the following individuals and organisations.

Janet Walford, Money Management
Hal Austin, Financial Adviser
Patrick Connolly, AWD Chase deVere
Ian Cowie, Daily Telegraph
Stephen Womack, Financial Mail on Sunday
Jeff Prestridge, Financial Mail on Sunday
Carl Emmerson, Institute For Fiscal Studies
The Bank of England
The Office of National Statistics
Members of the Russell Study Group
Members of the Midlands Professional Development Group
Hindsight
ICS
Deutsch Bank
Nationwide Building Society
Partners & Staff at O'Halloran & Co
M&G Fund Management
Invesco Perpetual Fund Management
Moneyfacts
Robin O'Grady DipPFS, Williams de Broe
Claire Markham DipPFS
Duncan Smart & Colin Smart, Walker Crips Weddle Beck Stockbrokers.
Stocks for the long run- By Jeremy J Sieger. First and Fourth Editions.
The Ascent of Money - By Professor Niall Ferguson
The Intelligent Investor – by Benjamin Graham
Chicken Licken
Mike Brown
David R. Kamerschen, Ph.D. Professor of Economics

Who is the odd one out?

Sir Fred Goodwin: FORMER chief executive, RBS

Andy Hornby: FORMER chief executive, HBOS

Sir Tom McKillop: FORMER chairman, RBS

John McFall MP: FORMER chairman of Treasury Select Committee

Alastair Darling: FORMER Chancellor of the Exchequer

Gordon Brown: FORMER Prime Minister and FORMER Chancellor of the Exchequer

Sir Terry Wogan: FORMER presenter of Radio 2's Breakfast Show

IF you're thinking

Sir Terry Wogan,

THEN you're right.

However, the reason may surprise you...

Terry Wogan is the only one out of this motley crew who actually holds *ANY* formal banking qualification.

Worrying, isn't it!

Introduction to the book

It would be very easy to trivialise *the classic market* ^{TM} by just stating blandly: "this is the way it works and here are the indicators and now get on with it." But it is not actually as simple as that. There are many myths and misconceptions which, if they are not explored, investigated, explained and put in their place still persist in the background to encourage the well known phrase "it's different this time" to prevail.

One of the primary objectives of this book is to prove that it is never different this time, or any other time. Fundamentals, it seems, prevail.

Much has been said about the political influence that can override economics and change the character of markets. Certainly political influence needs to be explored, analysed and its relevance noted. However, if politicians can use *the classic market* to their own political ends then the investor can do likewise by adopting simple analysis techniques and applying them in an appropriate way. *"Hindsight -The Foresight Saga"* endeavours to give you, the reader, the tools to make that work in your favour.

There may well be elements of the text that you feel are 'over the top' or irrelevant, hopefully they will be few and far between. If you do find any section too political, too forceful then all that is asked of you is: please persevere. A lot of thought has gone into the inclusion of every story, case history, political nuance, conspiracy theory and statistic. It is all there to ensure that "it's different this time" does not come into play in your thought process when it matters – at the point of investing or starting a savings plan (or at the conclusion of the investment/savings period).

The success of your investment and your saving for your future and the optimisation of the returns that you are able to achieve are here for you to take on board and profit from. Believe me, it is worth the effort to make your future a more certain and prosperous place.

Terence P. O'Halloran B.Sc.
Chartered financial planner
Fellow of the Chartered Insurance Institute
Associate of the Institute of Financial Planning
February 14th 2011 The 35th Anniversary of O'Halloran & Co

Other titles by Terence P.O'Halloran still available include:

Trusts - A Practical Guide (2nd Edition)

Mountains out of Molehills

You Sign (the little cheque and we sign the big one)

If Only Politicians Had Brains

Building a Business on Bacon and eggs

The Fight for our Post Office

CHAPTER 1

IT'S A FINANCIAL CYCLE – GET OVER IT: AND WIN

There is always a danger when setting out to change economic theory, or at least modify it significantly, that there is a bias towards the change that colours the view of the market overall. You will need to read *"Hindsight – The Foresight Saga"* to judge whether that is the case here. However, the figures are compelling and the three historic timescales used are sequential and confirmatory. The driving force of any advanced economic culture is the banking system. It is the pulse by which much of human economic activity thrives or fails.

What has been revealed in this book is the interrelationship between the property and equity markets and their indisputable effect on the banker's ability to lend. Those interactions and those interactions alone create a *classic market*^{TM} which is broadly a fifteen year cycle of equity and property movements that are brought about by the availability or dearth of the bank's ability to support property purchases or support the expansion of commerce. Couple that with the emotional factors of greed, fear and grief that attend every market rise and fall over time and you have the basis for a predictable financial cycle.

Does it take almost 300 pages to explain the theory? Certainly not, but it probably takes that number of pages to explain that there is no such thing as "it is different this time" because the conclusion that the research draws is that: it never is "different this time."

We have to conclude that politics is a powerful force which can accentuate the rise and fall, along with the duration, of any particular aspect of the market cycle but, what it cannot do and does not do, is change the cyclical integrity of the financial markets. The same 'pattern' emerges whatever the external forces appear to contribute.

If proof were needed then proof is here in this publication. The *classic market* makes financial fortune-telling a serious consideration with very real benefits in increased returns. What acknowledgement and, hopefully, adoption of the principles described here might also do is to smooth out the excesses in the movement of equity and property markets and thus lessen the effects of the 'boom and bust' syndrome that is associated with them. Bankers will become more pragmatic in their lending practices

There are pressures geared to performance and financial targets which manifest themselves in various ways, for investors and providers of financial products alike.

. . . .

The date was late October 2009. Autumn was closing in, the leaves were falling, the value of shares rising. The recession was in evidence (the longest recession since 1955) and the last 'structured product' liable to offer 7.5% per annum return as an income over the next five years was on my desk.

There are a number of trustees, with Family Trusts, desperate to find a reasonable return on their investments without 'undue risk'. There are quite a number of individuals who in September, 2008 were earning 5% per annum on their deposits with banks and are now lucky to achieve 0.3%. Where can depositors, investors, turn with any certainty?

The correct word might not be "desperate" to find a better return, but rather more "anxious;" (perhaps bordering on "desperate"). When you have a duty to perform, as trustees do, things can get 'anxious.' The trustees want to perform, however they are used to a 'status quo.' Banks provide deposit accounts and (usually) pay a reasonable rate of return to depositors. Banks are 'safe.' Capital is available on request. Deposit accounts are what you and I, and trustees, are familiar with. However, what happens, psychologically, when things change is inertia sets in.

Can you remember the euphoria as you drove around "the corner" and discovered the petrol station that had reduced petrol prices to below £1 a litre? How soon we forget that the price was 65 pence a litre and that the government is taking a huge 'turn' on our money. We got used to paying £1.12 per litre in a relatively short time span. And now? It is forecast to rise to over £1.30 per litre.

I was listening to Radio 4 recently and they were reviewing how they should accurately forecast the weather. The topic of the conversation centred on, "should we be stating Fahrenheit or should the temperature for the forecast be in Centigrade?"

The broadcasters raised an interesting point: the weatherman said, that whether the temperature was given in ° F or ° C only mattered at the extremes. In other words, when it was very cold, minus two (-2°C) Centigrade was more relevant to our psyche (how we understand numbers and relate them to reality) than twenty seven degrees Fahrenheit (27°F).

On the other hand twenty two degrees centigrade (22°C) did not relate to how warm it was when compared to seventy two degrees Fahrenheit (72°F). This is the result of perception despite both being the same level of coldness and warmth respectively.

So it is with market comparison. Many people are bewildered by terms that they are perhaps unfamiliar with and nervous of:

a) The FTSE 100
b) The house valuation index (Nationwide Building Society or Halifax Bank (HBOS))
c) The S&P GSCI-ER index (commodities)
d) The FTSE EPRA/NAREIT Developed Europe Index (Property)

From the sublime to the 'cor blimey' I had never heard of the last one until that late October day when the leaves were falling and my mind was racing to understand more about how an element of 'certainty' could be instilled into providing the returns people required to fulfil their obligations.

What had been placed on my desk was an opportunity to satisfy the needs of the trustees and those anxious individuals within a very brief window. Here was an opportunity to utilise my knowledge of the market. Here was the relevance of 'timing' and the certainty that an opportunity lost was an opportunity gone; not for ever, but gone, for probably twelve to fifteen years.

3

Let me explain.

This period of time (2009 – 2011) constitutes the last throes of a *classic market*. The *classic market* is something that I have defined personally in conjunction with many well rehearsed and learned economists and commentators 'giving forth' on market cycles. The *classic market* is primarily a relationship between property and equity price performance – they are inextricably linked, as this book will illustrate to your advantage.

A fundamental link also exists between the stock market and property values and the lending power of the banks.

When you go into a new town and you get off the train, (bus, plane, or boat) and you walk out of the station; do you feel apprehensive in a new environment - a kind of nervous feeling? So it is when a new financial idea is 'floated' for your consideration.

It is true to say that when you have been in certain circumstances once or twice you become quite confident in the knowledge of where you are, and how to proceed. However, what if it is some time since you have been to Mansfield or Dublin, Lewes or Newcastle, Edinburgh or Gibraltar? You know what I mean? The confidence evaporates and you look out of the car; or walk out of the station. The familiar territory has changed. That is what happens over the course of a *classic market;* familiar territory changes constantly, but as I hope to convey throughout this book, the changes conform to a recognisable and predictable pattern.

If you know where you are (in time) you can be confident. A feature of the *classic market* is that in some stages it is a 'capital' orientated environment. Investors are chasing capital gains. The stock market has usually moved ahead quite dramatically, like the January sales - everybody suddenly starts heading for the bargain basement except that the storekeeper has very often 'seen you coming,' waited for the rush and changed the products on the shelf.

The bargains are not that good value anymore, but still people buy them on the basis of perception rather than fact; after all it is a sale, therefore the items must be good value – better value because after the sale the price will rise. A bubble can easily be created and when the bubble bursts individuals, still convinced there are bargains to be had, look elsewhere.

Property is usually the target of a professional investor's attention when the stock market looks vulnerable. The experienced eye will detect any market alteration first. When the bargain basement of shares is shunned by the experienced shopper, the novice remains and even intensifies their position in that marketplace. They buy more shares because recent history shows the price rising to confirm to the novice that gains can be made.

The property market will have been static, for a long period perhaps four or five years and then it starts to rise exerting itself for reasons that we will discuss later on. However, the 'chase is on' and the 'bargains' become irresistible.

As the stock market careers downwards, so the residential property market initially, and the commercial property market in its wake, move inexorably upwards, supported, and even encouraged, by the banks - and of course governments, because both banks and governments love the people to have the 'feel good factor' that owning something of value imparts.

Does this all sound familiar?

Possibly not; because, as I will explain, a lot of people, a lot of the time, are just not in that mental space that makes any of this relevant to them. The stock market is not something that they, as individuals, consider themselves invested in, not consciously anyway. The residential property market is irrelevant to young adults who may still live with their parents or are content in rented accommodation because they may be involved in higher education or require the flexibility to move to a fresh location at short notice with their work.

There are many individuals who did "all that" long ago. They are firmly in their home; it is all paid for and everything else is irrelevant to them. Property values only become relevant when the *incumbents* want to move from their own home or they want to exercise 'equity release' and raise money from their home. Equity Release is something that we will discuss later.

The real driver in this leap for capital growth through property ownership, particularly where commercial property is concerned, is the rental income generated by the property through increasingly reliable tenants chasing low levels of rent for new or expanding business propositions that banks will support through short term loans and overdraft facilities (often secured on the private dwelling of the entrepreneur).

In this part of the *classic market* then, there is an inverse relationship between shares and property. As shares are going down in value the property market may be going up. Why would that be so?

The collapse of the stock market during this phase of the cycle is not about mainstream business failure. No, it is about the adjustment of the market value of the shares in businesses following a period of mild hysteria that drives share prices beyond their 'real (perceived) value.'

Businesses can function at a normal level in this environment because the banks have the financial capacity to provide them with financial support using their property as security not necessarily for individual bank customer loans but because of the collective, universal multiplying counterbalance of property values and the knock-on effect that has on bank asset ratios (the banks' solvency margins).

At any point in time a bank could multiply its cash asset base and lend out everything it had on deposit eleven times, and count the equity in real property in for the multiplier. The equity in this case is the difference between the loan (mortgage) and the underlying asset value.

As the property market rises the security held within the banking system grows in value. The bank has more and more resource (money) to lend out. Thus support or even an upward spiral presents itself as a mechanism of business expansion even though the stock market would be in free-fall.

Why was it different in 2008; at the other end of the *classic market?* The catalyst for that change of focus was linked to property values.

The UK banking system had simply lent too much secured onto a now shrinking value base.

It is perhaps at this point that it becomes apparent to people in authority, who really should have known better, that a reduction in property prices affects the ability of banks to lend money. It also affects the support for the banks' own balance sheets in the process (the banks' solvency margins).

Banks lend money on the basis of a multiple of their 'cash' asset base. In other words for every pound that the bank has physically, or by way of equity in security as a mortgage, or other collateral agreement, the bank could lend that money out eleven times, up until September 2008. The rules are tighter now.

By the end of 2008 the government was in the process of changing the rules. Basel III was on the table as Basel I and II had been held to have failed. The Regulator had tightened the screws, property values were sliding with increasing speed and businesses in difficulty found their financial support from the banks evaporating. Businesses during this phase of the market cycle were experiencing a shrinking market, shrinking asset values and shrinking support from the banks accompanied by panic at government level. Armageddon was imminent!

In reality it was not Armageddon. This was a normal, predictable set of circumstances repeating themselves, but who could remember that far back: to the last time. Hindsight had become 'short sight.' For every million pounds that property values sank the banks had to 'claw back' £11 million in cash to support their own balance sheets.

The result was a complete correlated drop in value of both property and equity prices largely due to the fact that banks headed the financial sector in the main share index and as the bank shares dropped, confidence in the market as a whole waned therefore other share values followed suit. The market sentiment changed so rapidly many institutions were caught out.

What has that got to do with a late autumn day in October, 2009? - Everything!

The opportunity that arose on that October morning stems from the fact that somebody had been smart enough, astute enough, lucky enough, to have put together a structured (we will talk about the definition of that later) product that had an underlying interest rate of 7.5% per annum paid monthly as a very tax efficient income source. The contract was linked to any one of three indices (measures of price movement within a particular market):

One linked to the possible fall in share prices, by 50% or commodities or property under the same terms.

What was on offer was a contract, paying 7.5% per annum on a monthly basis over the five years, subject to certain market criteria. The banks and building societies were paying less than 1.4% at the time.

Was there a possibility of any of those indices, shares commodities or property devaluing by half (50%) during the five year period?

The odds had changed the view of the future and the structure of the products was moving into a different regime. This was not gambling, it was a carefully calculated mechanism put in place, with a set of known returns being juxtapositioned against a statistically probable outcome in order to generate a defined return.

First of all: the structure was based upon a five year term. The second premise was the possibility of a 50% reduction in the FTSE 100 index (shares). This was unlikely but possible. Was the FTSE 100 INDEX still something that people could put some trust in? Let me explain:

In March 2003 and similarly in March 2009, the FTSE 100 index had 'bottomed out' at around 3250. In chartist terms 3250 was a very firm base below which it would be very difficult for the index to fall. That is the theory. The theory does tend to hold up in practice.

In October 2009 the index of 100 leading shares, the FTSE 100, was moving between 5200 and 5300 with every likelihood of it then moving ahead quite rapidly.

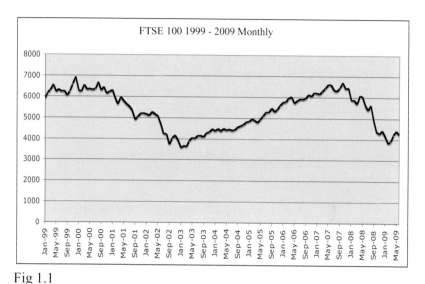

Fig 1.1

But what of property?

Commercial property reduced in value by half. Could it halve again? The great thing about property is that at the bottom of its market, it becomes moribund, it plateaus out. The graphic representation shows that property values become very flat, uninteresting, and a 'safe' but poor value as an investment, for a protracted period of time.

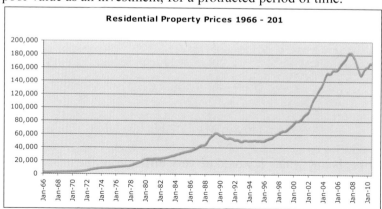

Fig 1.2

A great number of people lose extraordinary amounts of capital through the effects of negative equity, the forced sale of 'buy to let' properties of being caught in property funds that moved to a 'penalty price' so they were 'locked into' the investment for six or twelve months. Hence few people want to venture back into an inflexible environment. "Once bitten twice shy." The trust in property and the reliance upon the adage that; "one cannot lose money in property," are all but lost to a significant market influence.

Property prices

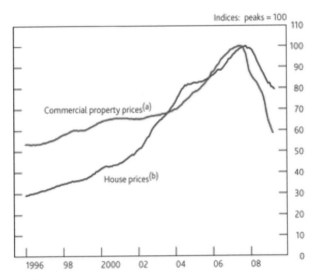

Indices: peaks = 100

Sources: Halifax, Investment Property Databank, Nationwide and Thomson Datastream.

(a) Commercial property prices are indexed to their peak in June 2007.
(b) The average of Halifax and Nationwide measures. The published Halifax index has been adjusted in 2002 by the Bank of England to account for a change in the method of calculation. House prices have been indexed to their peak in October 2007.

FIG 1.3 – property prices

This commercial property situation (a flat market) can last six to eight years, therefore the likelihood of a 50% further drop in value when that market is confirmed to be "at the bottom," is almost non-existent. The likelihood of any damaging reduction in the property index (REIT) over a five year period puts the prospect of a 7½% income per annum for five years, against the security of the European Property Index, firmly in the frame as a 'buy' signal.

As we go through this book I will expand on what I have tried to say in paraphrase in this opening Chapter. Hopefully the graphics will help and, as we progress, the jargon will become more and more familiar; and more relevant to your particular savings or investment situation. Please persevere, it is worth the effort.

The message that this book *(Hindsight – The Foresight Saga)* is conveying is that 'timing is very important'. Yes one can take a twenty, thirty, or forty year view and be invested for that length of time and allow invested capital to move up and down with the markets. That is okay, indeed it is a fundamental of how you should work your long term aspirations to build up funds in order to pay off a house purchase, create an income in retirement, and so on.

The short term view has to concentrate on where the markets are in relationship to where they are expected to go, and be 'of the moment.' The timing of entry into an investment optimises the return.

However, I shall illustrate that 'optimising returns' depends largely on what is happening with the property market and the equity market specifically. It is their inter relationship with each other over a twelve to fifteen year time span, that is really important in providing you with guidance and the "markets" with vitality.

Whether you are in a 'capital' orientated market; where people are running for growth and a quick return, or in the 'income' phase, where quite the opposite dynamic is in play; consolidation, comfort and a reasonable return with a medium to long term view, has to be decided – and adhered to - at the point where an investment or savings decision is made. Your future depends upon it.

Hopefully I have whetted your appetite. Simplicity is difficult, but I will endeavour to make the task of examining history and using it to improve and enhance your future, easy for you.

CHAPTER 2

PROPERTY PERFORMANCE ANALYSED

The market in 2004 was starting to 'overheat', residential property prices had doubled and doubled again - just as they had in 1971 to 1976. The circumstances were markedly different in 2004, there were low interest rates just starting to rise. There was also low inflation - and, according to Government sources, getting lower (a view not shared by the populace as a whole, and particularly the elderly). On the face of it there seemed quite a contrast to the 1970s yet at this same stage in the *"classic market"* as its predecessor the relationship between property values and equity performance was remarkably consistent. Could there be a link?

PROPERTY "BUY TO LET"

Whenever "Make some money by investing in 'buy to let' property" seminars appear along with a proliferation of glossy leaflets through the post, you know - or should know - that it is the beginning of the end of the viability of that particular market for future short to medium term returns on investment. And so it was – even the TV programme producers adopted the 'buy to let' and "make money" mould and produced a number of compelling programmes.

By 2006 the average landlord held 3 to 4 properties in the buy to let portfolio. Banks were joining the wave of enthusiasm for the capital growth projects based upon the (false) premise that the "rent will pay the loan interest and the capital growth would be the icing."

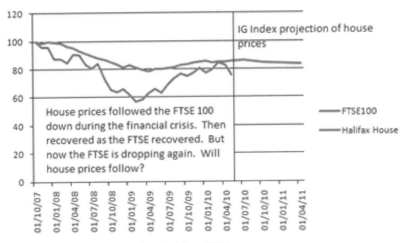

Fig. 2.1   property v equity 2000 – 2011

The stock markets were recovering strongly from the March 2003 low and financial institutions were making money on the back of property based lending.   Record profits and a re-discovered commercial property market pushed residential 'buy to let' and commercial properties to higher values and excited the "me too" people who - by now - were certain that the 'gold rush' was passing them by, even when they had little or no capital of their own to commit to property purchases. They were right - the 'gold rush', had all but gone, however the financial institutions were still offering multiples of rental income on 100% or even greater mortgages.

Why is it that 90% of investors invest at the top of the market? Any market?   The quest for certainty is perhaps the rationale, but, TIMING IS EVERYTHING. The situation in 2006 had started to look ominous in 2004, but few viewers were in evidence. Few people appear to be watching the signs and even fewer taking any notice of them.

There are some interesting factors that played a massive part in the eventual outcome of this manifestly crass farce.

The banks and building societies' upper/middle management were aged between 34 and 44 in 2009. What age would they have been in 1992-93? 17 to 27 say. Many of the mature managers had been 'retired early' under a specific redundancy programme in the mid 1990s, to allow 'progress' in a new age; Oh! and to save the senior managers' higher salaries.

What experience of the effects of the "propped up" property market (1989-93) and the after-effects of a direct assault on bank solvency margins caused by collapsing asset values (that constitute a large portion of bank asset value through individual "charges" held against lending as security) would those managers have?

The whole thing about financial forecasting is much like predicting winter in the previous spring: we still get snow in April or June. Life has a habit of 'throwing up' the unexpected.

Having spent the largest part of my life (40 years and more) anticipating rather than predicting the financial trends, and generally getting them right, noting the odd spectacular exception, I do feel confident about anticipating the future in a reasonably assured way. War wounds do heal but they leave scars and provided we learn from those scars then I guess that one can say they were worth the anxiety and pain acquiring them in the first place. Hindsight is a learning tool.

Many years ago now I identified and named a specific phenomenon in the financial market as *'the classic market.'*

In that 'market' there are four major primary players:
   a) Equities, (company shares).
   b) Fixed interest (gilts [government loans], and corporate bonds).
   c) Property (both commercial and residential) together with
   d) Cash.

There are of course many sub divisions and non correlated oddities which sit outside of those four generic 'heads' but those four are the main players for the majority of people. The two main 'players' in my book are equities and property because they tend to inter relate; a fact which most commentators appear to have missed, or ignored as irrelevant.

The intricacies of any inter relationship are not to be explored in any detail at this point but it suffices to say that the second market slide of equities in this *'classic market'* is invariably brought about by the collapse of asset property prices. Residential properties lose value first and then, historically, commercial properties follow by what can be 12 to 18 months. In 2005 through 2008 both markets went into decline at around the same time.

Let us assume that you are a banker at the point at which the first stock market downturn was occurring, noting that the property market had been subdued for some 7 or 8 years and was starting to exert itself. Would you perhaps anticipate that values were going to rise significantly giving you really good 'cover' as an asset base for any mortgage that you might agree - and therefore be tempted to lend 100%, or even 110% or 120% of loan to value to stimulate the market and drive the economy forward?

If you were that same banker some 2-3 years later with a burgeoning property market and a resurgent stock market running behind it, would you not think it prudent to gradually ease back your lending criteria to 'dampen' the property and possibly the equity market, and protect your own asset base by reducing the 'loan to value' from 100% to 95%, to 90%, to 85% and down to perhaps to 80% loan to value for any new mortgages?

The housing market would slow gradually; the bankers' own asset base (which is crucial to their solvency margin) would be protected from at least a 20% drop in the underlying value of the properties the bank had lent money against. Shares would also probably just ease back a little as funds could be diverted to commercial property to support businesses in building their own asset base for longevity.

What happened in reality was that bankers started off in 1970 and the mid 1980s and in 1997 with 80% loan to value and then as the underlying asset value in residential property powered ahead, the banks then lent 85%, then 90% then 95% and then 100% and, in the latest round of confused optimism; up to 125 % of loan to value (LTV).

Not only was the LTV increased, instead of cutting back, as one would suppose, on the amount of salary that could be made available from the borrower for the house purchase in order to create a balancing effect on the mortgage structure; the lending institutions actually moved the income criteria from 3.5 as a multiple of earnings to 6, 7 - and in the worse case that we know of; 8 times earnings, (EIGHT!) to allow people to buy their own house, OR WORSE to rent to someone else!

Wouldn't you think that an intelligent regulator, made up largely of ex-bankers, Bank of England bankers, charged with protecting the public, would have made the same observation that we have made for the last 3 years of the upward moving property cycle, that the latter model was untenable and the former far more desirable?

STATEMENT OF MORTGAGE ACCOUNT

Nationwide Anglia Building Society

FOR THE YEAR ENDED   31ST DECEMBER 1989

If you made any mortgage payments through a bank or agent in the last week of December, you may find that these transactions are not shown on the statement below. However, they will have been recorded on your account and will appear on your next mortgage statement. If you disagree with any of the information that is shown below, you should write direct to the Mortgage Liaison Manager, Nationwide Anglia Building Society, Moulton Park, Northampton NN3 1NL. Please enclose this statement

Anyone's guess

ACCOUNT NUMBER
0830/ 99 019 901

DATE	TYPE OF TRANSACTION	CHARGES £	PAYMENTS £
	BALANCE BROUGHT FORWARD	60,235.12	
09 JAN 89	PAYMENT		558.86
07 FEB 89	PAYMENT		593.26
07 MAR 89	PAYMENT		593.26
06 APR 89	PAYMENT		593.26
05 MAY 89	PAYMENT		593.26
03 MAY 89	PAYMENT		10,907.00
07 JUN 89	PAYMENT		469.91
06 JUL 89	PAYMENT		469.91
07 AUG 89	PAYMENT		469.91
07 SEP 89	PAYMENT		469.91
06 OCT 89	PAYMENT		469.91
07 NOV 89	PAYMENT		505.41
07 DEC 89	PAYMENT		505.41
	INTEREST CHARGED	6,297.05	
	FEES AND CHARGES	15.00	
	BALANCE CARRIED FORWARD	49,347.90	

INTEREST RATES APPLIED	
01 JAN 89	12.750%
01 FEB 89	13.500%
01 NOV 89	14.500%

It is important that you retain this statement for future reference.
A charge will be made for any duplicate statement provided.

CN04N (11/89)

'Ah, but, interest rates and inflation were lower,' they said.

Interest rates in 1991 were 12-15% - inflation was still high but reducing. The dynamics were the same: it was the ambient forces that were different, in quantum. The over-used and over-simplistic expression that: "It is different this time" was repeated "ad nauseam."

The truth is that the *classic market* fundamentals were no different with interest rates at 3% and inflation at 2% per annum because property prices had moved beyond sensible borrowing limits with regard to the average home owner's earnings. The 'buy to let' market was also 'suspect' to say the least - especially when rental incomes dropped. There was an over supply of rental properties and many were too expensive to run, especially after government tax changes which included a levy on landlords.

Professional landlords had started off-loading (selling) their portfolios in 2003-2004 to naïve investors - some in their early 20's, for instance university students (or their parents), or perhaps those disenchanted with the equity market crash that sought a more certain investment future; many at, or near to the top of the market.

After all: "You can't lose by investing in property; can you?" Buying a property near to a university worked for some. However in the general market, some (including people I know, in London) lost considerable amounts of money for others.

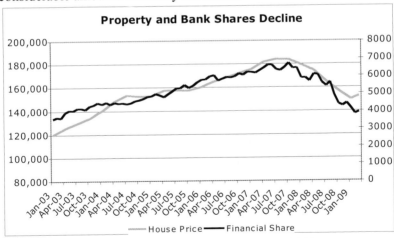

Fig 2.2 Property Decline; and Bank Shares 2003 - 2010

There are number of real 'giveaways' as evidence of the impending reversal, at the tail end of a *classic market* if one cares to observe carefully what was going on.

Official statistics work on the sale price of the property. But is the sale price the whole answer when you get to a situation where you perhaps have an £180,000 home which you are looking to sell? A builder has a £280,000 home on a development site that he needs to 'shift', because the bank is pressing him to get his overdraft down. The builder takes a £50,000 cut in the price of the property by discounting it to £230,000 and takes the purchaser's house in part exchange. What has actually happened? Fran and Stewart felt that they had worked this to 'their advantage' to obtain a larger home.

The property probably cost the builder £150,000 to erect, equip with a kitchen, put carpets down and present as a new home (not a house). It is that £150,000 that is 'out' to the bank, as the builder's overdraft, secured by the builder's development properties.

At £280,000 he could put £130,000 into the bank but he knows that the market prices have collapsed by at least 15%. By collecting £50,000 from the purchaser, plus their house, the builder still has a house to sell, but it is a cheaper house, further down the market chain on an established estate that he can discount.

The builder has received £50,000 that he can put back into the bank, reducing the £150,000 that he owes to the bank, to £100,000, easily secured by the exchange property which stands him at £180,000 which he can now discount to £150,000 and sell reasonably quickly, paying off £100,000 to the bank leaving him £50,000 profit, on the double deal.

The effect of the foregoing is to reduce the market value of new houses (£50,000 on £280,000 - a reduction of 17.8%) and also to discount the houses in the next tier down; £180,000 to £150,000 a 16.7% drop.

That is one of the mechanisms that pushes the market down (deflation) and the buyers think they have got a good deal. And possibly they have. The bank has its need for 'money in' satisfied, however, it is a deflationary exercise, and eventually affects the property market as a whole until the margins become too thin for the ruse to work effectively, or the market grinds to a relative halt.

It is when the market gets really tight and there is no mark-up to be had, because nothing is selling, that 'the builder' really does get into trouble.

The bank is happy to support the style of activity that has been outlined if only in the short term, in the hope that the bank can recover at least a portion of the indebtedness that runs into millions of pounds from property developers caught in the market downdraft. It is only at the last minute, when the builder has exercised all the options and the market has finally given up, that the bank will move in, repossess the second hand properties and sell them for whatever price it can make. It is not rocket science, but it does take thinking through.

The rental market is also adversely affected. As the capital value of properties fall one would expect rents to rise but at this point in the market the opposite happens - second and third homes come back into the frame from naïve 'buy to let' landlords.

	Rent	Capital Value	% return
April 2006	£650/mth	£300,000	2.6%
June 2009	£475/mth	£210,000	2.7%
	Capital loss	£90,000	-30% (minus)

In 2006/7 the 'tide' for property was going out and by 2008 (September) it was taking the financial sector - especially the banks, with it. How could that happen?

Easily.

Just look at and consider, get a feel for, the contracts in the early "CAPITAL GROWTH" driven market dynamic of the property and equity elements of *the classic market*.

In the opening stages of the *'classic market'* - every time - the driving force for CAPITAL GROWTH is the stock market. As the stock market becomes more and more reliant upon a small "driver" sector it collapses (well actually confidence collapses and with it share values across the board), where would seasoned investors, wishing to protect their money, invest at that turning point in the stock market?

Property had been in the doldrums since 1993 and barely moved in capital value or market prices as for practical purposes the market had flattened out and rents had initially stagnated.

By 1997 however rental incomes were improving, 2.5% had grown to 6% and that growth became 18% on capital values.

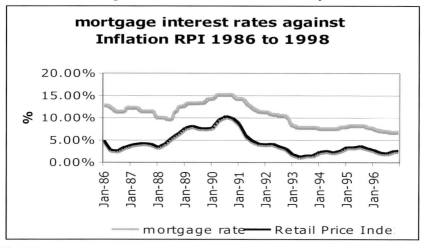

Fig 2.3

Interest rates and inflation had started a downward trend as shown in Fig 2.3, and both just kept going. The stock market rise may well have responded to that.

Individuals have long(ish) memories and the negative reaction to the property collapse of 1991-1993 and over ONE MILLION in negative equity held sway. But then - memories fade and new participants enter the arena.

In 2000 the stock market slide got underway. There was a need for a 'new' investment market and property presented the ideal solution.

Over the next three years house prices moved forward and shares moved down.

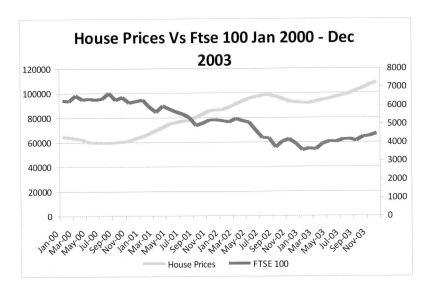

Fig 2.4

Contrast that graphic with the 2005/8 picture.

In Figure 2.5 it is quite clear that BOTH PROPERTY and EQUITY values are going down together as property undermines the banking system and thereby equity values just as it had so many times before. For every £1 million of property value decline the banks had to find £11 million to maintain their solvency. It is a simplistic view but science and higher maths are wasted where emotion drives the response.

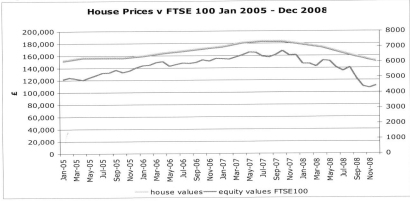

Fig. 2.5

Whilst home ownership has become a mantra, and ostensibly a good and beneficial mantra, there is a myth that needs to be erased and that concerns 'rent' being "money for nothing".

What is the difference between rent and mortgage interest? That is not a trick question. What is the difference between rent and mortgage interest?
There is no difference. NONE.

What is rent?

Rent is an amount of money paid to a stranger, paid on a regular basis at an agreed sum unless the rent changes, in return for the privilege of occupying a property.

What is mortgage interest?

Mortgage interest is an amount of money paid to a stranger, paid on a regular basis at an agreed sum unless the interest rate changes, in return for the privilege of occupying a property.

In return for rent: there is no share in the change in value of the underlying property. Short notice is required to leave.

In return for mortgage interest: the payment allows the payer to share in the change in value of the underlying property. Leaving can be difficult.

In other words if you exclude the value of the underlying property then rent and mortgage interest are synonymous. Individuals merely pay 'rent' to a building society or 'rent' (as interest) to a bank at a given rate based upon the amount of capital value mortgaged and interest charged.

I well remember a young man of 23/24 years of age coming to me for advice:

"I got to the point where I realised I just couldn't afford the payments that I had to pay for a mortgage," he said, "So I went to the building society, threw the keys on the desk, and said I can't deal with it, you will have to; I just can't afford the repayments. I turned on my heel and walked out. That was 2½ years ago," he said, "And now they have sent me a bill for £32,624. They have sold the house but they didn't get enough to cover the mortgage plus the outstanding accumulated interest, they say, therefore I have got to pay the difference. That can't be right; can it?"

Well actually it can be right, and it was, and it affected over a million people, it was called negative equity and it arose in 1992/1993. In Britain the mortgage is linked to the borrower. In the USA life is different – the mortgage is linked to the property.

Why wasn't negative equity a feature in the 1970s? It was. I suspect that fewer purchasers were affected because the rules regarding 80% loan to value were not altered until later on in the market growth phase. Also mortgage guarantee insurance was available.

Greed had not outwitted common sense quite to the extent that it managed during the late 80s early 90s and with even more devastating effect in the period 2004 to 2008.

The early 1970s were marked out in history as a time of change and therefore make a useful and pertinent starting point for some analysis that might just convince you that there are cycles; and they are predictable.

The general awareness of average earners acknowledging that saving could be done profitably outside of the government National Savings scheme was increasing in the early seventies.

The late sixties had been described as a period in time when the average Brit had "never had it so good". School children had learnt early on in their lives to purchase a savings stamp each week at school, with either a Prince Charles or a Princess Anne photograph emblazoned on them; 1/6d (7.5p) and 2/6d (12.5p) was the weekly amount to be saved and the proceeds helped the treasury to refill the nation's coffers after World War II had ended. The government was re-stocking its coffers, and doesn't that sound familiar?

Adults were familiar with operating a Post Office Savings Book, into which they would deposit cash at the end of a week (when they got paid) in order to build up a reserve fund for personal emergencies, or perhaps a holiday or special purchase. Even Building Society accounts appeared a little risqué. The Post Office and National Savings ruled the market for savings and the modest investments of the average individual. 2% to 4% per annum return was the "norm."

Certainty and guarantees were the order of the day.

Gerry and Linda had never saved. Gerry had lived up to his income and had a meagre £4 in the 'new-fangled' Premium Bonds that allowed him to keep his capital safe and have the hope of a big win. The big win never seemed to arrive; despite the 1961 'investment' date!

The win still did not come until, in frustration, in 1974, Gerry wrote to the Premium Bond office to enquire whether the 'bonds' that he held were actually in the draw. A £25 win came within three months of his letter and made headline news in Gerry's domestic domain. Was it a coincidence? Probably. There has certainly been no further 'winner' cheque since, despite increasing the 'investment' level.

Financial Planning was at that time traditionally the province of the wealthy, whoever they were, but it was starting to 'roll out' into the middle classes, an expanding group with aspirations for their future. The aspirations were given life through a rising and enthusiastic growth of 'service industry' group-orientated sales organisations, and inflation.

Those groups of 'independent' and single company sales teams expanded rapidly, primarily under the umbrella of life assurance companies or life assurance related commission salesmen and women, working full or part time, and drawn from the teaching, medical, police or military service professions, where earnings were above average and the regard for property ownership and share ownership, through a variety of channels, was growing.

Many had elected to enter 'the park' and get 'warmed up' on 'the boomerang'.

Excitement and quick profits seemed to be so available, so close, so immediate!

Figures show clearly that the stock market had generated an expectation of (almost) immediate gratification. The insatiable appetite for capital growth eclipsed the security of deposit based savings and caution was thrown headlong "to the winds." The only way (for markets of any kind) was perceived to be "UP." Average savings would have been between £2 and £5 per month. Earnings were £40 to £100 per month for this group of professionals (no, there is not a nought missing, inflation since that time has had a tremendous effect).

A three bedroom detached house, in Lincolnshire could be purchased for £4,650 (£10340 in London) in 1976 and the stock market equivalent of today's FTSE 100, DAX or Dow Jones 50 was at an "all time high". Christmas was promising to come big time – all year around – for a lot of people. The FT 30 index of leading shares moved ahead spectacularly as the 'middle class' investor stoked the 'fires' beneath it. A most significant change was taking place.

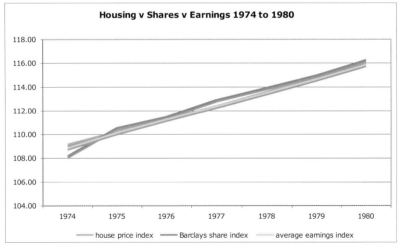

Fig 2.6

As the graph shows, there was plenty of room for optimism

CHAPTER 3
A PICTURE AND A THOUSAND WORDS
EQUALS CONFUSION

The problem with graphs is that they are deceptive. It is alright showing alpine contours as they appear on post cards but just how relevant are they?

Take a look at the graph (Fig 3.1) similar to that produced by the popular press to illustrate the movements in the stock market during sequential political phases of Parliament. The extreme left hand of the graph imparts very little real information until you study the graph **of that time** in perspective. And that is what graphs do, or rather can do, they can distort perspective.

What I will endeavour to do throughout the ensuing chapters is to restore that perspective to allow you to understand the real movement and the volatility and expression of that movement in genuine comparative terms. Each time period will be comparable with another even though the underlying data may be many times a multiple of another.

Fig 3.1

Just as a tester let me ask you a question: as a homeowner with a mortgage, which would create most distress for you in terms of your monthly outgo:

a)   A movement of interest rates from 12% to 15% per annum ?
or
b)   The movement of interest rates from 3% to 6% per annum?

Many would plump for a) as the bigger problem because the numbers are bigger representing high interest rates moving to even higher interest rates and therefore higher costs begetting higher costs still. £600 per month @ 12% would become £750 per month at 15%.

However the arithmetical fact tells us that a move from 3% to 6% is actually doubling your outgoing interest payments; £600 per month will become £1200 per month. Although the actual interest rates are lower, the capital borrowed is much higher. Hold that thought as we go through the next Chapters.   It is important.   It is called 'perception', and very often, in fact more often as not, it perverts genuine commentary.

NOTE: £600 per month @ 3% would become £1200 per month @ 6%

"Do not confuse me with the facts; it is what I perceive that is the truth" is a quote from *'Mountains out of Molehills'* published in 1992. It is my quote; a universally true observation about human instinct that is born out of experience and observation.

There is no deception intended on behalf of the creator of these particular graphs.   They are genuinely trying to convey trends or movement, but of course they are restricted because if they use the same scale throughout then the result at the right hand end of the graph using a continuous analogue scale would be 6ft high.

The second graph illustrated is one that I have used in virtually all of my presentations since Invesco Perpetual produced it in 2003.   I superimposed, in pencil the (not to scale) property prices graph as I saw it, in order to explain my theory of relativity between property prices and stock market movements.

As we will see during the next few chapters the relationship holds firm and is the more understandable for segmentation of the data and an analogue based presentation as opposed to the logarithmic, compressed, features of this example.

The interesting thing for me, and I believe to those that I was presenting to, was that the graph that had started to be formed at the extreme right hand end of this pictorial view of the markets when presented in non logarithmic form (in other words it was not scrunched up) was starting to look scarily like the graph from the 1970s. I believe it is therefore worth examining the 1970s in order to see what would emerge.

If we took that historic data would we be able to foretell the future in other words, history, 'hindsight'; would give us 'foresight.'

Just compare the two graphs. The first 'Telegraph' lookalike, Fig 3.1 is an analogue graph which highlights the movement of the market at its greatest – shown on the right hand side of the graph.

The 'Invesco' graph, fig 3.2 is logarithmic - in other words the scale scrunches up the graph line the further up the scale one progresses which makes the historic left hand side appear more as we would expect.

Now compare the two extreme ends of the graphs right and left respectively; a spooky sameness in the shape of the graphic representation is evident and will become even more evident as we progress.

This book does not review earlier market conditions prior to 1966. However the graphic later may well be viewed as 'interesting' with reference to the shape of the 1930's graphic representation.

This was a graph that I used in my presentations in the 1990s

It was Simon that said: "Where do I begin?" The question is probably answered by an old Irish reply when asked the route to somewhere:

"Sure; and if it were me; I wouldn't start from here".

But, where does saving and investment start but from where you are? You are where you are, and you are required to act accordingly.

My task is to provide you with a route map that will allow you to start from almost anywhere with a degree of certainty of attaining your final financial destination; no matter how many diversions or obstacles get thrown into your path.

The journey starts with an understanding of the markets and their relationship to *The Classic Market*. The most logical place to start is with cash deposits but is that really where you, if you are representative of 'most people', want to start?

How many individuals head for the theme park with a view to going on the swings or the seesaw?

OK. In reality the cry at the theme park gates, having paid the entry fee would more likely be: Let's head for 'the boomerang' or, if the queue is too long, the 'Double Dipper' and really get started.

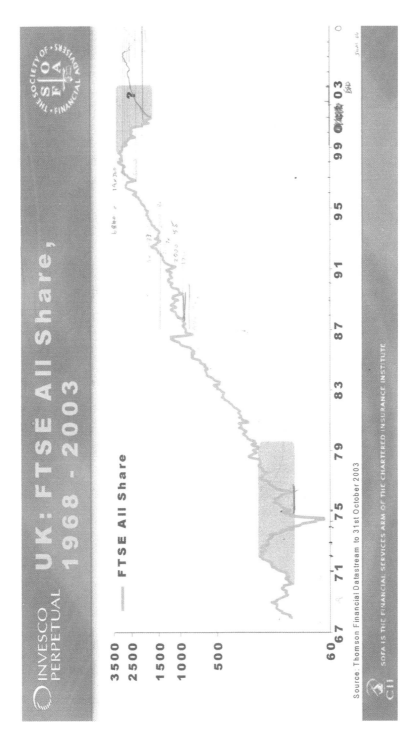

Believe it or not, that is precisely what most people do - they jump in - both feet – '**** or bust'; and usually because of peer pressure and/or experience of others. Don't be a wimp – it was great when I went on (even if I was sick!).

Gerry and Linda are an ordinary couple, who used to live in a small estate bungalow. The rent was reasonable and the two bedroom accommodation acceptable. In 1971 they were both starting out on their 'life journey' - not yet married and earning a modest income between them.

Please – don't stop reading because it is 1971. 1971 could easily read 2001 or 2031. Interesting stories are timeless, as you will discover.

Gerry had a part-time job selling "Kleeneze" brush ware door-to-door, as well as his full-time occupation. Neither of them aspired to the 'high life' and little in their lives was forcing any issues, yet their situation was changing in the way they saw life. It was subtle and yet forceful. The feel of life was different and their appreciation of aspects of property value started to play on their minds.

The stock market had grown rapidly from the mid 1960s, dived, and had risen to reach a peak in 1972. The subsequent 73% collapse of the market's value in the United Kingdom, and the reverberations around the world, was of little consequence to the majority of building society investors.

Bank accounts and the payment of regular bills by standing order were a relatively new idea in 1971. Cash - that is real money - was the order of the day in most households. "Only buy what you can afford" was the mantra given down by parents scarred by the deprivations of the 1930s and the uncertainties of the 1940s. The Barclaycard was yet to become a household expression.

Life assurance premiums were often paid by cash at the offices of the company; as were mortgage repayments and savings plans. Life assurance commission salespeople changed all that over a very short space of time.

A stock market crash meant very little to the average individual - it was perceived to be the province of the very wealthy. "Nothing to do with me then?" Linda's complacency was matched by Gerry's total disregard.

What was affecting both of their thinking was the growing pace for home ownership and the subliminal increase in not only awareness, but also desire; a subliminal desire NOT TO BE LEFT BEHIND.

Left behind what? They were not quite sure. The pressure was building, but from where was indiscernible, it was a gut feeling, inexplicable, but real.

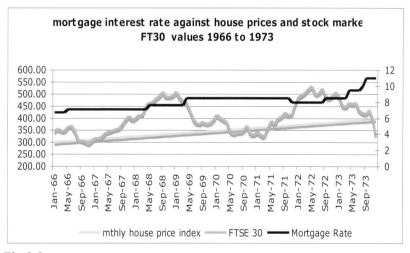

Fig 3.3

House prices had doubled in a comparatively short period. The rent that they were paying could just about transpose into a mortgage repayment if they 'got in quick'. That was the pressure, but what was the 'promise'. What was the WiiFM factor that was so tantalising? (WiiFM? – What's in it For Me!). Incidentally; they had no money in savings! None!

They could not lose money on property, because, well, you cannot lose what you have not got – property always 'went up' in value over time and they were setting out on a long-term 'journey' together from the stable roots of a fixed location. They could take a long-term view.

Does this sound emotional, 'airy fairy', where is the logic, to you?

What the story of Gerry and Linda raises rests in the perception of:

(a)   market performance; and

(b)   personal relevance.

The residential property market had already experienced house prices that had doubled. The price of a three bedroom detached house outside London had moved from between £2300 and £2600, to £4650 over an eighteen month period. Annual incomes were £800 to £1200 per year. Inflation was just entering double figures and was continuing to increase along with interest rates.

The majority of mortgage lenders in the early 1970s would have been 'building societies' with a history of giving priority for mortgage loans to those that had a savings or investment account <u>with that</u> society. But, things were changing.

Fig 3.4

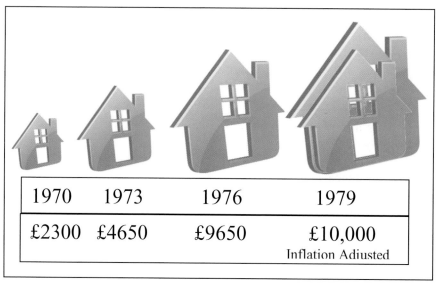

1970	1973	1976	1979
£2300	£4650	£9650	£10,000
			Inflation Adiusted

Building societies were constrained as to how much they could lend on any individual residential property through their Building Society Association rules, which had to be strictly followed.

History had shown that a safety margin between the loan and the value of the property being used as collateral, the loan to value (LTV) ratio, was essential to protect the Building Society investors if there was a housing market value reversal and a spate of bad debts.

At least with a safety margin in the LTV ratio the forced sale of the property could be conducted in such a way as to achieve the best price and hopefully a recovery of at least the full amount of the mortgage amount outstanding. The industry norm for the LTV was 80%.

An interesting side issue was that a building society was obliged to obtain the best price on a repossession sale, and return any surplus to the mortgagee.

Banks were not prevalent in the domestic mortgage arena. However, where a bank had a 'charge' (a mortgage equivalent charge) it, the bank, was only required to satisfy its own debt recovery from a loan redemption sale and could therefore place the property on the market without regard for the full market value being achieved. This proved to be a pivotal point in the market as we progress to subsequent *classic markets*.

Some of the smaller societies were offering to support mortgages beyond the normal 80% of property values. This uplift on normal lending criteria was achieved by Linda and Gerry insuring the balance of the money lent above 80%, with an insurance company. The policies of insurance were known as Mortgage Indemnity Policies and Eagle Star, a major insurer of the day, underwrote the majority of them.

The insurance industry, in its turn, was quite happy to insure the balance over and above 80% because the market was rising and the underlying demand to purchase one's own home was gathering momentum. House building was booming. You couldn't lose money in domestic property, could you?

Five million people were being exported from London out to Peterborough, Chesterfield (with the Post Office relocation and expansion programme), Stevenage and Milton Keynes (new towns), Gainsborough and many more locations were declared as London 'overspill' centres.

Other major centres were encouraged to do the same, a mass migration by government diktat was under way, brought about by the re-location of major government departments – move or lose your job. New towns were fashionable too.

Home ownership was what politicians desired. Home ownership became what the people wanted and the financial service industry was encouraged to support and grow alongside that emotionally based desire.

The effect of the property market boom was predictable. Like Gerry and Linda, individuals who had once sought a home now sought a capital return on a property investment. The first phase of any bull market, and this had all the credentials of a bull market, is greed, and there was greed aplenty. NB chapter 4 contains an explanation of the term 'bull market'

'Gazumping' became a new addition to everyday language.

Sellers no longer shook hands on a deal with a buyer, as the norm, and stuck to the bargain: no, a higher bid meant a broken promise. The highest price submitted, even a day before contracts were signed, and often several times as prices rocketed, won the day.

The movement of populations from prosperous 'city' locations to previously low price suburban towns and smaller city locations with modern 'new build' estates growing from previously 'green field' sites put building firms like Gleesons and Wimpy on the map.

These new firms of mass market builders, anxious to sell their products were, in turn, putting pressure on to the building societies to 'ease up' on their lending criteria. Mortgage 'broking' came into fashion and the banks picked up the scent of a profit in a new area of the broad market place that they (the banks) had hitherto ignored.

This was a cocktail that would make Molatoff green with envy.

The explosive nature of the mix and the redefined criteria would come home to roost with a vengeance, but not before thirty years or more had elapsed and the process had repeated itself a couple of times.

The real 'problem' started in 1973 which was the year that witnessed the introduction of the 100% LTV mortgage. The 100% mortgage was the catalyst to propel many into house purchase for the first time, but it also became the seed corn of a type of universal greed that consumed common sense. It gave Gerry and Linda an opportunity that they were to be thankful for over many years to come. Their timing was perfect.

The major financial criterion for acceptance of a mortgage application was also altered quite fundamentally. The principle wage-earner's income could now be multiplied by more than the previous 3.25 times to give the maximum mortgage amount that could be lent – and a second wage-earner's income could be taken into account. (This is not always a good thing as it assumes the second wage will continue – but a second wage-earner may soon become a non-wage earner as the borrowers start a family)The result was to increase the borrowing power of the individual and through that mechanism alone to inflate house prices through 'affordability'.

Inflation was rife.

By 1975 the rate of inflation had risen from 11% to 24.6%. Interest rates had also escalated. Wages had increased alarmingly as RPI (the Retail Price Index) galloped ahead and monthly uplifts became the norm. Government employee salary-related pensions became RPI linked for the first time (1974) and soon retired officials were receiving a pension as large as their employed contemporaries were earning! (So rumour had it).

The winter of discontent and the second phase collapse of the stock market made for interesting times. Property was at the very heart of the whole financial debacle, as we shall discover.

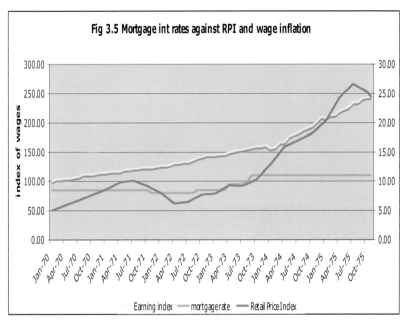

Fig 3.5

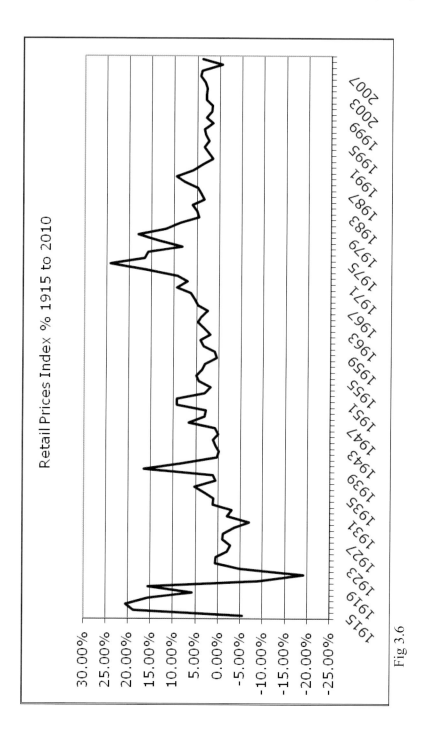

Fig 3.6

CHAPTER 4

Financial Relationships in history

The only connection between the common 'man' and oil prices in hindsight was "at the pump": the petrol pump that is; (4/11d in UK per gallon) 25p per gallon – under 6p per litre. The price of oil "per barrel" meant nothing until the "Arab crisis" took hold and the continual upward surge of the stock market (a bull market) came to a

halt. I refer, of course, to the 1970s. The situation today, in the 2010/11 era is strangely the same.

A "Bull" market is an upward trending market. The term "BULL" is easily remembered by the bull attacking with his head down and moving the head in an aggressive upward sweeping movement.

The triggers for market changes are many and varied – for the stock market in the 70s it was apparently oil prices, 28 years later (2000) it was reputedly terrorism. The root cause of ANY market change is **emotion,** i.e. confidence. When confidence fades, as it did in 1972, there is no stopping the downward drift. The 2000 adjustment was merely awaiting an excuse, and it came with the terrorist destruction of the World Trade Centre (the twin towers)

1972. This then was Gerry's first taste, at 28 years of age, of a rapidly declining market, a bear market.

A "Bear" market is a downward trending market. The term "BEAR" is easily remembered by the bear attacking with his head up and moving his arm in a downward sweeping movement with his claws extended. A defensive gesture.

The newspaper headlines were of 'ARMAGEDDON', we are 'all doomed'. The international stock markets were in turmoil and yet:

> In Gerry's world; there was no real change to everyday life - it just carried on as if nothing had happened.

Elsewhere, however, Charles was breaking his heart. As a sergeant in the Royal Air Force, Charles had £50 per month to spare to save for his retirement from the services in order to fund his travel plans. The graphic rise of Equity values in 1969 had drawn him into a ten year 'unit linked' savings plan. His statements of account had been a constant increase in value, reflecting the stock market's upward trend.

The 'bull market' was doubling his money over time and he was part of the phenomenal capital growth in equity investment that so many were then chasing. Charles had little capital to invest therefore he chose to save on a regular basis. Many of the professional workers from teaching, the police, the armed forces and so on were doing the same. That in itself was driving the market prices higher as a wave of new capital from their cumulative savings entered the quest for good value equity investment.

In *'Classic Market'* parlance this was a growth phase which was driving expectation beyond what was evidently reasonable in the short to medium term.

By 1974 Charles' vision of wealth had been shattered. The stock market (EQUITIES) was a 'spent force' to his understanding. The Financial Times (FT) FT30 index had dropped by 73%. Small wonder it made a mature man cry. All of his savings seemed to have dwindled away.

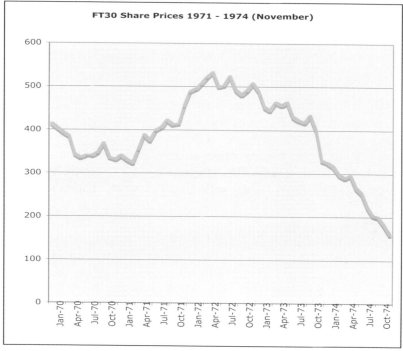

Fig 4.1

Well, they had at that point in time, but only if he crystallised the loss by encashing the savings plan - See Fig 4.1

The value of the stock market dropped by just less than three quarters of its capital worth.

In the meantime Gerry's new found passion, property, was showing exceptional capital growth.

In a 'classic market' the first phase or stage is in pursuit of CAPITAL GROWTH. As one market peaks and starts to decline another market sector starts its upward journey. Investors, particularly professional investors, move their capital to where the potential growth is to be found.

As the stock market fell, the second phase of the Classic market manifested itself as the property market's capital growth kicked in. Mature investors led the way by moving their money from the

EQUITY market into PROPERTY DEVELOPMENT. Land prices accelerated, new residential estates grew and expanded beyond belief. Thousands of new homes were being built and sold to a new generation of home owners. The property market got its second wind and quickly doubled again.

Existing home owners in the more affluent south of England sold properties at £10,000, then moved north with their mortgage repaid and purchased a new property outright for half the price and very often, with double the value in terms of space, garden and so on. Supply and demand quickly took hold.

The lenders had 'a field day'. However, borrowing money was made easy - too easy, some would say. The lending criteria for building societies had been very strict. As the market developed more 'lower earnings to value' individuals, like Gerry and Linda, were drawn to the market, yet they had little or no savings for the 20% 'mandatory' building society deposit. Something had to change to accommodate the 'feeding frenzy' for people like Gerry and Linda; and it did.

Enter the insurance industry with 'Mortgage Guarantee' policies. The policies of insurance were otherwise known as 'Mortgage Indemnity' policies. These policies indemnified the lender against loss if the property value dropped below the lender's required LTV threshold and the borrower defaulted.

Thus the policy effectively guaranteed that the building society's exposure never exceeded 80% of the 'purchase date' loan to value and therefore allowed lending beyond that criteria without breaking the very sensible building society rules that had operated successfully over many years.

Banks had no such constraints and 'smelling' a lucrative market the banks joined in the fray.

Linda and Gerry enjoyed the privilege of a 100% loan in order to purchase their first house. They had now joined the capital market foray, they, like many, had been carried away with the changing tide of popular perception, and for them, because of their timing (a fluke), it worked. One could argue that the accident of chance set them, and many like them, up for life.

Residential property, rather than just providing a place to live, became a capital investment in its own right. Just at the time when Gerry and Linda were entering the property market came the relaxation of the rules accompanied by the availability of, particularly, new houses on massive estates propelled in part at least by the movement of several million jobs out of London into the midlands in particular, and north in general, pushing house prices and personal aspirations even higher.

The mortgages that were available to individuals without a deposit were very few, up until the early 1970s. The maximum mortgage that a Building Society released from its own capital availability, reliant largely on the savers using the society, was, as has been said, prescribed at 80% of Loan To Value (LTV) secured by the property being purchased. Many societies only gave loans to existing investors.

Inventive brains, and the aggressive avarice of the banks, plus the increasing demand from would-be purchasers, and increasingly active property developers, created a totally new dynamic. The developers were also borrowing from the banks to purchase building land and fund their development activities to the tune of £millions giving the banks a further incentive to link the production and sales ends of the process.

Sales people were actively engaged in what was a precursor to the 'total' individual financial planning facility that would become the normal practice of later years.

Life assurance and savings firms employed salespeople who became engaged in opening bank accounts in order to facilitate the payment of premiums plus building society savings accounts in order to build the necessary relationship with a building society in order to have a mortgage application agreed at some later date. Life assurance premiums had historically been paid by cash at the home of the individual policyholder or by cheque (or cash) at the local office of the life assurance company. That process was changing dramatically, and the initiative was led by those same sales people.

Payment by 'standing order' saved a lot of journeys by policyholders with life assurances and mortgages paying their monthly dues and also valuable time taken for the money to get into the accounts at the 'life office'. The advent of bank standing orders also reduced defaults.

It soon became apparent that banks and building societies would pay commission for the introduction of new accounts from professional advisers. Interest rates in the high street were outstripping those of the National Savings movement. 'Greed' was taking over in the nicest possible way - in fact, it took over - and the property market, with inflationary wage rises supporting it 'took off' once again. In 18 months the valuation, and, as it proved the selling price, of Gerry's house doubled to £9,650. But, inflation was also on the rise.

Where else could an ordinary individual make so much money so easily?

Bank managers had insurance agencies in their own right leading up to the late 1970's and well into the 80's, at which point the banks decided to take the commission cake and cream for themselves. What had been a business expansion perk at branch level became a national target-driven addition to the 'banking service'. If external salespeople could make a good living why couldn't the bank?

Indeed a number of creative salespeople 'set up' deals with the bank managers of the time and taught them the finer art of selling financial services only to find that they, the advisers, as the bank managers before them, had been relegated to 'the bench'. It is sports terminology that implies that the individual is no longer counted as being in the game, no longer required in the active team, only to watch from the side lines.

Building Societies were lending 3.5 times a borrower's earnings, plus one times the earnings of the spouse, up to 80% loan to value. Then came a realisation - people were generally short of initial capital to place a 20% deposit on a house - why not insure the element above the restrictive limit. With the addition of that insured facility up to 100% loan to value could be offered to borrowers. And so it was, after all, "You cannot lose money on property".

The background to this 'breaking down' of barriers is essential to allow a full understanding of how commerciality, without prudence, can create a market demand that simply escalates out of control. Myths abound, like the forgoing quotation. Of course money can be lost on property investments, if the investment is made at the wrong time, using inappropriate criteria.

Mortgage lending is and should be restricted, as it was back then, (in the 70s) to ensure that the lending institution's assets are in line with its liabilities. Every loan is a liability backed up by an asset - the property being mortgaged.

£5,000 house - £4,000 loan = £1,000 EQUITY. If the property was subject to repossession, due to non payment of the mortgage, then the Building Society or bank could carry a loss of capital value on a forced sale and also, if the sale was for full value, receive interest on its capital.

The mortgage Indemnity Guarantee insurance policy was designed in order to make good to the Building Society any shortfall; as an indemnity package - this was the start of a second doubling of the property market. What could go wrong? After all; who could lose money invested in property? The answer turned out to be; a lot of people, including the lenders and insurers. It all but bankrupted Eagle Star.

Gerry and Linda were in their three bedroom detached house for just 18 months, thanks to their 100% mortgage. They could not have entertained the idea of house purchase in any other way. But, then (in 1976) their property had risen in value to a massive £9,650.

It was sold to a policeman moving into the area, just before the top of the market. The significance of the policeman? He, like a lot of public service employees, was no longer tied to a 'police' house. A full rent had to be paid for 'service' accommodation, choice had been introduced and for many a transient lifestyle for the whole family in all of the public services was becoming ancient history.

Roots were being set down by those in once transient occupations and the purchase of a lucrative, long term, and secure property, was part of that strategy. The newspapers were full of encouraging articles. The difference between the cost of owning and renting had narrowed to nothing.

Then the market stagnated; thus giving credence to the notion that **timing** is important.

Date	Actual Value	RPI In Year	Real Value
31 Dec 1968	£4,010	5.9	£3,742
31 Dec 1969	£4,222	4.7	£3,767
31 Dec 1970	£4,480	7.9	£4,054
31 Dec 1971	£5,106	9	£5,143
31 Dec 1972	£6,959	7.7	£6,320
31 Dec 1973	£9,044	10.6	£6,461
31 Dec 1974	£10,077	19.1	£5,917
31 Dec 1975	£10,846	24.9	£5,041
31 Dec 1976	£11,866	15.1	£4,605
31 Dec 1977	£12,804	12.1	£4,759
31 Dec 1978	£15,261	8.4	£5,790
31 Dec 1979	£19,820	17.2	£6,023
31 Dec 1980	£23,288	15.1	£5,113
31 Dec 1981	£23,954	12	£4,697
31 Dec 1982	£24,851	5.4	£4,817
31 Dec 1983	£27,622	5.3	£5,197
31 Dec 1984	£31,076	4.6	£5,676
31 Dec 1985	£34,737	5.7	£5,677

Fig 4.2 actual against real values using 1966 as a base (see Glossary 'Real values'). Source data: Nationwide B.Soc.

At one point the housing market was so buoyant, and sales agreed so quickly, that sale boards were hardly necessary. Prices were agreed and then a fresh purchaser would offer more. Gazumping was rife.

Then a more routine structure was re-established, until the 100% mortgage became common - even life assurance companies started lending their own money, nobody wanted to miss the excitement and easy profits. The second phase began to 'burn out' when confidence waned and fresh purchasers dried up - the reason? Inflation and interest rates were blamed, but, penury was a better bet. Property had simply become too expensive to service, financially.

What was the difference ?

Inflation and interest rates had effectively priced the first time buyer out of the market and northern house values had caught up with those in the south to the point where "moving north and discharging the mortgage" for many southern based potential buyers was a thing of the past. For the time being at least, the 'boom' had 'bust'. Another 12 to 15 years would see it all again – but don't let us jump ahead.

Graphically, the effect is to flatten out the property curve, as we would expect, in relation to the equity curve as their profile joins together.

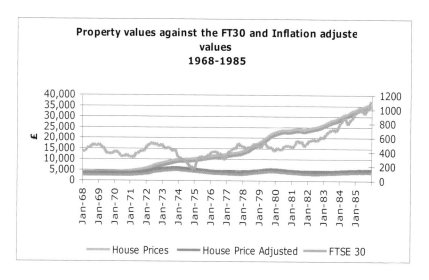

Fig 4.3

Factually the figures reflect an average market which is more akin to values in London and the south of England; and in 2010 they still do.

CHAPTER 5

ASSET RATIOS AND SOLVENCY MARGINS EXAMINED

Whilst all of the residential property growth was going on, the commercial lenders, sometimes bankers, were becoming more and more interested in the returns being generated and the exceptional levels of asset values that could be 'captured' to bolster their lending power. Banks make the most money from lending money. In fact it could be said that lending money, in order to give a return to depositors, is the banks' reason for being in the marketplace.

Banks, as has been stated, are required to keep a level of assets that maintains their liquidity and provide a safety net for their depositors and shareholders should there be a 'run' on the bank, or the underlying assets of the bank reduce in value. A bank could in 1970 lend the same pound out <u>fourteen</u> times, latterly reduced to 11 times, therefore if the asset base over which the banks have a charge rises then the money that can be lent to those seeking credit can also increase.

Question:

If you had £100 to invest; would you invest it with an institution that directly matched its assets against the firm's liabilities:-

£100 to £100,

or would you choose to invest in an institution with £8 of assets against your £100. That is what a bank's current account is:-

£8 to £100.

And what if we return to poor Charles and his unit linked savings plan - NO real ASSETS?

£0 to £100

The ratio of assets to liabilities in the banking sector is a very pertinent element of the conditions that move the critical values within the framework of *The Classic Market,* as we shall discover.

You may well be wondering: whatever happened to Charles?

'Pound cost averaging' is what happened to Charles. The company that he invested with provided no guarantee of a return, it merely undertook to invest Charles's regular payments into a particular 'unitised fund' or market place. The company providing the plan did not provide a reserve to back the capital invested other than the shares purchased within the fund. In this instance the contributions (premiums) purchased units in a balanced equity fund investing, on Charles's behalf, in the stock market.

During the last week of 1974 and the first week of 1975 the stock market indices rose by 50% from the bottom of the 'crash' (INDEX 147 at the bottom) in a remarkable resurgence of confidence. What that really means is that the big investors bought into the market in a bargain sale and pushed the value of extremely cheap shares (against the assets and earning power of the companies comprising the 'index') up. That was a genuine January sale from a bargain basement personified.

Charles' equity units rose with the index to restore a little of his faith; but he was still very hurt. The 'drop' had comprised two years of decline and the resurgence was only half of the loss sustained during the previous drop. The interesting thing is that it happened when everyone was least expecting it - over the Christmas/New Year holiday. Charles was maintaining his £50 per month payment by direct debit - another new computer driven phenomenon that had replaced the manually processed standing order. He started paying into his plan in 1969 and, as any 'chartist' will tell you, experienced more than one 50% retracement until the index hit 'bottom'.

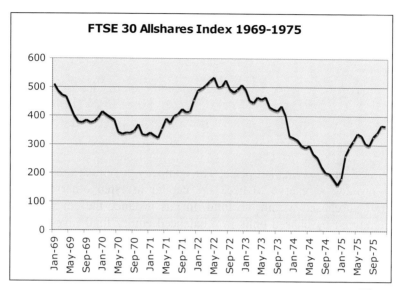

Fig 5.1

Here is the really interesting question that stems from the foregoing observations:

If the market had dropped 70% from May 1972 to December 1974, how much would the market need to grow in order to return to its previous level of 533.7?

For those interested in arithmetic the low in 1974 was 160.1 therefore:

160.1/533.7=0.3

0.3 x100= 30% which is the percentage value of the index at the bottom (ie: the index lowest value).

Therefore the loss is 30%-100% =

-70% loss.

Formula : ((value 2/value 1) – 1) x 100 = percentage gain or loss. Therefore:

in order to regain an index level of 533.7 the sum is:

533.7/160.1 = 3.3335.

3.3335 x 100 = 333.35% which is the percentage value of the gain when the index has reached the target figure of 533.7 .

Therefore the gain is: 333.35% - 100%=

233.35% gain.

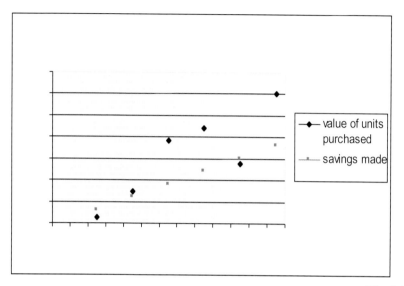

Fig 5.2

Provided that the index returned to its previous high Charles was in the money, because of £ (pound) cost averaging. All of the contributions to the savings scheme made whilst the market was in deep decline would now reward Charles's patience with real palpable growth.

His £50 at the top of the market was buying, say, 100 units, at the bottom his £50 was buying 273 units. In the interim stages each £ would have been buying incremental increases in the number of units purchased. The average would be 24 purchases of 167 units or 4008 units instead of 2400 if the price had merely stabilised.

The 233.35% market rise would have restored more of that perceived loss than Charles realised. That is the effect of **'pound cost averaging'**. Charles would still have some way to go to recover the loss of capital value built up between 1969 and 1972 (when the equity markets collapsed) but a future rise would claw that back too - over time, and, to his advantage. The negative market was, because of its timing, working for him even though he perceived quite the opposite. Charles was keen to know when it would recover but there were more twists to come in this *classic market* than he could comprehend.

As the typical *Classic market* progresses the investors' focus shifts from CAPITAL growth to INCOME provision. Income is invariably perceived as secure and rather more assured. Having been caught napping themselves; or having shared in the experience of friends like Charles' disappointment, investors and savers look for safety, value and a reasonable level of income.

So, what about Government stock?

Mike had been investing for a long number of years in what he considered to be safe investments: government stocks, (gilts).

These are 'loans' that are created by a government department, either the Treasury, or the Exchequer, to raise money from public subscription. The money is initially raised through an auction usually via the institutions such as Insurance Companies, Pension Funds, Friendly Societies and the like, in order to secure a long term financial facility for the government in return for a fixed income facility for the Institution together with a known return at the redemption date.

Take for example Treasury 5% 2025 stock, the inception date of which was Jan 2002.

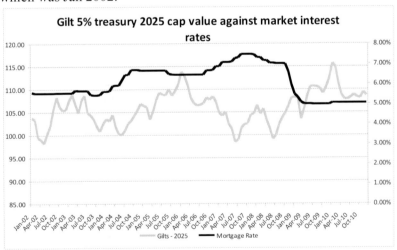

Fig 5.3

The name tells you everything there is to know apart from the issue date which was Jan 2002. The Treasury wanted to raise money, they will perhaps have offered a several £ million tranche of loan stock inviting investors to lend the Treasury money until 2025 when it will be repaid, £100 per £100 of stock, guaranteed. In the meantime 5% interest will be paid every year to the investor, usually in two half-yearly instalments, in this instance March and September.

By carefully choosing a portfolio of six different stocks, with distribution dates selected to make payments in sequential months the adviser can create a regular monthly income from a portfolio of government loan stock.

Now; the last time we had interest rates at 5%, would have been in the early 2000s. If the underlying rates in the market place were around 5%, then the stock would be valued at £100 for you to buy (or sell) on the open market, ignoring extraneous costs.

However, what happened over time and into the late 90s/early 2000s was that interest rates were decreasing in the market place. Inflation was low and therefore it was a factor that could virtually be ignored.

Question:

If you could buy a guaranteed return of 5%, underwritten by the government with a guarantee that you would get your £100 (per £100 invested) back at the end of the loan stock period (2025) would you jump at the chance? Most would, but, wait a moment, in order to buy that fixed rate of return, promised by the government; in September 2010 you will have to part with £118.13. 18.13% more in capital outlay for the same fixed income. The Bank of England base rate is 0.5% per annum.

If underlying interest rates were rising, you might well be nervous of committing yourself that far forward, 16 years is a long time. However if interest rates were falling and you could 'lock in' the 5%, you might take a chance on 16 years, or even longer.

What if you could 'lock in' to 5% as a guaranteed income, with a guarantee of getting your money back in 2025 and underlying interest rates were between 0.5% and 3%? Would you be tempted to pay more than £100 to buy into that 5% return? Strange as it may seem some people would actually do that. It does make sense doesn't it?

This might be particularly useful if you are the investment manager for an institution and you are promising a return, or providing guarantees, such as you would with, say: annuities and pension payments? A fund manager might well lock into a regular income against the future guarantee of the £100 known return. What happens to the 'capital value' the capital purchase or sale price of the investment in the intervening period, is wholly academic.

An investing body would need to know that you are getting sufficient income every year without having any underlying worries about performance being required to meet your obligations. If the 'contract' that is being invested in is underwritten by the government, a professional manager may well be tempted to buy into it; and pay a 'premium' for the 'deal!' And that's exactly the way the market worked.

That is why the gilt market (the market dealing in government loan stock) is priced daily, or even more frequently, to allow for market interest rate fluctuations.

How does the foregoing analysis of gilt edge securities or the general principal of fixed interest investment affect you the reader? The answer is: in just about every aspect of your provision for your future financial welfare.

For the elderly, and this may be your elderly parents or a relative, the effect can be profound and confusing.

Edna was in her 90s and needed advice on her capital

The intriguing thing about the Edna story is that we were asked to evaluate the capital value of Edna's free Estate following the sale of her house so that income could be provided to cope with the residential fees at the nursing home that she was going into.

Harping back into that 'unfamiliar sight from a familiar destination' metaphor that I used earlier on, one look at the capital immediately suggested that it could not possibly produce the sort of income that was necessary to support this lady in her old age. How wrong could I be?

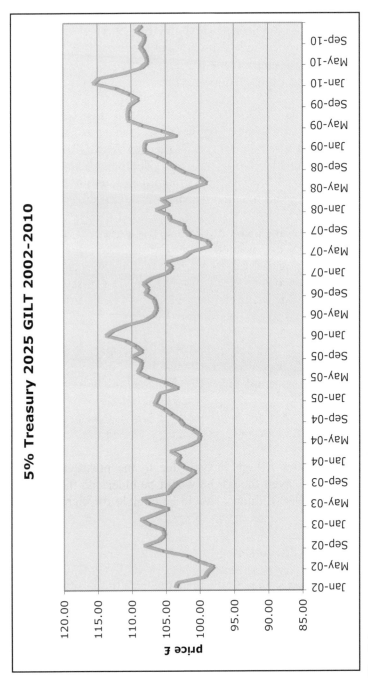

Fig 5.4

The whole point of putting this particular case study into the book is that the capital value was to a great degree irrelevant. What Edna had purchased when she made her investment in a fixed interest 'open ended' investment company (OEIC) several years before was the income that this particular investment was producing - and it was rising over time.

Interest rates had risen considerably, in fact they had doubled from 3% to 6% over just a couple of years in the post millennium decade. The effect of a 3% rise in interest rates was a mere 20% drop in the capital value of the fund. The point here is that the income was fixed. In fact it was more than fixed, it was subject to increases because the fund managers had done their job.

They were pursuing income at the expense of capital value which was just what Edna wanted. She was not interested in capital value just so long as the income wasn't eating away at the capital and creating a problem for her future. Needless to say there was no need to change the investment strategy in that particular case, the situation was as near perfect as it could get.

At a younger age approaching retirement the situation can be just as confusing. I was on the telephone a few days ago to a client in his late 50s. We were talking about his personal pension contract.

Charles had read in the Sunday paper that now was a good time to buy annuities because, if Charles waited, the amount of income that his capital would purchase (the annuity rate) would not provide such a high income due to the prospect of lower annuity rates - even though he would be older and therefore, in the normal order of things, should be eligible for higher rates of annuity (pension income) due to age.

Was the journalist correct?

Perhaps the easiest way to illustrate the truth of the situation is to consider the effects of interest rates on annuity rates. Is there any correlation between the movement of Bank of England (BoE) base rates from time to time, and the income that an insurance company will pay you for the rest of your life?

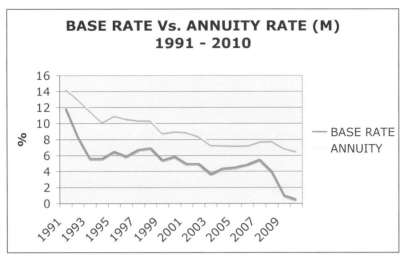

Fig 5.5

The relationship appears to have a very positive correlation in historic terms, so what can we expect for the future?

We know from the table that interest rates have fallen and we can attribute a great deal of that fall to a concerted international endeavour to reduce inflation. The following graph picks up on that relationship.

What conclusions can be drawn that must surely apply to the future?

The analysis of interest rate performance appears to rely upon inflation and the prospects for inflation are in the balance, but trending upwards. Invariably and inevitably some pundits will say interest rates will have to rise. Certainly if government wants to attract capital investment in an inflationary environment and in consideration of longer dated stock, the return on fixed interest offerings from commerce and government have to be more rewarding

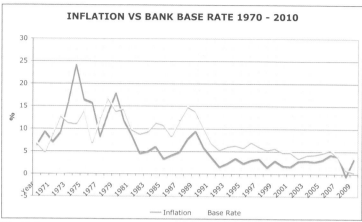

Fig 5.6

Interest rates, as at October 2010 are at a significant low point and, in all probability, can only rise. Indeed, the argument goes that interest rates HAVE to rise in order to contain inflationary effects; if of course inflation gets 'out of hand'.

If the prognosis for interest rates is for them to rise then, from the historic evidence, and not withstanding improvements in mortality rates, annuity rates should improve rather than, as was reported to be the case in Charles' newspaper, be poorer value. Better value was in prospect from a larger fund, which would hopefully be achieved if the fund was left to grow, plus an increase in age would also conspire to improve Charles' position if he leaves well alone.

Are interest rates likely to reduce? Quantative Easing (QE) is a form of interest rate reduction without the outward signs of published lower BoE base rates, but the effect is the same.

It is perhaps interesting to note that, due to low yields (the lowest for an eternity) the British government is finding it difficult to sell £50 billion of new issue gilts that it needs to sell to fund the Government's deficit. The Government needs to 'reschedule' maturing gilt edged stock. Just like you coming to the end of a fixed term, fixed interest mortgage without the funds available to 'clear' the debt.

Foreigners are, apparently, reluctant to buy British low yield gilts because of the fear of inflation driving interest rates up and thereby the gilt capital values down. This is perhaps a view that many can understand.

The remedy, we are informed, is for the Government to lean on the banks, which are struggling to restore their solvency margins, to force them (the British banks) to buy the British fixed interest stock (Gilts) in order to bail out the Government who have just bailed out, and continue to support, those same banks.

The plot; she has been lost!

We all understand mortgages; or at least we believe that we do. The average person's life expectancy after retirement should be about twenty-five years from aged sixty with improving mortality and all the other good things. Bear in mind that those who are in pension schemes are select lives and have a different mortality experience to the average population. They live longer.

I chose to use twenty-five years because the average mortgage is twenty-five years and therefore the comparison becomes a little easier to make with annuities. If you are so inclined you can go into your Lotus software or Microsoft Office suite and you will find a little programme for repaying your mortgage.

If we assume a 7% interest rate and create a mortgage for £100,000 we can establish how long it takes to repay half the mortgage. You may be surprised at the acceleration that occurs once the capital value of the mortgage starts to reduce. By the end of twenty five years of course there is zero capital outstanding and the £100,000 that you borrowed would have been paid off.

With an annuity we would demonstrate the reverse. The annuitants start off with £100,000 plus a willing life assurance company. If the life assurance company get the sums absolutely right then at the end of twenty-five years they, the life assurers, end up with zero capital and the annuitant will have received all of their income 'entitlement' (the equivalent of the mortgage repayment amount) month by month for the full twenty five years. That of course represents perfection. Unfortunately, or perhaps, fortunately, it is not what happens in reality.

The difference, of course, is that if, like many these days, some people do not die at their scheduled time, that throws the calculations out.

Other people are generous with their funds. Those people die early and leave the legacy in the life assurance company coffers; which a number of linear thinking individuals imagine disappearing out of the back door of the life assurance company office and into some Swiss Bank for the Chief Executive to go on his holiday. Realists know different.

If we bear in mind that we are dealing with a cohort of say, ten thousand people, then other members of that group wishing to get better value for money than they are absolutely entitled to just keep on living. It is a selfish attitude, I know, but nevertheless the life assurance company have to cope with it and what is more they have to cope; with a smile on their face.

The smile, if they have got their sums right, is produced from the excess of the people who died early funding the people who died later than the average expectation (in our case the twenty five years). It does save the life assurance company writing letters to people at aged eighty five to say: "We are sorry but your funds have run out, your fund is now down to zero, tough luck, you are on your own." And the income of course ceases.

Mortality is an inexact science and therefore one tends to err on the side of caution. Life assurance companies are providing guarantees where annuities are concerned and those guarantees usually last for life. Most individuals have difficulty forecasting investment returns over two years let alone twenty-five years. Miracles are not the province of Life Assurance Fund Managers.

There is a debate at the moment, within the Financial Services Industry, for a euthanasia Society so that we can establish more precise figures: but thus far their findings have been inconclusive. The FSA will no doubt report shortly.

I made that bit up, sorry.

There are quite a number of people who do feel that they can do better than the life assurance companies. After all somebody somewhere is making a profit, but that is to miss the point. You may or may not understand the term 'drawn down'; however a 'draw down' facility allows individuals to look after their own financial funds, at least for a period of time. Just imagine what would have happened to their funds in 2008 if they were on cash deposit when interest rates dropped from 5% to 0.5%.

What would have happened to their funds is as happened with someone of our acquaintance, drawing an £8,000 a year income, only to find that there had been no growth in their fund and their £88,000 'draw down' fund had reduced to £80,000 from which they still needed to withdraw their £8,000 per year. They were panic ridden, and they were right to be so.

'Draw down' is a much publicised concept. The linear thinker immediately identifies with the £100,000 lump sum (if we can continue to use that figure as an example) because rather than 'giving it' to a life assurance company and experience a loss of funds on death (assuming that they die before the twenty-five year calculation period for average mortality expires) they can pass the money on to their beneficiaries.

We will not get into the argument of: "It is not their money anyway." The individual **purchasing** the annuity will pay their contribution to the life assurance company to do a job, which would be to provide income in retirement for the rest of that individual's life, therefore, the annuity 'purchase' money is no longer the individual's money. Under current legislation, individuals can utilise that money through 'draw down' to build up their own capital base, whilst drawing income, without committing themselves to an annuity. It may be that using the investment techniques outlined in this book: that some advantage can be gained. The often painful difference is that they have sole responsibility for their own 'annuity income'.

The thing to remember is that whereas with the mortgage we are paying an element of capital together with interest; with the annuity we are doing exactly the opposite; we are drawing some capital out plus the interest earned on the capital. As the capital reduces, the interest earned provides less and less income and the proportion of capital increases over time.

As a mechanism to provide a known income in return for a fixed capital sum, over an uncertain period, there is much to be said for the certainty that an annuity provides.

When asked, most people like guarantees and security where future income is concerned. No doubt the debate regarding whether or not compulsory annuity purchase for pensions should be maintained will go on. The more important debate is whether those who elect for the alternative, including those who advise the government, really understand what they are letting themselves in for?

To guarantee or not to guarantee, that is probably, on analysis, the real question.

CHAPTER 6

PERSONAL INSULATION FROM THE MARKET FORCES

We have observed that Gerry and Linda took a chance on the purchase of their first property, they had no other investments; in fact they had no money.

The market allowed them to take a 100% mortgage to purchase a modern house and get themselves established.

There were peripheral opportunities as well.

Credit had become easier through bank loans for personal items by way of 'cheap' and easily obtained hire purchase and bank loans. Credit had adopted the face of respectability. The lessons of the thirties were old hat. Buy now, pay later, because tomorrow it will not be affordable. Just look at the interest rates coupled with inflation rates and you might understand the 'buy now' mentality.

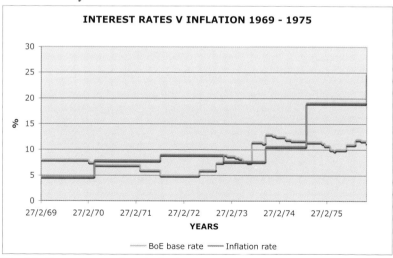

Fig 6.1 Base rate against inflation

The system was awash with money as savings grew and bank asset ratios   (7.14%ASSETS to 100 LIABILITIES) and the growth of underlying property asset values geared up that formula.

Bank initiated property re-valuations became commonplace. The greater the asset value secured against existing mortgage loan equity, (the difference between market value and what was owed to the bank) became the more the banks could lend. An eternal stairway to the stars: UNTIL IT ALL STOPS. 'Fourteen times' was the multiple that the banks could lend for every £1 they held.

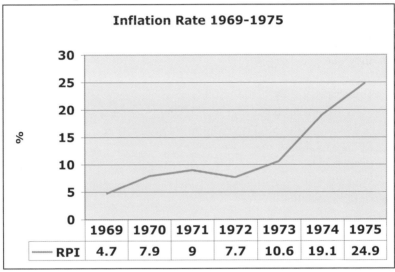

	1969	1970	1971	1972	1973	1974	1975
—— RPI	4.7	7.9	9	7.7	10.6	19.1	24.9

Fig 6.2 inflation figures PLUS graph

In other words; the bank regulator, the Bank of England, allowed banks to assume that, at any point in time, only one in every fourteen depositors would ever require their money from the bank at any one time. Assets would comprise not only money, but property both residential and commercial, and once the barriers started to be removed, (or ignored) other property such as plant and machinery, shares and gilts could all be added in, but only for assessment purposes.

Second hand furniture – really good quality, but old – was being chopped up – why have old when you can buy new (on credit)? The situation sounds familiar in 2010, however, times and views do change, as we shall witness.

The answer for Gerry and Linda was to furnish their three-bedroom home for a very modest outlay from the second hand furniture market and enjoy time together painting and 'tarting' it up to look more respectable.

Linda and Gerry had found a way to make capital – they had no ties to the property they owned. Relatives were far distant. Schools were not a consideration, however they needed to move to the other side of the city due to work requirements. Because travelling time to work was wasteful and expensive there was little to lose and plenty to gain from reduced travelling costs.

Linda and Gerry had the opportunity to sell the property that they had purchased only 18 months before, at double the price that they had paid for it.

If necessary they could move into rented accommodation with a view to getting back into the housing market when 'the dust had settled'. The strategy would have worked. The residential property market went 'flat' shortly after they sold their original property in 1976. Building new houses, particularly large housing estates, had been a national undertaking in villages and right up to smaller cities. Indigestion had set in.

During the mid 1970s interest rates had risen along with the cost of living – people had no extra cash - and the banks and building societies had tightened their lending criteria, their underlying asset ratios were now in reverse.

Inflation was creeping up and undermining incomes.

Interest rate rises had a crippling effect on mortgage repayments. Few mortgages were 'interest only' style contracts unless accompanied by an assigned endowment policy or other repayment mechanism. The trend to interest-only mortgages was becoming more and more popular, however.

Commercial property valuations were also experiencing a slow down.

It was June 16th 1978 and an auction was taking place for Victorian (or maybe Georgian) terraced property in a major City.

It was a good location; the property was in sound condition and had been on the market for some considerable time at £35,000.

At £35,000 it was far too rich a proposition for Gerry and Linda, however, if they could 'pick it up' for something considerably less than that, then it would certainly become an attractive asset which would house their embryonic business and perhaps even accommodate a tenant or two. It was a four storey building with plenty of room; it just needed 'a bit of work doing to it'.

On the night of the auction Linda and Gerry were prepared to celebrate with their friends or commiserate whichever way the auction went.

They set off to the auction room expecting a crowd. When they arrived they were the only ones there with the auctioneers and the rest, as they say, is history. The hammer came down at £13,500 for a four storey City Centre property with twelve car parking spaces to the rear. Gerry and Linda could not believe their luck; put in perspective £13,500 in 1978 plus the extras on top which included pots of paint and paintbrushes and a three week 'out of hours' painting session, was a bargain.

The point being made is that the market had just collapsed. Properties were sat idle in most major locations. Interest rates had got out of hand, inflation had got out of hand, and in fact the whole economy seemed to have got out of hand. Over the next few years a new damp-proof course, major work to the basement, attention being paid to the plumbing, the roof which needed sealing, put the property into good order.

Was this unusual? In 2010 the economic backdrop looks just the same, the fundamentals have not changed

It is not the property that looks just the same: the situation looks just the same; there are properties due to come on the market which people will pick up as bargains. Large companies have collapsed one such company born of the 1992-1993 economic debacle. That company's directors' ability to buy heavy plant cheap at the auctions (much the same as Gerry and Linda purchased their property) created a whole multi-million pound business that was built out of bargain hunting and thrift.

Not a lot can be said for PLC's (Public Limited Companies) with too much money, over ambitious CEO's (Chief Executive Officers) and a business plan that does not exhibit commonsense, but it is as ever was, the way that the world works. That company born of thrift went bust in 2008 along with the banks who exhibited similar avaricious traits. We shall talk about that more later.

Memories are short; too short. History teaches us so much; if we allow it to.

For Gerry and Linda the whole situation concerning property purchase and 'timing' as opposed to 'time in' was working well for those who had an insight into the market or, as in Gerry and Linda's case, just happened to be in the right place at the right time.

Among a plethora of new 'Property Bond' offerings in the market place Abbey Life set the seal of greatness on the sector by purchasing the first £1m property in the UK into its property fund. Centre Point was the property's name and it became a centre of attention for all the wrong reasons, along with many other office blocks in major conurbations because it remained empty for a decade or more.

A white elephant born of greed? No, just very bad, some would say unfortunate, timing.

Property had assumed the status of being a long-term investment; because, if anyone wanted to get a 'decent' price from their initial purchase, either directly or through a Property Fund they had to wait a long time (years) to get it. Property is not a daily traded investment medium like shares and gilts.

For very good and valid reason, the statistics of the time do not reflect the marketplace that well. Computers were relatively new and still unsophisticated.

As we shall discover the property world statistics are skewed (distorted) by London and the south in general. Regional variations however hold one of the major keys to the timing of property purchase across the UK.

As prices rise in the south there is a movement of retirees or those wishing to consolidate their finance and improve the standard of their accommodation whist doing so by moving north. The further north (or generally away from London), the wider the price gap, with the notable exception of the South West. Holiday homes also started to become a much sought after investment as the middle class expanded and became more affluent.

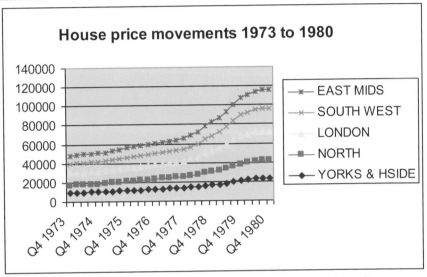

Fig 6.3 The relative rate of escalation in property values in different regions over the period 1973 to 1980

The expansion of home, and other property, ownership spawned another revolutionary idea, equity release. The ability to release the equity value in one's home without having to move or make monthly payments meant that a private income could be generated or capital could be available for repairs or alterations, particularly, and specifically for the more 'mature' home owner.

There is a huge misunderstanding as to what comprises an Equity Release scheme. So here is a pocket guide.

The generic term 'equity release' merely means taking capital out of the property value in order to utilise it for another purpose. The ways that can be achieved is broadly under three headings: A Lifetime Mortgage, a Home Reversion scheme, or an Equity Release scheme.

1.   A Lifetime Mortgage

This is a mortgage for the over 60s, sometimes older ages, dependent upon the lender. Anything up to 75% of the value of the house, subject to there being no other mortgage, or any other mortgage being repaid, can be taken up on a fresh Lifetime Mortgage with interest only being paid to the lender until the death of the owners of the property (the mortgagees), sale, or downsizing following which, the house would be sold, the debt repaid and any balance would be paid to the borrowers or the beneficiaries.

Interest rates vary, but they are normally at the market rate, currently they would be around 7%, and the interest would be payable monthly.

This type of release programme might be used where there is existing debt, even credit card debt, or loans at exorbitant rates of interest where an older couple have got themselves into a little bit of a financial mess where cash flow is a problem but income is not.

A Lifetime Mortgage can be used to consolidate the debt at a lower interest rate, therefore, far lower monthly payments would ensue, which fits in with the income that is available to the mortgagees and, voila, a problem is solved. That is precisely what Bill and Mary did. The exercise saved them expenditure of the order of £500 per month, which they then had available to spend on other things; with first consideration being themselves.

2.   A Home Reversion Plan

A Home Reversion Plan, quite simply; is when you sell all or part of your property to a third party. They own that portion of the property and, therefore, also the equity that is in that part of the property.

It may also be that the agreement provides the underwriter of the schemes, normally a bank or pension fund, with an increased portion of the equity increase in the property in lieu of interest against a direct loan on the property. It is just another way of achieving the same thing. The risk is with the mortgagor because if the property value diminishes then the interest level that they achieve is negative. Similarly, if the market climbs very slowly their return would be not too great.

However, in a burgeoning market such as we have had over the five or six years ending in 2006, the short term aspects of that type of mortgage can be very beneficial to the lender in the event of the house owners' early death and the reversion of the title to the property passing to the underwriter.

Over a normal valuation period, say 20 years, the whole thing should balance out into a more acceptable mean return that is in line with market interest rates. It can often only be carried out once, although there are schemes which allow top ups, which are now not always available in the marketplace because the underwriter has to anticipate a rising market in order to get a return.

The home owner on the other hand usually retains a larger proportion of the house value with no repayment necessary than would otherwise be available under an Equity Release schemes, as described next.

3.   Equity Release Schemes

Equity release is merely a mortgage provided by an specialist lender where the interest is declared at usually a fixed rate and the cumulative interest rolls up over the period of the mortgage, usually, until the owner or owners have died and then the property is sold, and the initial loan plus the rolled up interest is repaid and any balance of value falls to the residual estate of the owner(s).

It is usual to find Equity Release and Home Reversion schemes are used by individuals who have a need for capital but have insufficient income to pay interest, or the property owner needs income or capital to invest to produce that income, or a mixture of the two.

Helen and Len, Marjorie on her own, and Mary (well into her eighties) all needed not only cash for repairs for the house but a significant income lift to make ends meet. All benefited from these types of schemes. It is the significantly higher amount of capital released from Home Reversion and Equity Release mortgage schemes that makes them attractive at any particular point in time.

The graph, below, has been shown a number of times in the O'Halloran Gazette, and we regularly use it in reports, but it does give a fairly clear indication of the normal pattern for domestic house values over time in real terms.

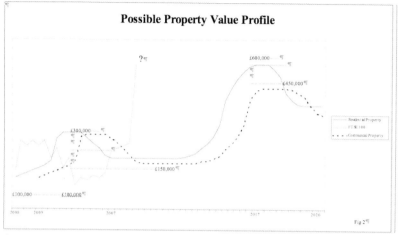

Fig 6.4

Using the Rule of 72, one knows that at 7.2% per annum interest rate the capital value of the principle would double over a 10-year period ($72 \div 7.2 = 10$).

Similarly, at 6% it would take 12 years ($72 \div 6 = 12$) to double the principle.

Therefore, taking the recent past, a £100,000 property has, say, doubled in value to £200,000, and let us assume the home owner can extract 35% value from the house. That is £70,000 capital that can be uplifted. At 7.2% interest rate that £70,000 loan will accumulate interest and become a £140,000 debt against the property in 10 years time.

However, even if the property price collapses by, say, 30%, the residual value would be £140,000. Therefore if the market does not increase during the whole of that period of time, then the beneficiaries will get nothing because the debt and the property value would equal each other. At no time can the debt be more than the residual value of the property.

We would expect the value of the property in 10 years time to be double, or at least start moving that way, therefore, the £140,000 property becomes a £280,000 property with a £140,000 debt against it and beneficiaries have something to share. Once again 'timing' plays an important part in producing a balanced return for the lender and property owner alike, over time.

The residual value available to any beneficiaries of the estate of the deceased property owner will vary over time as property values ebb and flow.

The same graph shows that Home Reversion schemes will deliver a varying amount of capital to the underwriters, and they would hope to achieve a broad rate of return that would equate to 6% or 7% per annum interest rate.

Each type of equity release scheme has its day.

The forgoing resume is not extensive however, in summary, there are three main types of mortgage for more mature people to extract capital from their property, and one does need to consider which is the most appropriate at any particular point in time.

That decision will vary from one point in time to another dependent upon the variables that I have described and in particular, from a lender's perspective whether the facility is being offered in prospect of a rising or falling property market, in order for a commercial return to be achieved.

Even providers get the timing wrong by ignoring the fundamentals. Out of interest, does inflation have an effect on the property markets?

Inflation 1973 to 1980:

1973	1974	1975	1976	1977	1978	1979	1980
10.6	19.1	24.9	15.1	12.1	8.4	17.2	15.1

See how the effects of inflation, particularly outside of greater London, can give the impression of a flat property market from the mid 1970s. The 'real' value of property north of Watford fell dramatically.

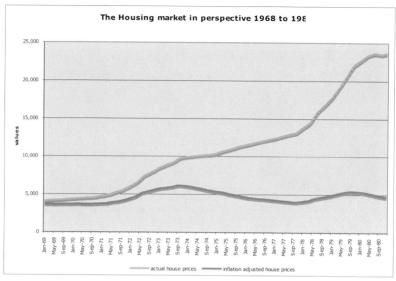

Fig 6.5 Actual property, compared to inflation adjusted, prices

Commercial property showed a physical reduction in 'street' values. Few buyers were in evidence as the cost of borrowing and an acute oversupply of bricks and mortar, reined in the buying and building spree that had resulted in a world shortage of plasterboard!

Property auctions, normally expensive to run in a seller's market, became the order of the day with ever dwindling interest in what was being sold.

Interest rates and inflation had both reached double digits and by 1975 the rate of inflation peaked at 24.9% per annum. House prices froze at best and dropped 20% to 30% in real value at worst over the ensuing years.

Commercial property sales stagnated. Bankruptcies and liquidations increased as banks worked hard to restore their liquidity by revoking overdraft facilities. After all, if the banks had insufficient assets to match their £7.14 to £100 liabilities they themselves would have to stop trading. Some of the smaller commercial banks did cease trading.

What had happened between 1969 and 1979/80 was a prime example of a *classic market* in operation.

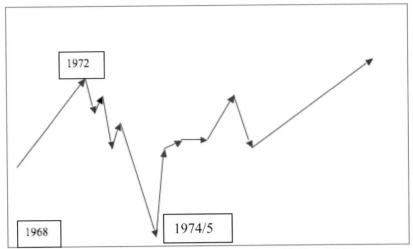

Fig 6.6 a consolidated overview of the markets 1968 to 1982

How does the foregoing help you today?

Because of the high levels of inflation the graphs are not as explicit as they might be.

Perhaps if we look at the graph at Fig 6.5, in order to get the housing market in perspective when considering the period 1968 to 1982 we can get an impression of the real value of property prices and how inflation actually devalued what was a very significant upward trend in actual house prices in the marketplace. 1975 is clearly represented with house prices moving ahead at probably 10% per annum and inflation at 24.6%.

The market is, therefore, distorted somewhat but the real clincher is the fall in house prices from 1978, 1979 through 1980 because inflation had started to ease off by this stage and the stock market can clearly be seen to have levelled off and then fallen before starting to rise again towards the end of 1981 and into 1982.

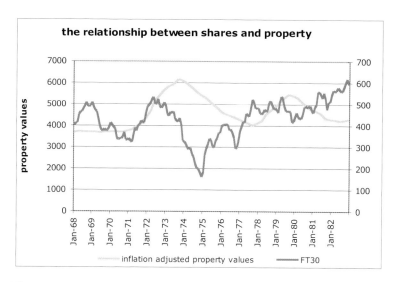

Fig 6.7
Graph showing interaction of the above table in 'real' terms.

That relationship is clearly shown in the graphic above, Figure 6.7. That period marked the end of my first experience of a *classic market*.

It was felt that this graph should be included for comparison with the other two graphics just to allow you to draw your own conclusions. Are the figures being fudged? Is there some relationship that can be picked up later in the book? We shall see. One just has to hope that we never see inflation in the UK quite like that again.

CHAPTER 7

THE DIFFERENT STATEGIES FOR INVESTMENT AND SAVING

Charles ended up cheering. You will remember the concerns that he had when the stock market collapsed in 1974 taking his savings with it.

His tears of despair in 1974 turned to tears of joy by 1980 because the stock market grew in value to recover all of its losses and presented Charles with a fine return for his diligence. By the mid 1980s the situation for Charles would have been even better as the share values that his unitised fund was invested in moved ever upwards towards their 1987 peak..

The savings strategy known as *pound cost averaging* exemplified the value of the saving ethos that he had adopted, albeit by accident rather than design.

Charles may not have known that he had adopted such a 'strategic plan' for the future. He had £50 per month spare in 1969 and merely put it away, by way of a standing order, and latterly direct debit, as a means of financial storage for his retirement – 'savings' in order to supplement his pension. Luck played a huge part, but, arguably, so did the emotional motivation of the marketplace.

How does 'the marketplace' work?

If we roll the time frames forward we will find the same parallels working as the emotional guide between:

GREED

FEAR

and   GRIEF

These three elements not only take their place in the hearts and minds of the investing public; but, they are also to be found in the dynamics of institutional fund management.

The terms are used in the most benevolent way to highlight how we, as human beings, work where savings and investment are concerned. Sometimes a strategy pays off. Other excursions into the financial markets fail spectacularly. Timing is the key, every time.

If history is used purposefully to develop a strategy then every one wins.

Gerry and Linda wanted a house and a home. The house proved to be a worthy investment: the home, a deliberately thought through meeting of minds and scarce resources. Gerry and Linda **invested** into an **upturn** in the property market.

Charles wanted security for the future; yet he chose a volatile and risky route to get there, his timing, unbeknown to him, was perfect. Charles bought into a market **downturn** through regular **savings**.

Year	Bank Rate	Long term gilt yield	RPI in year	
1970	7.00	9.3	7.9	*Base*
1971	5.00	8.3	9.0	*Rate*
1972	9.00	9.6	7.7	*Analysis*
1973	13.00	11.9	10.6	
1974	11.50	17.0	19.1	
1975	11.25	14.8	24.9	
1976	14.25	15.0	15.1	
1977	7.00	10.9	12.1	
1978	12.50	13.2	8.4	
1979	17.00	14.7	17.2	
1980	14.00	13.9	15.1	
1981	14.50	15.8	12.0	
1982	10.00	11.1	5.4	
1983	9.00	10.5	5.3	
1984	9.50	10.6	4.6	
1985	11.50	10.5	5.7	
1986	11.00	10.5	3.7	
1987	8.50	9.5	3.7	
1988	12.00	9.3	6.8	
1989	15.00	10.0	7.7	
1990	14.00	10.6	9.3	
1991	10.50	9.8	4.5	
1992	7.00	8.7	2.6	
1993	5.50	6.4	1.9	
1994	6.25	8.6	2.9	
1995	6.50	7.6	3.2	
1996	6.00	7.6	2.5	
1997	7.25	6.3	3.6	
1998	6.25	4.4	2.8	
1999	5.50	5.3	1.5	
2000	5.88	4.7	3	
2001	4.96	5.0	1.8	
2002	4.96	4.4	1.7	
2003	3.67	4.7	2.9	
2004	4.375	4.5	3	
2005	4.5	4.1	2.8	
2006	4.875	4.7	3.2	
2007	5.5	4.5	4.3	
2008	3.95	3.4	4	
2009	1	4.2	-0.5	
2010	0.5		3.4	

Source: Barclays' Capital

31-Dec	EQUITY FUND INDEX	INDEX RETURN %
1973	1382	-28.1
1974	690	-50.1
1975	1719	149.3
1976	1759	2.3
1977	2614	48.6
1978	2839	8.6
1979	3165	11.5
1980	4268	34.8
1981	4846	13.6
1982	6227	28.5
1983	8019	28.8
1984	10552	31.6
1985	12680	20.2
1986	16139	27.3
1987	17536	8.7
1988	19552	11.5
1989	26498	35.5
1990	23947	-9.6
1991	28936	20.8
1992	34672	19.8
1993	44207	27.5

Statistics can lie. Well, not exactly lie, but certainly mislead.

You have to know the truth to be able to lie, to deliberately mislead; but statistics by their very nature know the truth, it is just whether that truth is displayed in the correct, or should I more accurately state, appropriate manner or not, and that is in the hands of individuals responsible for the data's compilation and display. Believe it or not, the individuals handling the data may not know that they are misleading those that they are presenting the data to. How so?

You might well ask.

I am sure that in the 1980s Target Life would not have wished to mislead anyone with their advertising campaign. Advertisements for the Target Life Pension Equity fund illustrated the exceptional growth that took place within their equity fund. It was genuine. The advertisements were merely displaying the performance of the equity fund without perhaps drawing attention to the fact that a large proportion of the Target Life Pension Equity Fund was eventually, because of the share growth of that one stock, invested in one company that was performing incredibly well; Polypeck.

You may remember Polypeck? North Cyprus? Fruit Importer?

The company, 'Polypeck', went into liquidation and Target Life stopped advertising as their performance figures went into reverse.

The managing director and principle shareholder of Polypeck has just returned to the UK for his trial.

We, you and I, need to be more in tune with regard to statistics and their ability to mislead us as individuals. The crucial element stems from when data is assembled, i.e. over what period and with what spaces in between datum points: is it a daily grid, a weekly, monthly, or annual grid. Is the data taken over a period of one year, two year, five year, ten year, or a longer twenty year period? That is the sort of thing to establish.

Just refer back to 1987, October 19th; where does the annual statistic give you a clue to the real volatility of performance in that year?

Please, keep reading, this is where it gets really interesting. "Oh look more graphs", I hear you cry. Please; just look at the lines or study the data.

Some people like lists of numbers and can understand the list in much the same way as some of us like to see data in pictorial form.

I would like to think that the end product is broadly the same in the way the figures affect how you feel about the data and how it might relate to your own circumstances. We become emotionally involved with the numbers; unwittingly, of course.

The period 1985 to 1988 is a classic case in point. 1987 is the central area that I wish to concentrate on for this example and if we take annual data, just annual data, in other words the 31st December for each year 1985, 1986, 1987, 1988 and 1989, the graph created is shown as Figure 7.1 and is a tad outside a straight upward moving line and depicts a market without problems.

That illusion is created because the stock market in 1987 ended up with the FTSE 100 index higher at December 31st than it was on January 1st 1987. A 'cautious to balanced' investor might be tempted to invest in such an index.

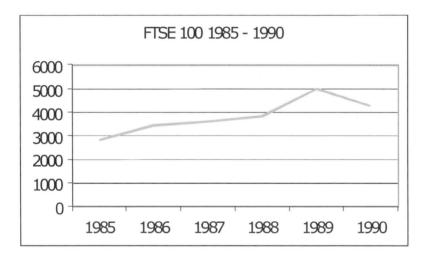

Fig 7.1 Year on year data 1985 to 1990 FTSE 100

If we now create the same data but on a monthly basis, you can perhaps start to appreciate the point that I am endeavouring to make.

Now we can see some quite perturbing 'lumps and bumps' and these would certainly start to raise some questions in the investor's mind as to whether the potential returns were going to be within that 'cautious to balanced' range or would they be more towards a 'balanced to high' risk expectation

The 1980s presented a *classic market* with a 'soft centre'. The volatility depicted in extreme graphic representation that is presented from 1997 through to 2009 and also the 1969 to 1980 period are harsh by comparison. Nevertheless the general pattern still pertains for this less volatile period between 1982 and 1996.

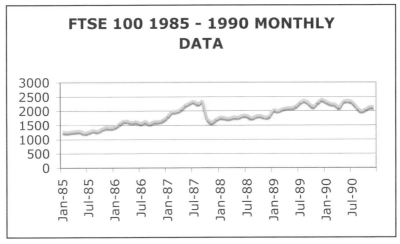

Fig 7.2 Monthly data 1985 to 1990 FTSE 100

Jan-87	Feb-87	Mar-87	Apr-87	May-87	Jun-87
1808.2	**1979.2**	**1997.5**	**2050.5**	**2203**	**2284.1**
Jul-87	Aug-87	Sep-87	Oct-87	Nov-87	Dec-87
2360.9	**2249.7**	**2366**	**1749.8**	**1579.9**	**1712.7**

Table 7.2

The daily data would help to illustrate the feeling of complete desolation felt by many as the stock market lost 30% of its value in just a few days. (see Fig 7.3 on the following page)

October 19th 1987 was certainly a day for most of us in financial management to remember.

I, and my colleagues were managing a portfolio of unitised funds referred to as a 'Broker Fund' at the time. Fig 7.3 is one of my crude slides of the time. How technology has advanced.

In the June of 1987 we had moved our client investment portfolio out of equities completely; anticipating a correction in the world stock markets. We moved into fixed interest and cash, a poor choice with hindsight. Perceived security and guaranteed returns

drove that decision. That was the point at which we should have
moved into the property fund.

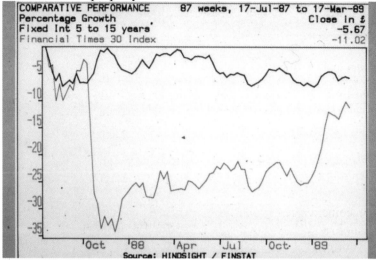

Fig 7.3 Daily figures from 1987 and the crash.

Investment success is all about timing, and whilst the wrong
decision might not be a disaster, it can delay a rally in one's
fortunes or the continuation of reasonable returns on investments.

Our monthly performance dipped and our investors immediately
sought to complain that the stock markets were rising in value
and our funds were doing anything but. We were failing in our
task of keeping up with the growth in stock market values, even
though we were managing a managed (diverse market) fund.

By early September peer pressure had pushed us back into the
equity market and by October 20th the damage was inextricably
done.

A valuable lesson had been learnt. 'Don't let your heart rule
your head', but of course, it often does. Do not let others dictate
to you to do what you know is wrong. We should have known
what was going to happen, indeed, arguably, we did know that
was why we came out of the equity market in June 1987.

We should have been in property. Look at the *classic market*
profile. The insight is there if we had merely had the courage,
and perhaps the 30 years experience to observe it.

We discovered the sequel, the second phase of the *Classic market* the hard way as well. Just have a look at the property market on the graph. The signs are all there to tell the informed investor exactly what is going to happen with the equity markets and latterly the property fund that our clients were invested in.

By 1991 the banks, and other financial institutions would bring the property and equity markets down. It was at this point that my clarity of vision concerning the inter relationship between the stock market and the market value of property really took shape. Statisticians and financial writers up to this point in history (2010) have ignored, or failed to realise the correlation between these two asset classes to the investors' detriment.

The coincidence of property growth in value and its eventual collapse and the relationship with the timing of the downward movement of the stock market is well documented, if we look at the statistics, yet few observers, writers or analysts seem to connect the two, in terms of a growth continuum.

Given market conditions where was a good place to run after the stock market had fallen apart in 1987? Property was bounding ahead, and we were in the 'secure' embrace of Gilts and fixed interest funds.

The actual answer was 'switch into property funds dealing in real property (not property company shares) rather than a panic "let's get out of here before it goes down even further, or, where can we find security?"

Property was bounding ahead with commercial property funds increasing in value at a good steady rate, and it had done so for a few years. We delayed that move into property rather too long. Instinct in 1989/90 was, 'go there; catch the upside (it cost nothing to move as the investment vehicle was a Broker Fund) and all will be well'.

By 1990 all was not well at all. Certainly the property fund had moved upward and risen in value quite dramatically but now the property market had stalled and a twelve-month moratorium had been imposed on the property funds that contained our fund's investment money. Why the moratorium? Because everybody wanted to be out of property funds and property just cannot be liquidated to accommodate the process of repayment of invested money quickly enough. There was a lack of liquidity.

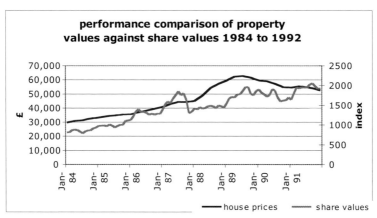

Fig 7.4

We, and our investors, just had to stay put and 'sit it out'.

Reading the markets is not that easy. Fund Managers have to give the impression of being 'at ease' in order to create and maintain trust and I do not doubt that we, as fund or portfolio managers, generally feel 'at ease' most of the time. The dis-ease comes when the fund manager, and it may have been me, gets it wrong. In 1987 it was, in hindsight, so easy to get it wrong.

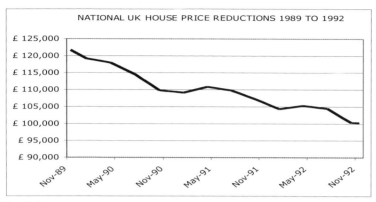

Fig 7.5

The Thursday before black Monday (19th October 1987) I was returning from a very successful presentation as a respected and well thought of Broker Fund Manager; from The Moat House hotel, Telford. Our re-entry into the stock market had been heralded as a brilliant move and investments were once more starting to flow into our funds. The journey home was uncomfortable, but only because of the wind and rain buffeting the car.

Friday morning was 'mayhem'. A hurricane swept across the south of England bringing down trees and with them telephone lines. One of our Broker Fund providers was NEL (National Employers Life) a small boutique company in Dorking. Our phone calls only raised the caretaker whose words still ring in my ears as we tried to relieve ourselves of already plunging equity market stock:

> "No-body here mate. All the trees is down across the drive. Nobody can git in!"

If nobody could "git in" then nobody could do any deals and that meant that we were stuck in the equity funds, not only for the weekend, but as far as any fund dealing was concerned, probably a lot longer because nobody from the dealing department could "git in" for quite a few days.

Consequently we could not get our investors out of the equity funds, we just looked on as helpless spectators. As far as

Scottish Mutual, our other carrier, was concerned they had similarly been caught.

Everybody wanted to shift out of equities at the same time and the dealing rooms in London and Edinburgh were in total disarray with a large proportion of their staff unable to make the journey in to the City of London because of the disruption with road and rail transport. In financial terms it was a 'bloodbath'.

The market dropped 30% in 24 hours and there was nothing that most people could do about it.

If you were investing from 1998 onwards could you have used past statistics to indicate what might happen?

Well; you could, provided you looked at the right statistics. If you merely looked at annualised figures showing December 31st each year, you would probably not have picked up on the disaster that occurred in October of 1987 or the magnitude of the disruption.

If however you had used the monthly figures taken at the end of each month you may well have picked up on the disturbance.

With weekly figures, you would most certainly have been aware of the speed with which the market collapsed and if, as you can now observe from the historic data that you might compare to the figures from the 70's and late 80's, or overlaid the graphic with residential property details, you might also have known, had you been invested in equities, where to go for safety, and how long to stay there.

Once again the value of timing had presented itself as the all-important criteria.

Chapter 8

THE IMPORTANCE OF TIMING PROPERTY TRANSACTIONS.

Is there a good time to 'buy' and is there a good time to 'sell' as far as actual property is concerned? The purchase of a home, a 'buy to let', an office or factory space can all be timed to advantage using *classic market* principles.

"Boom market periods will go on for ever, is the common perception; after all, you cannot lose money on property". So went the modern fallacy that accompanied the late 80s and probably every other Property boom in history.

The alternative observation that I would like to consider works along the lines of, "the property market is stable at present therefore it really does not matter whether you rent or buy."

Somewhere between these two extremes of emotion lies the truth and there is no better way of exemplifying that truth than considering what actually happens in peoples' lives. Gwen isn't a 'make believe person' she is a real widow. She became a widow at a relatively early age.

Gwen lived in a village, in a very nice house with all sorts of development potential, some of which had been partially exploited by converting a barn into 'part commercial' and 'part residential' property.

The first phase of her rehabilitation was to finish the conversion of the second half of the barn into a fully-fledged semi-detached residential property, which, after separating the title deeds, was subsequently sold.

Within two years it became very apparent that Gwen's future lay a good five hour journey south of where she lived and therefore the sale of her main property, together with the other half of the converted barn, had to be committed to the market place. The

95

timing of her <u>need</u> to sell was close enough to 1992 to create concerns in Gwen's mind. It was less than 10 years prior to her husband's death.

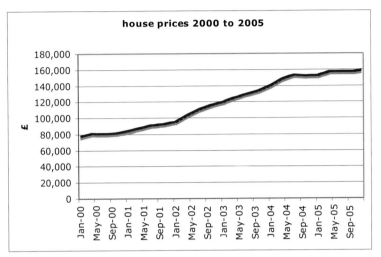

Fig 8.1 Graphic of property value movements. 2000 - 2005

If we refer to the graphic representations that run throughout this book, we can establish that in 2000 the property market was developing 'a head of steam' and a good price could perhaps be achieved for the two properties if they were sold independently of each other. The money from the sale could then be invested in a replacement property 'down south'. That was the theory: what was the practice?

Gwen was fortunate because the timing of her circumstances, coupled with the financial security provided by her husband's life assurance enabled her to do what she wanted, or to feel comfortable doing what she wanted, when she wanted. The property market valuations had been rising, but the stock market had fallen, rapidly.

Properties were selling, although prices were faltering at the stage that Gwen made her decision to sell (2002/3). There were some concerns that perhaps the market had peaked. The truth is that it had peaked on its initial rally, but it had some way to go on its second. It was the stock market that was unstable and that factor was adversely influencing the perceived relevant values regarding house prices.

96

At this point we also recall that the subliminal reference point in the property slump of 1991 to 1993 was that it was accompanied by the collapse of the Bank of Credit and Commerce.

The property had been valued on her husband's death. The numbers that were written on a piece of paper amounted to £450,000 and two years later, Gwen had to decide whether to 'let' the property (rent it out to third parties) and hope that she would have a continuing tenant who would produce a reasonable return on the capital value of her erstwhile home, or sell. The options for selling created difficult decisions as well because of different points regarding the process to achieve a sale, one might use different strategies:

Should Gwen:

a) Sell through an agent and wait for the right person to come along and buy from Gwen at the right price? And would she achieve a good price using that strategy?

b) Should Gwen go to auction with the property? Then at least a reserve could be set and if the bids were in the right price range on the day she would either get what she was asking, or a little bit more maybe, or, the property would be withdrawn because it failed to meet its reserve. Gwen would incur costs that might prove to be unnecessary.

c) A relatively new introduction to the English market was the "closed tenders" mechanism that seemed to find favour, or at least become a temporary fad in the early/mid-year 2004/2005. This was an interesting mechanism - a 'half way' house between an auction and a direct purchase. There would be an inherent commitment on behalf of the person placing the tender, and of course, the most appropriate tender submitted by the closing date and time would achieve the purchase. Once again the house would be sold: or not, if no tenders at the appropriate amount were forthcoming.

With the market in the ascendancy and a relatively good flow of enquiries regarding the house emanating from the local estate agent Gwen followed the advice of a local Chartered Surveyor;

Gwen put the property on sale in the open market. As we know the semi-detached barn properties were the first to be sold; they were more modern, up to date, and so on.

The main house was a large family house and well established. This kind of property situated in the countryside tends to have a very specialised market and therefore potential purchasers are a little less frequent, yet more discerning, however a buyer came along and the sale was completed, but not without that element of concern that has already been mentioned.

Had Gwen elected to sell the property some two years later, the situation would have been entirely different; indeed an auction may well have been the main chance of achieving <u>any</u> price. In the event roving purchasers had all but dried up. Deals were being "looked at" closely by purchasers; it had the appearance of a buyer's market rather than a seller's market. This was not a market for the 'faint at heart'. Even rented accommodation was feeling the cooling affects of a 'market in retreat'.

Gwen was fortunate in more than one respect because with the market cooling and with speculative builders reducing their workforce, a lot of proficient tradesmen were thrown back onto the job market to do jobs at a more competitive price, and 'turn up' to do them, for private customers.

In that regard then Gwen was able to benefit twice, once from the rising market and the sale of the property in good market conditions in the midlands and second, the building of her new house and fitting it out in the south of England. Good hourly rates were available and of course discounts were also the order of the day on the fixtures and fittings.

Timing, it seems, is everything. So, how does one deal with a market that has 'topped out'?

Mike & Val were selling in 2006 and they were looking to move to the Midlands. Their stated objective was to buy a property as soon as possible in their new location. They were having problems selling the house that they had in Eastern England and they were moving into a more expensive area in the central midlands.

The market had only just started to cool. How could they entice a buyer and yet still purchase a more expensive property? In the long run they could be flexible. The strategy suggested was quite straightforward:

a) Reflect on the 'top' market value that had been achieved between 2004 and 2006, discount that property value by 20% and put their current property on the market at that price. The caveat to the prospective purchaser was that they had to complete the exchange of contracts within four weeks to achieve the substantial discount that was "only being offered because Mike & Val needed a prompt sale".

b) The next stage was to move into **rented** accommodation. The object? To stay in rented accommodation for between one and four years (I will explain later). Place the capital realised from the sale on deposit so as to achieve a reasonable rate of return and for the capital to be available when the property of their dreams came along at an appropriate discounted price.

c) An alternative to waiting 'too long' was to get involved in the excitement of 'repossession' auctions, taking time and trouble to assess the properties available and possibly take advantage of the huge discounts as the number of people attending auctions 'tailed off' and the number of properties being auctioned rose (an eighteen months to two years 'window' of opportunity should exist, probably in 2009/10).

Mike & Val took the advice. They discounted their property by 20% and had sold it within three months, despite a very difficult market. It is worth noting the contrast to most other sellers of property who insisted in holding on to their perceived market price.

The money from the sale was put on deposit and was accessible. A superb rented accommodation was found in their proposed new location, Mike and Val moved in. The interest earned by the capital paid the rent on that property.

Sure enough twelve to eighteen months later (2008) bank repossession and property auctions were in full swing. Many people were having problems with their mortgage repayments, particularly on 'buy to let' properties and reasonably 'silly' offers were actually being accepted. Mike and Val were cash buyers.

Mike & Val now live in their own property, which, as forecast, had discounted even further than they had discounted their original east of England property sale price. There was no need for them to take out the mortgage that they had expected to have to take up, the 'new' property in the midlands was reduced in value and fell within their cash budget.

The plan worked a treat. Timing was, and remains, important. In fact, it was essential. But more important than timing, was the commitment to take the chance to do what was necessary. If the move is made too soon or it is left too late to make the move, then the opportunity can well turn into a disaster.

A constant reappraisal of the market circumstances has to be engaged in. That premise applies to every market in every case.

In order to do ultimate justice to the situations that arise out of a variety of circumstances, then you might like to consider someone who not only got the timing wrong once, but managed it twice, to illustrate the downside risk and the penalty of poor timing.

When the disaster was linked up with personal health problems and a redundancy, the world of the couple concerned could well have fallen apart.

Brian and Julie were newlyweds in 1989. They had just moved into the East Midlands determined to purchase a home to cement their new circumstances. House prices were booming; they really couldn't go wrong. They bought a 3-bedroom house on a new estate just at the turn of 1990 for the princely sum of £120,000. The mortgage lender had provided a 100% loan over 25 years to help them set up their new home.

Within 18 months Brian and Julie were £30,000 in negative equity.

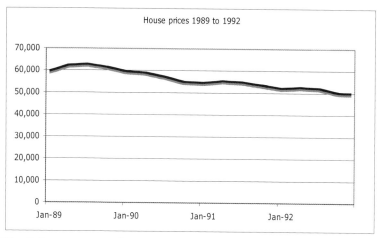

Fig 8.2 property price movements 1989 to 1992

They eventually sold their home, delivering a loss of £32,000 (that is £32,000 less than their mortgage) after three years of the house being on the market and having moved out of that property two years earlier because the journey to Brian's new job was just too far away to justify the cash flow cost of travel.

1992 heralded the collapse of the U K property market.

The 1992/3 values dropped by 20% to 30% against the 'top of the market' values. Brian and Julie found themselves extremely disadvantaged as they endeavoured to move nearer to Brian's place of work 40 miles or more to the north. As was stated; the negative equity on the home that they were obliged to sell amounted to £32,000. In other words: when the house was eventually sold Brian and Julie still owed the provider of their original mortgage £32000.

They were fortunate in moving from a relatively expensive area to a cheaper area. However, moving into rented accommodation left a 'bitter taste'. But should it have done? Their circumstances left them with little choice in the matter, but, did they make their situation any worse?

It is worth reflecting on the definition of rent and interest. Just what is the difference between rent and interest?

They are both amounts of money paid to a third party for no particular gain other than the ability to live in a property to which either the lease or a mortgage is attached.

If you can separate the environment from the rent and interest payments, then it is the environment, in other words; what happens to the property or what you can do concerning the property that varies. I would contend that: in a property market that is slowing down, rent and interest are virtually synonymous, and rent can be a preferred medium.

Eventually the mortgage outstanding on the Peterborough property was repaid and by this time, around the year 2000, a bungalow way out in the country had been found and purchased and the couple settled down to their new life. Ten years on Brian and Julie started in the housing market again.

Brian's high paying job and Julie's higher than average salary, with bonuses, got them back 'on an even keel'. They even saved some money for a deposit on their new house 'in the country'. Life was great. They settled down, and had a baby.

By the time the child, Mark, was 4 or 5, they were running him backwards and forwards, every weekday, to his new school 22 miles away in Lincoln. It was now 2002 and the ideal house 'came up', near Lincoln, at the right price to allow a move. The 'new' property was a family home that just needed 'a bit of underpinning', it had suffered from subsidence, but it was 'cheap' at £230,000. When the work was completed the house would be worth 'double' or maybe 'triple' what they paid for it.

The country property, a bungalow, had sold well, at a good price, within a matter of weeks of it being placed on the market.

We have already discussed the fact that the stock market was collapsing throughout 2002 and 2003 and that created some problems in the commodities market, the focal point of Brian's income. There were changes in his employer's circumstances and the knock on effect created worry.

As often happens in these situations the way out of the plan was far removed from that envisaged. Brian and Julie's game plan was to buy the property with a subsidence problem in a rising market, 'cheap'. They achieved that.

The next step was to 'fix' the subsidence problem, add value to the property, which in turn would add to the resale value (in a rising market) which would restock the coffers and allow the mortgage amount to be reduced on the purchase of a fresh property, in a good area, to be their longer term 'family home'. The period during which this took place was 2002 – 2004.

To cut a very long story short, the whole saga could well have ended in a complete disaster because when the house went on sale, with only one income coming into the house because of illness (another 'unforeseen' complication) house prices had overshot their maximum (2005-2006) and the market was slowing considerably. Property values were tracking down, and purchase timings had moved from 3 weeks (no sale board) to 3 years (and include everything that could be included).

The one redeeming feature of the problem property was, and remains, that it is in a desirable village location that demands a premium, at every point in the market cycle, well, almost every point. By the time the four-year selling period had elapsed (2004 to 2008) the surrounding property values had escalated sufficiently to leave a very desirable residence at a very acceptable, discounted, price.

By 2008 the negative equity barrier to a long life of unhappiness nearly caught the couple again. I am pleased to relate that the decline in property values did not catch them completely the second time, they sold on the cusp, to a buyer seeking 'a bargain' which released Brian and Julie with a sale receipt of £380,000 which included the mortgage, which they skilfully transferred to their new purchase.

Brian and Julie had spent £100,000 plus on the property with the subsidence defect. You can add the figures up. They did not "double their money" as they thought they might, however, market timing, or luck, which allowed them to sell when they eventually did, is the reason for their experience being entered here. They purchased a fresh property and have a reduced mortgage of 70% loan to value.

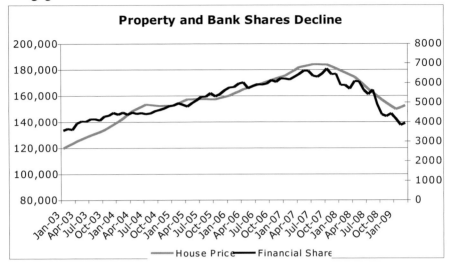

Fig 8.3 Property values (left axis) compared with share values (right axis) source: Nationwide B.Soc. and FTSE100 data

All of the foregoing, genuine case histories should be a lesson or two, well learnt, for us all.

How does an individual know when the housing market is topping out? There are well known and established tell tale signals such as those that follow. The typical property pattern appears to be:

Stage 1. Approaching the summit. 2-3 weeks to sell – hardly time to put boards up – 3 to 6 months (no agent) own boards.
  a) Valuation/prices moving upward by x% per month.
  b) Completion –is quick and mortgage money freely available
  c) Gazumping is rife.
  d) New developer houses – no extras – the house, that's it.

Stage 2. On the Plateau
   a) New developer houses
        introduce free 'legals'+ white goods+ carpets
   b)Second-hand homes – 6 months to 2 years to sell (agents – tender – auction (difficult or specialised)

Stage 3. On the Down-slope
a) Developer – House exchange programmes

b) Second-hand homes – 12 months to 4 years (auction/tender)

Stage 4. In the Foothills
a)Developer – sites close/sites sell (knock down)
Everything including the 'kitchen sink' PLUS a discount (via the deposit) (auction) High discounts
b) Second-hand homes – 12 months to 4 years (auction–desperation) High discounts

Stage 5. The Bottom of the Market Rent. It is cheaper and safer.

Bide your time.

The time to sell, or move out of a commercial property fund to safety is around stage 3 at the latest, preferably, stage 2. Ease out of property funds, say, 20% at a time.

CHAPTER 9

DIVERTING YOUR SAVINGS TO THE GOVERNMENT'S COFFERS

If we believe that hindsight can give foresight from which to accomplish personal dreams - your dreams - then, as with anything, the theory and practice should be compatible in use.

Here is an example of how hindsight was, allegedly, used against you. Can that be possible?

In 1997, when the Labour government came to power, Gordon Brown the Chancellor of the Exchequer at the time said that he wanted to 'stimulate savings.' If that was so why then did he reduce the amount of money that savers (you) could put into tax free investments?

Very often one can discover that the voice says one thing but the body does something entirely different. The last thing Gordon Brown wanted you to do in 1997 or any subsequent period was for anyone to increase their savings or even to start to save. What Gordon Brown and his cohort desired, indeed needed, to accomplish their goals WAS your savings. That desire resulted in an entirely different dynamic. The resultant strategy would enable his government to spend.

If you want to know why pension funds still have a shortfall in 2010 look no further than Gordon Brown and the Labour government administration, coupled with Stakeholder pensions, a hangover from the previous administration.

Socialism works by undermining freedom and exerting control by using hard earned 'people' based funds to purportedly achieve public good, 'by the people and for the people'.

There is one thing UK residents love most and defend least, freedom, of either speech or action. Let us just have a look at the effect that the 1997-2010 Labour government had on savings and reflect on the two *'classic markets'* that we have already described in this book.

I will refer you back to the Invesco Perpetual graph that I use in my presentations to individual and corporate clients and talk you through the cycle as it has actually emerged.

The Labour administration in 1997 needed to change the way politics works in the United Kingdom, therefore financial reserves had to be identified and relieved of sufficient 'excess' in order to carry the long laid plans through.

The 'new' government had a plan. That plan has actually used your savings to give you the illusion that you were somehow getting something out of 'the system', where in fact you were losing control of virtually everything that you had ever put away, in part or whole "for the greater good."

Consider the fact that Civil Servants and many government employees (in particular the Police, Fire Brigade and Armed Forces) were, and still are, perceived to have "free pensions." They are all members of "pay as you go" schemes (in other words there is no fund for the future being built up.) This is different from the schemes relating to Teachers, National Health Service workers and local authority employees whose pensions come from the members and the employers contributing to an invested fund.

Midway through the administrations thirteen year tenure the government introduced the requirement for the members of the 'pay as you go' schemes to pay towards their pensions by way of personal contributions although previously the pension liability had been solely that of the employer, ie the government.

But did the employees actually contribute? Certainly the contributions were deducted from their pay, the question remains, was it actually the government still footing the bill? (for government read you and I).

Statistics show us that public sector pay rose by 6% per annum every year from 1997 whilst the private sector rose by a mere 3% per annum over the 1997 to 2007 period. In other words the government used your money, your savings, your tax, to pay higher wages to government employees so that those employees could be 'seen' to 'pay' for their pension benefits. 'Smoke and mirrors' come to mind.

Please, if you are a government employee, treat these comments as they are meant. The situation is not of your doing.

The result of that action was higher taxes and higher National Insurance rather than a meaningful contribution from public sector employees who, of course, pay tax and National Insurance on their earnings which goes back to paying their pensions which are 'index linked' in retirement. Fact always, it seems, gives way to perception. Deceit is the word that many may be looking for.

Consider a pension seminar in 2003 at the British Academy, which I attended. One of the presenters of learned papers was Baroness Hollis. At question time Baroness Hollis was asked; "where is the £31 billion surplus that is purported to be in the National Insurance fund?" (The National Insurance fund is the 'fund' which enables the State to pay old age pensions). Her reply was short in the extreme:

"You don't expect it to be in a deposit account do you?"

"Well yes ma'am; we do", was my response. Not that my response drew any attention, vocal though it was.

£31 billion is a lot of money. 31 thousand million is:

thirty-one billion, with twelve noughts: **£31,000,000,000,000.**

In 2010: a billion **seconds** ago was 1959

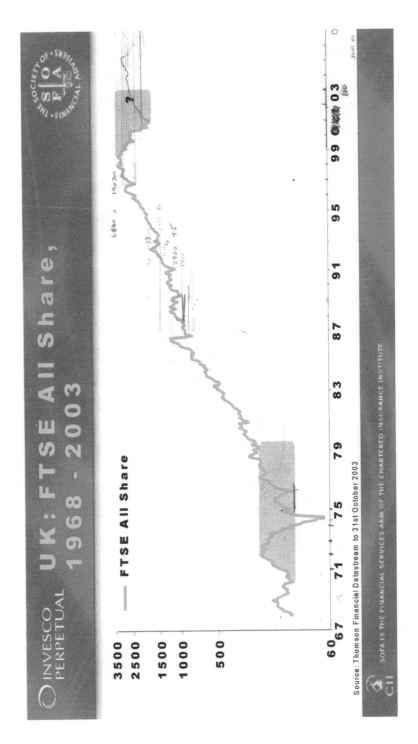

That should put a billion in perspective. One **billion pounds ago** was **thirteen hours and twelve minutes** the way the UK government of the day's administration was spending money in 2009. That too should put **things into perspective.**

£31 billion was a huge amount of money and incidentally the National Insurance fund provides for pensions, State Pensions in 2009 <u>was</u> in surplus and liable to stay in surplus for fourteen years at least; because, more was being 'paid in' than was being 'paid out.'

The UK state pension works on a 'pay as you go' system which means that the government has the excess money to 'play with', totally unaccountable, it seems, except for those in authority.

Baroness Hollis **confirmed that there <u>is</u> a surplus** and that it is somewhere: but, where? We were not informed? What we did ascertain was, and remains, that the money is not in a deposit account, obviously. Nor was the money in gilt edge securities attracting interest, which to my arithmetical mind, is where it should be.

The point that is being made here is that - if the government can predict, and make capital out of market cycles, then so can you. If they can observe their own inability to give you value for your savings, they have no right to criticise the private sector and manipulate it in the way that they have.

Just as the government has the possibility to use that 'cycle' *(the classic market)* as they appear to do, to create a market storm by feeding money through tax allowable instruments into the 'dot-com bubble' therefore could they utilise a three year duration 50% stock market crash that ended in March 2003 to redirect your saving into 'cheap' (for the government) gilt edge stock, (i.e. long dated government loans) at very low rates of interest?

This could well have been achieved in The Treasury's almost certain knowledge that the stock market would rise and that the capital value of pension funds would re-establish positive balance sheets for occupational schemes and thereby repair the damage. It is easy to forget the private sector pension miracle that, in 1998 for the first time in history, was paying out more money in benefits to a grateful public, than the State.

We can call the success of private pensions 'capitalism.' Whatever slant is adopted private pensions are your savings and when government undermines the value of shares it undermines the value of every commercial pension scheme; it undermines the value of the savings environment, and in so doing it is undermining what you have done to look after your future; and it does so with impunity.

In 2003 the 'Real Accounting' regime was introduced by the financial sector's regulator the Financial Services Authority under guidance, I suspect, from the Treasury (perhaps Gordon Brown).

Is there any good reason why the government would not take any notice of 'long term' gains that have the potential to be made in the recovery of the stock market, rather than use the weakness of the stock market in the short term to divert money held within institutional funds, your savings, to their own use by way of government loans? The Treasury may state that such loans (e.g. 5% treasury 2025) are guaranteed (aren't they?) and share values are not.

As it has turned out, government loans are only as good as the government that has the ability to service the interest payments on the loans and eventually repay them.

Government loans, gilt-edge investments (Gilts) are guaranteed, but, only at a pre determined date in the future (2025 in the example shown). Consider the volatility in the capital value of those gilts in the interim period. See Fig 9.2.

What actually happened, as far as one substantial source of personal savings was concerned, was that £7.4 billion (there is that-easy off the tongue 'billion' word again) of Standard Life's investment fund money was moved (sold and then reinvested) out of equities and into gilts without disturbing the market, a wonderful feat of financial management, over a period of ten months and during that ten months the stock market rocketed up by over 40%, interest rates rose and the capital value of the government's stock that money had been transferred to, reduced by 10%.

In simple terms in March 2003 if you would have had a billion pounds in a Pension Fund then ten months later had it stayed in equities, you would have had £1.4 billion, a £400 million gain. That same money transferred to gilts turned a £1,000 million fund into £900 million and made matters a lot worse under the new 'Real Accounting' rules.

Rolling the clock back a little further we witnessed an administration so intent on bringing money into the Treasury coffers as quickly as it could, that Gordon Brown's second most contemptuous, and at the time, talked about action (following the raid on pension funds) was undertaken; to sell the country's gold reserves, giving 6 months notice and arguably ensuring that the sale was completed at gold's lowest price for years.

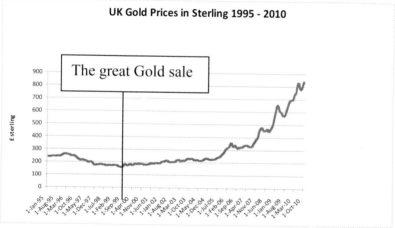

Fig 9.1

The sale of the UK gold reserves was such a contrast to the skill displayed by the fund managers at Standard Life Assurance cited above. Gold was circa $283 an ounce, over the six month period that gold was sold. The price of gold now, in 2010, is over $1,000 an ounce.

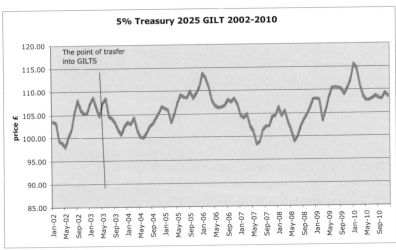

Fig 9.2

This Graph shows 5% Treasury 2025 gilt edge loan capital variation over time. In 2025 the gilt will be worth £100 at maturity.

The point of the transfer into gilts marks the enforced movement of institutional funds from shares into gilts.

This is not higher mathematics, this is fairly basic arithmetic. The savers lost even more of their investment's value and the government then had the use of those savers' capital. Clever.

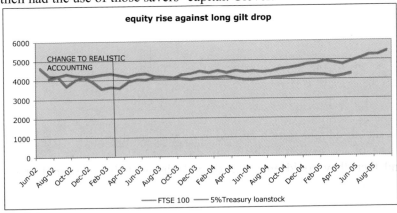

Fig 9.3

Who were the recipients of the gold largess? India, Russia, China?

Coincidence? Opportunism? Design? Your choice.

A friend in need is a friend indeed.

In 2004 the stock markets recovered to their 50% retracement levels, as expected.

In 2005 as the share and property markets moved upward the Labour government had every reason to be genuinely concerned. Having survived one election during the collapse of the stock market, but on the back of rising house prices (refer back to Fig 8.3) (70% of households in the UK are owned by their occupier), escalating house values would provide widely felt 'comfort' to voters.

Those in Government knew that if the housing market 'came off' the top too quickly with a general election in the offing, they would be in a difficult position.

As we know from reading the 1970s experience together with the historical data from the 1980s and early 1990s period: in the second phase of the *classic market* if the housing market collapses the stock market collapses with it.

If that situation predated the general election the incumbent Labour government would have a very difficult time getting re elected. If in doubt, gerrymander the markets. They would not stoop to such a thing, surely?

The key to the stock market collapse in the second phase of the *classic market* is always with the financial institutions. If the stock market collapse happened on Labour's watch, they would lose the General Election. There was already disquiet in the electorate. What the labour administration needed to do was get through that transient phase of the market without any disturbance from property values and then they could enter the crucial phase of their declared plan, which could answer their 1983 declaration of intent in their election manifesto of that year: to nationalise the banks.

Please remember that during this phase in the *classic market* the banks are flush with money and asset security. It is the peak of the bank's affluence and influence. The banks' senior management would be on a 'high' – "anything is possible" frame of mind. The AMRO Bank (RBS) and HBOS (Lloyds) acquisitions may be seen to prove the point.

The financial institutions would, at the point under discussion have a huge amount of mortgages on their books many of which would have substantial equity against market value on current valuations which the banks in particular can effectively use, by 'claiming' all of that equity to have a 'cash' equivalent, achieved by allocating a certain amount of the mortgage equity to reserves to support their solvency margins thereby allowing the banks to keep lending money.

The banks primarily make money from lending money.

With government's encouragement and lax regulation (a government Quango in charge of regulation) the banks started doing the most outrageous thing that has ever hit the British financial markets. The housing boom was starting to slow; builders were starting to offer 'free legals,' inclusive white goods or carpets, exchange deals, and other incentives to buy. The banks joined the perceived rally by offering 100% mortgages and in some cases (Northern Rock) 125% mortgages. HSBC were offering mortgages to 'you' plus 'three of your friends', others were offering six to eight times earnings (because interest rates were low?).

Commonsense and sound financial principles had been abandoned.

Just as President Clinton in the USA had done, to save his hide, in the early 90s so it was that the UK equivalent of Fanny Mae and Freddie Mac's strategy was adopted by British banking; lending mortgage money to those that simply could not afford the risks involved. Fortune favours the bold and understanding the market place carries the bold over the threshold and it certainly carried Labour into its third term of office.

Interest rates doubled between 2003 and 2008.

It was at this point that the spending really did start, but, by 2007 everything was starting to crumble. Interest rates had moved up as we have already noted therefore the capital value of gilts had moved down. Some very low coupon plus RPI index linked government loans were issued, again long dated; '0.⅝%' over twenty years plus inflation of course. The situation became almost surreal.

The government had taken on six hundred and eighty thousand new employees since 1997. There was no more room for non-jobs.

The 6% per annum pay increases to Civil Servants and government officials started to slow. Occupational pension schemes had all but ceased to exist other than in the public sector; their funds undermined by Government diktat.

Builders and developers were frantically trying to find ways of shifting their housing and even their land stock in order to reduce their debts with the banks. The banks were reassessing their overdraft levels back from 75% loan to value to 60% loan to value.

In the meantime the value of the underlying assets was dropping by half. All of the foregoing loss of value was foreseeable. Everything that happened, not withstanding the gerrymandering and diversionary tactics, was in line with normal market practice. It is commonly called 'indigestion' and it could have been controlled so easily, if tackled competently and early enough.

In 2010, a General Election year, it was interesting to see just what came to pass. I would state my reputation on a stock market that moves into high gear and moves forward on the back of climate change and 'cheap' green energy and the associated technologies that government is pouring money into, despite the fact that it cannot afford the expenditure (or is it investment). Either way, it is a future bubble inflating to eventually burst.

The property market will collapse back to 50% of its top market value for commercial property and at least 30% of the market high of 2005 and 2006 for residential property.

Those values will stay at their new levels, in real terms, for seven or eight years, London may prove to be an exception. Interest rates will have to rise from their 0.5% position in December 2010 and there is a very good chance that inflation will create the environment for that to be necessary.

Is there any relationship between how shares and bonds perform during a General Election year? Well, Ian Cowie, of *The Daily Telegraph*, (Apr 10 2010) thought that there was when he wrote the article that I have quoted from verbatim here:

"Election years tended to be good ones for shareholders, who enjoyed gains on more than two thirds of these occasions (elections), or 68% of the time. But bonds issued by the British Government –known as gilts – lost value in nine of the election years. (out of 17 considered)."

It is really quite interesting.

If we look at Figure 9.4 which is the graphic that I have been drawing for my clients ever since 1997 with minor modifications to the time scale of the *'classic market'* and you super impose it on the effect of 'political affiliation' in the stock market, you will probably find that the cycle takes account of most of it and politics all but none of it, other than the extension of the property peak.

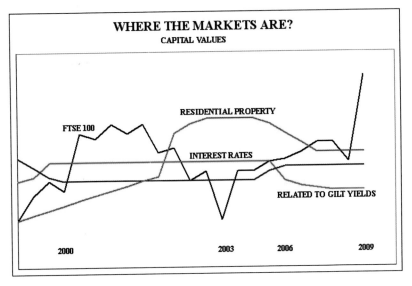

Fig 9.4

Politics as I hope I have shown can use the market cycles to its own advantage, driving its own political agenda. So can you. What politicians invariably fail to do is disturb the overriding rhythm of the *classic market*.

CHAPTER 10

THE PLEASURE OF THE DOWNHILL RUN

(Pound cost averaging explored)

The conclusion that I have come to, after careful analysis of my own actions over the past 40 years, plus the actions of many other individuals and organisations, is that experience counts for a lot where financial planning integrity is concerned. Innovation often defies the rules that experiences of the financial markets prove to be eternal.

What experience does a 35 year old have?

This is a genuine question put into the context of the 'collapse' of a number of the high street banks, closely followed by Lehman Brothers and other investment banks in 2008.

In 2003, house prices were burgeoning and "there was no other way than up." The housing problem that arose in 1991 when a (2003) 35 year old was 23 and having a good time, probably at university, the last thing on their mind, perhaps, was home ownership (unless their parents were buying their 'university house' as an investment). The current cost of houses, the start of the collapse of the residential market values, and the personal consequences of one million homeowners being in negative equity would have been lost on most, if not all, at that age group cohort.

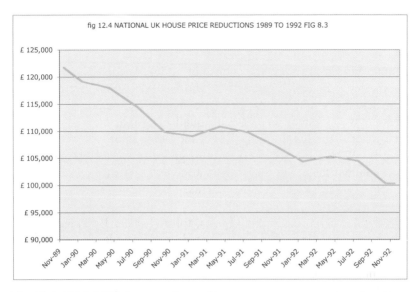

Fig 10.1 1990-1992 house price collapse

Notwithstanding the lack of understanding of the intricacies of mortgage defaults, and repossessions, coupled with the personal dilemmas facing families: the knock on effect of property value reductions on the solvency margins of the lending institutions responsible for lending to those home owners would have been even further from the experience of a 23 to 33 year old at that time.

The people making decisions regarding mortgage lending and the lending criteria, as managers for the various banks in 2003 would have been graduates, aged between 35 and 45; innovative, fast thinking, hungry men and women with great ideas for corporate growth and improvement.

Upon their entry into a career in banking they would undoubtedly be brimming with theories and 'new' best practice. These were the new generation leaders pumped full of "it's different this time," "make hay whilst the sun shines," bravado. Inflation was lower than it had been in decades. Interest rates were similarly lower than they had historically been, and by a huge margin. The market place has to be different if the Bank of England base rates are 2 or 3% instead of

10.5%. After all everyone can borrow four times as much for the same monthly interest cost as they could in 1991!

Many would say, with hindsight, that these were careless, inexperienced, easily led novices who were 'bucking' the principles that actually got the bank to where it was, at that time. The old guard, well established, well qualified and, moreover, well experienced to recognise the trends and nuances of potential disaster had, by 2003, largely been put out to grass. The "new model" bank management team were in charge, an average age (at a guess) 35 to 45. If only we could check the records.

What is for certain is that the banks, following the 1992 debacle, did what they always do, they repeated the formula for reform by executing a substantial redundancy program of management personnel and branch closures associated with those redundancies. Redundancies show immediate 'book' savings, improving the bottom line.

Redundancies also release the very expertise from the payroll that will be needed in the next financial cycle. Cheaper new generation freshman managers would have to learn the practical lessons from scratch with few, if any, experienced mentors to guide them and even fewer employed by the regulator to contain their enthusiasm for change.

These young bucks were determined to make a difference therefore the cry would inevitably go up, 'if we don't do it, our competitors will'. Commercial innovation tells us –"let them have their head – it is different this time". The only problem is, like Northern Rock, sometimes their "run" can last 25 or 30 years until they really do go 'too far' for them to bring themselves, or the institution that they manage, 'back on track'.

There is a thirty year cycle as well as the *classic market* 14 -15 year sequence to contend with.

Having examined the reason for the slide in property and equity values is there a way to capitalise on the outcome that proved so painful for investors (and the bankers)?

There is if you are a saver. Let me introduce you to 'perception,' and Cyril.

John was talking with Cyril about investments.

"Well, if you put £60 per month away, Cyril, you will generate about £8,000 to £8,500 at the end of 10 years."

Cyril's response was disdainful. "Can't you do better than that John?"

"Well, yes, you could put £600 per month away, then you would get between £80,000 and £85,000 at the end of ten years."

Cyril's hesitation was measured in milliseconds. "Well that's more like it," he said. "Now that's real growth!"

There is a moral to the story; which is, incidentally, true: perception is always more impressive than fact.

The fact is that both of the saving plans outlined by John grow at the same rate and are merely in direct proportion to each other. One is no better value for money than the other; it is just that the larger amounts saved produce larger amounts of money delivered and are, therefore, more impressive. The perception, therefore, is the achievement of a better return.

Why do I tell you that?

I tell you that true anecdote in order to tell you this further anecdote.

George was looking to make his income work for him to generate capital value for the future. As we have seen, in 1999 stock markets were bubbling along quite happily with extraordinary capital growth and value being produced by 'dotcom' shares displaying extraordinary multiples of their price earnings ratio (p/e ratio). Most of the 'dotcom' companies were earning a negative profit.

A stock market crash was on the cards. It was a matter of *when* it was going to happen rather than *if* it was going to happen.

George, along with many others, was convinced of two things:

a)   A crash was coming and:
b)   The power of 'pound cost averaging' could, because he was told so, improve his rates of return in the medium to long term (between 10 and 20 years).

By March 2003 George was less convinced by the second, but had experienced the first.

The stock market had certainly crashed; by some 50% of its value. The FTSE 100 had dropped from 6932 down to below 3600 and Armageddon was just around the corner.

"Is this right Terry?" George said. "I've got this statement from my regular savings plan and it says I've paid £30,000 in (George was paying £1,000 per month and this was the fourth anniversary of his contract) and the value (of the plan) is just over £17,000. Is that right?"

"Absolutely George," was Terry's retort. "It's doing exactly what it should be doing. That's great!"

"You're joking" said George.

Fig 10.2 Graph 1997 -2003 FTSE 100 performance

"No" was the instant response. "You are witnessing the principle of 'pound cost averaging' George. You remember, I explained it to you. As the market goes down you buy cheaper and cheaper units. When the market comes back up, that's when you see the real value and over the 10 to 20 years of your savings plan, probably between 12 and 15 years from the date you took it out, that is when the enhanced value shows through."

It was at this point that Terry felt compelled to redraw the graph that he had drawn so many times for so many people to illustrate how the market might be expected to perform and how that performance would enhance the returns on George's money.

"You see", he began, "It's all about a chartist's view."

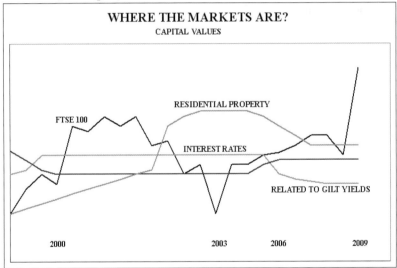

Fig 10.3 schematic of the financial markets (to save you turning back to the last chapter.

The market in 1997 was burgeoning forward. The dotcom revolution was taking hold, share prices generally, but dotcom's in particular, were accelerating apace. This was where easy money could be made and 'greed' was the fashion.

"The problem was," Terry explained, "that people were expecting to make capital growth on increasing share values in the short term in a volatile market. What the medium to long-term investor is required to do is to make the most of the returns available. The mechanism to override the downside risk is to <u>save</u> rather than <u>invest</u>."

Saving has been described as investing in instalments. The result can be quite spectacular and the proof of that lies 12 to 15 years before 2003 and the year that followed 2003.

"You started saving here Simon, on the 16th November 1999, the level of the FTSE 100 was 6503.2".

"We are now here Simon 30th March 2003 and the FTSE100 is 3708.5. You are now purchasing twice as many units per payment as you were at the beginning. Now what we expect the market to do is rebound – it will '<u>retrace</u>' by around 50%. It is during that period that the unit price will rise".

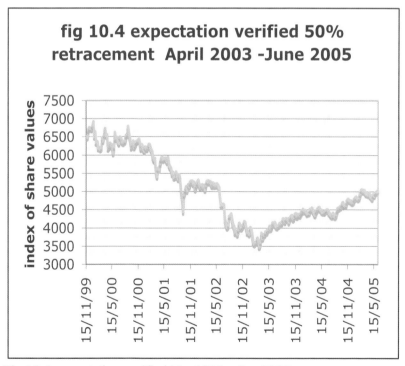

Fig 10.4 expectation verified Nov1999 – Jun 2005

If we look at the performance of unitised savings plans from 1985, 1986 and 1987 and compare the 10 to 15 year performance of that group of policies against others, there is a marked enhancement in the returns available from a volatile market, or low value market. That enhancement is created by 'pound cost averaging.'

In 1987, just as in the year 2000, the stock market faltered, and for those people with capital invested the result was that their capital value reduced with the market indices and rose again, slowly, as the market recovered.

For those who were saving, in other words those who were taking part of their income and, over time, converting it into capital, the drop in unit price month on month as the market fell was transformed into the purchase of a greater number of units at the lower price. £100 at the top of the market in the year 2000 purchased, say, 100 units in a particular investment fund linked to, say, the FTSE 100 share index.

By 2003 the FTSE 100 index had reduced in value by 50% (half) therefore the £100 monthly saving amount was then purchasing 200 units (double) for the monthly £100 saved in the fund. The principle was discussed and illustrated in chapter 4.

The profile of the 1987 crash was quite different from that which took place in 1972 and the year 2000. 1987 was a rapid deteriation in the stock market's value and took a shorter time period to bottom out. Therefore, the effectiveness of the 'pound cost averaging' principle was diminished because, in a constantly rising market (taking 1987 as the bottom and 1997 as approaching the top of a savings cycle) the unit price differentials are not as widely spread.

March 1999   Eric started saving £400 /month

Each monthly contribution is buying more units in 2000 to 2003 which would eventually, hopefully, rise. That possibility does not arise in the counter cycle from 1987 to 1997. In a *classic market*, that rise can usually be anticipated with some accuracy.

It is the precise timescales that are not necessarily that predictable, but with a flexible savings platform and a means of shifting the investment environment for the accumulated capital value, within the plan, the diversity of market selection between capital on the one hand and contribution on the other becomes quite apparent.

By 2005, six years later, Eric had saved £28,800 and the underlying value of his fund was £38,464.

The market had increased in value by over 30% between March 2003 and March 2005, but if you add 30% to £28,880 it does not quite appreciate to £38,000. There has to be something else going on and that has to do with the number of units purchased.

By December 2009: the plan had accumulated a value of £55,046.90; against a total of £48,000 paid in. At that point the FTSE 100 index was 5412 and rising.

The interesting thing at this point (Dec 2010) is that if the FTSE100 continues to move upwards over the next 2 years, as is anticipated, then by 2012 on an assumed index of 6500 the plan will be worth £75,713.24: a return on contributions made of 3.85% per annum compound.

If the plan runs to 2014 and the index attains 7500, then, the plan will be worth £99,537: a return on contributions made of 4.34% per annum compound.

If we compare that with a lump sum of £48,000 invested over a period of that same 15 years and using the same FTSE100 growth figures it would have grown to £72,000 after 10 years rising to £99,360 after 15 years and all of that capital would have been tied up for the full period of years assuming that you had the capital available.

Pound cost averaging has distinct advantages the most important of which is the reduction of risk over time.

Does the phenomenon of *'pound cost averaging'* only work with the stock market? Certainly not. 'Pound cost averaging' works in any declining, or moribund, already declined market where future growth is expected, such as in 2010 the real commercial property (as distinct from shares in property companies) unitised funds.

Savings plans, started now (2011), using the Equity Income funds for the first 12 months and then switching the regular savings element of the savings contract to the Property Fund with a 12 to 15 year forward plan should reap extraordinary returns for the saver.

The Equity Income fund element would require a switch to Property in, say, 4-5 years time (2015-16) to consolidate the gains of that small part of the plan.

An ISA or Maximum Investment Plan would give a totally tax free return. Pension Plans would also benefit from the same strategy, as would unitised life assurance or Critical Illness policies of assurance, where the owner of the policy has control over the underlying investment medium.

Your knowledge of *The Classic Market* will carry you through the process quite comfortably.

What about George? He got cold feet and stopped paying into his savings plan. He could have done as well as Eric.

Does the phenomenon of "pound cost averaging" only work with the stock market? Certainly not. Whilst the stock market was reducing in value between the year 2000 and 2003, property values were rising quite dramatically.

An astute investor at this point of time would recognise that the trend that had made 'pound cost averaging' so effective was that the stock market was wearing thin but re-manifesting itself in the property market. What the property market offered that the stock market did not was a smoother ride with less volatility.

Just as in 1997, 1998, 1999 and 2000, the principle of engaging with the stock market and a regular savings plan in anticipation of a drop was an attractive proposition for the twelve to fifteen year investor. So it was in 2003, 2004, 2005 and 2006 utilising the Commercial Property Funds within unit linked savings plan contracts.

Indeed the property market offered an even better mechanism for operating 'pound cost averaging' because once the property market had collapsed it stayed collapsed on a fairly smooth line and that lack of spiky volatility meant that the saver was buying cheap units right the way through the accumulation phase of the contract with the expectation of propelling itself upwards at the end of the first quarter of the next *classic market* to come along. It is a case of 'all aboard' for the next runaway train.

But timing is important; that two to three year period on the run-up to and at the crest of the property value relationship really allows the saver to optimise their gain by using the full period of progress through the *classic market* phasing.

Does it work for gilt edge securities? Not for me it doesn't:

a)   The volatility is not there and
b)   The prescription is not there.

Gilts are not necessarily held by ordinary individuals and interest rate volatility is not that profound or predictable, in my view, in the gilt market.

Gilts certainly have their day and we need to examine when that day is in relation to the period when both equity and property values collapsed together towards the end of the *classic market* period.

Chapter 11

A GILT TRIP

The interesting situation that presented itself in the latter part of 2008 and the beginning of 2009 was that interest rates fell very quickly and with that quick fall, the capital values of gilt stock and corporate bonds rose from the depths of despair that they had been wallowing in.

Corporate bonds fell back just as quickly as the fear of commercial collapse and therefore corporate loan default engaged with the psyche of fixed interest rates and fixed term loans.

With the benefit of hindsight, one would have moved out of equities in 2006/2007, also a move out of property altogether would have proven prudent. The agile and foresighted investor would have then moved that money into gilt stock in anticipation of the banking crisis which happens every time the classic market reaches this stage.

In the cycle (and it is a cycle) there is no doubt in my mind that all of these attributes occur at the same point, under similar conditions, on a recurring basis.

As interest rates dropped away from their lofty 5% that should have provided a stimulus for the stock market to recover its composure using economic theory. But that did not happen because the banks were in such dire trouble during this phase, as their asset base withered in line with property value reductions. The financial sector shares are invariably the catalyst for a market collapse. Check the history.

For the inexperienced or plain unwary, the symptoms of a share price reduction can be confused with the position that would, and did, pertain in 2000 to 2003 when the interest rate stimulus appeared to work. Property, at that time, was in the ascendancy: a diametrically opposing position to that pertaining in 2008.

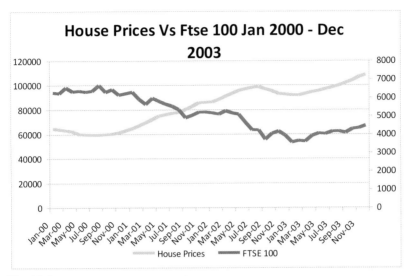

Fig 11.1

Fig 11.2

In the period 2000- 2003 the correlation between property and equity price variance was negative. Property was moving in the opposite direction to share values. During the period 2006 to 2009 the two were moving in unison, a positive correlation of almost 1 – perfect.

In précis: in 2003 the property boom was assisting the stock market recovery through enhancing solvency margins at the banks. In 2008 the property price collapse was detracting from the banks' ability to stay in business, let alone lend to their customers, because their solvency ratio was shrinking at a rate of 11:1 against the equity in their mortgage 'book'. Simplistic? Yes. True? Yes.

The banks' problems swiftly started to bite into the commercial market as bank managers found excuses to alter overdraft facilities by either reducing them, calling them in altogether or more likely, at that particular point in the market, increasing the percentage rate above base that an individual has to pay for the privilege of the facility.

In the most 'severe' cases, the banks imposed a monthly administration fee - which could all but double the levy on the company against its borrowings. The whole idea, for the bank, was to get money in quickly to compensate for the effect that reducing property values had on its solvency margins. This started as early as 2006. The primary recipient of 'the treatment' was the Construction Industry.

As the stock market and the property values continued their decline, so interest rates were reduced in an endeavour to stimulate the market, as has been mentioned, to bring cash back into the system. If the 'asset to loan' ratio has reduced to the poor levels that it achieved in 2007 and 2008, much of the stimulus of the interest rate cut is used in absorbing the asset value reductions. Mortgage loan rates, other than trackers, stayed high to further facilitate the bolstering of cash reserves within the banks through improved and increased margins.

What the process outlined above does provide, of course, is a mechanism for banks to increase their margins significantly, while not necessarily inflicting even more pain on the borrowers. As the base rate shrinks, the banks increase their percent over base to the borrower and the borrowers' costs remain much the same therefore both bank and customer are, to some extent, satisfied.

Domestic mortgages had become cheaper in these circumstances, at least for some they had where the facility provided is a fixed percentage over bank base rate. However, as in the 2006/2008 period, interest rate increases will have already pushed the cost of borrowing up, therefore any reduction will only result in bringing the cost down to the 'norm' that people had experienced prior to 2006.

A further element in the cost equation, which many borrowers ignore at their peril, is the arrangement fee that accompanies most 'fixed rate' short duration mortgages. Financial stress for the individual is often created as a result of the absolute need to find a new mortgage against a reduced property value in a further declining environment when banks and other mortgage-providing financial institutions are endeavouring to reduce, rather than increase, their loan to value exposure.

This happened in 1992

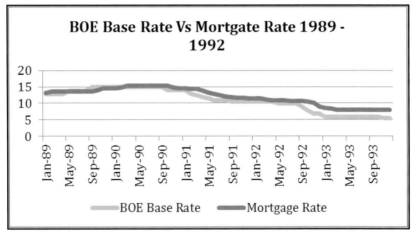

Fig 11.3

As far as income is concerned, it is fair to say that gilts are guaranteed if held to maturity. The capital return is also guaranteed – but not necessarily the price that the mid-term investor paid for the gilt.

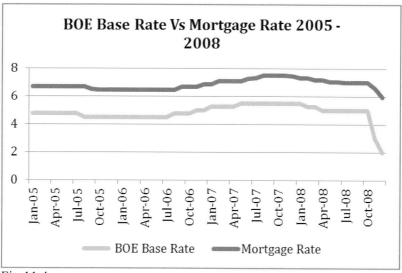

Fig 11.4

Fixed interest stock - (Government GILTS) is spoken of in **near guaranteed** terms.

Back in the real world things are never that straightforward.

> Edna was 82 and her need was for income. She had most of her life behind her and having built up a useful reserve of cash she invested in Fixed Interest stock through a collective investment that delivered a steady level of income. Just what Edna required.
>
> However, the outside interest rates had been steadily rising and that had a very significant effect on the capital value of Edna's investments because that capital value had decreased by a huge margin; this was 2007.

If the rate of interest from an investment is fixed; as it would be with Government Bonds (short-medium or long term fixed interest loans to the Treasury or Exchequer) or corporate bonds (the commercial equivalent of Government Bonds in many ways); then the only variable can be the capital value. The capital value is known at redemption; however these gilts (gilt edged securities) are freely tradable instruments with a daily price for buying and selling. Fixed Interest Stock has a market price just as shares (equities) do.

What governs the price of anything can be said to be supply and demand but, in the case of fixed interest financial instruments the price (capital value) is primarily affected by interest rates, especially under certain market conditions.

The inverse correlation is not perfect by any means but the relationship between interest rates and gilt or corporate bond capital values is very significant. They are inversely related because as market interest rates rise the capital value of fixed interest stock normally declines at a rate of approximately 7% for every 1% rise in interest rate return.

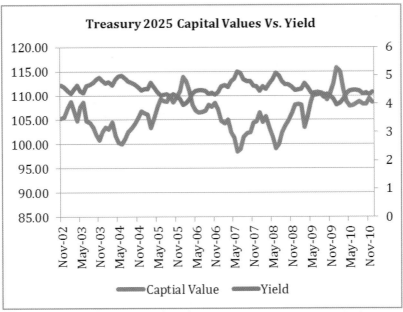

Fig 11.5 - Actual capital value changes against interest variations

You can buy the fixed interest 'stock' at a cheaper price because it is only by doing so that the yield, the return, can equate to what is available from a bank or other institution, on deposit, at the time of the transaction.

As an example, it might be that Edna wanted to secure an income of £3,000 per annum for the next five years when interest rates are 5% in the market place. However, Edna needs to be certain of the income that she receives NOT the yield, in other words, the income return on her investment to pay her nursing home costs, is, or rather was, her only criterion. The capital return after her death, or even, in her view, for the rest of her life was irrelevant. As long as her overheads were met, for certain, Edna was happy.

If £3,000 per annum represents a 5% return and Edna can obtain a fixed interest annuity or investment bond at 5% she will require £60,000 to secure her desired outcome.

If, however, she can only obtain an investment delivering 2½% per annum she will require capital of £120,000 in order to deliver the same £3000 per annum level of income.   Simples!

Nobody said understanding finance was easy. If Edna had invested her £60,000 to obtain £3,000 per annum and subsequently wanted to sell the bond to someone else and the market interest rates were now at a 10% level then the purchaser of the stock may only pay £30,000 for the fixed interest stock, but the <u>physical, receivable income</u> would not vary.

Imagine that the market interest rates available from the building society or bank are a little over 5% and you are offered a fixed interest payment from a five year bond at 7%: TAX FREE. It is 1974.

The stock market has collapsed - no solace there then - far too risky.

The property market has already doubled and appears to have levelled out - not liquid enough – you are a bit unsure.

Would you go for the 7% bond, fixed interest, guaranteed?

Deposit rates are around 5%; therefore you feel comfortable. Gordon did - he was over the moon UNTIL 18 months later the market had changed and bonds on offer were delivering 11% pa.

We are always happy until the market changes - so what changed?

In this instance interest rates, inflation and annuity rates all 'improved'. Again this was the seventies but does it have a modern counterpart?

The answer is assuredly yes: and it has had a further manifestation in-between those two points in time.

So, can we use these foibles of the market to create personal wealth with the best possible chance of a good outcome? And if so, how?

Where would we start? If it were me **I wouldn't start from here:**

<u>BUT</u> …..**We have to start from where we are: whatever we do.**

The question to ask oneself, is; can I do what I need to do safely, or so as to be relatively well assured of success?

Is income the priority to the exclusion of capital value?

Is capital appreciation for the future the investors' goal?

Perhaps a combination would be the focus of their thoughts?

Each individual would present a differing viewpoint from which a decision must be drawn. The question is then; is there a formula for success and can you access it?

Yes there is.

Yes, you can; if you follow the market timing for trends.

In the1970s inflation was a killer, it was also a saviour.

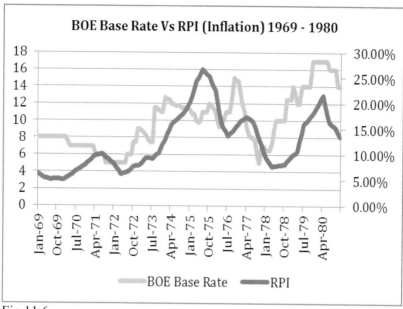

Fig 11.6

Gilt growth can reverse as quickly as it is created. As interest rates stabilise and investors abandon low coupon income, to perhaps re-enter the stock market for relatively high dividend yields in good quality companies coupled with growth potential. Also, of course, in anticipation of interest rates rising again, as inflationary effects start to bite; the capital values of the corporate bonds and gilts once more subside into a downward trend. Yields rise.

The only specific 'no go area', because of volatility and uncertainty, at this particular phase in the market would be a move into foreign currency fixed interest funds; although, of course, on this occasion, 2008-2009 offshore investments of any kind captured 30% growth from currency movements alone. Timing was the major contributor, and luck.

The brave may well favour the premise that equity income stock, blue chip shares, might present a relatively safe haven for the major upside promise and a minor down side risk. They would be right. Due to the high level of overseas investment earnings for many companies the currency 'dividend' is factored into any returns.

Capital value growth coupled with good dividend yields, even if a company halves or quarters its dividend, offers a far better environment, looking forward, than cash or fixed interest investments. Deposit and fixed interest facilities in January 2011 offer the prospect of poor interest rates from deposits and a high likelihood of capital loss from gilts as interest rates inevitably rise.

Chapter 12

THE MONEY CYCLE TO RECESSION

Stating that you have lost money because the value of an investment portfolio has gone down long before its target date is like putting an umbrella up in a bus because it is raining outside the bus at Peterborough and your final destination is London. Why would people do that?

Whilst talking to Julian, we remarked on his journey; not by bus, but his personal financial journey from 1973 to 2009 in the retail electronics industry. In 1988 Julian moved from rented commercial accommodation, in a town centre location to purchase a commercial property 'out of town', but on a reasonably busy main road.

Recessions are not something that happens once in a lifetime, particularly if you are in business for yourself - they happen every so often. People merely stop spending money, and life goes on. At every level, people, private and business alike, just stop spending money. When enough people stop spending money, the whole cycle of money exchange slows down. That makes sense doesn't it?

People don't always hold their money in a bank account either. In fact at some points in history, notably post September 2008 through to 2009, people put a complete block on putting money in a bank account. Not everybody, but a significant number of people, had 'rolls of notes' under the bed. Where better to put it, particularly when the banks are paying 'investors' 0.5%?

Well; there were a lot of better places to put money in order to achieve a return and a lot safer on occasions, however, the boycott principal (nothing to do with cricket) is the way peoples' perceptions work.

There was an email doing the rounds in mid 2009 and the email story went something like this:

The Money go-round

A man walked into a hotel put £100 down on the reception desk and said, "I would like a room until this time tomorrow, do you have something suitable". The landlord said he had, thanked him for his deposit and had one of his staff show the gentleman the room and the facilities attendant to it. Whilst the man was gone, and assuming the sale was secure, the landlord nipped round to the butchers where he owed £100 and discharged his bill.

The butcher thanked him, and when the landlord had left, the butcher went to the plumber who had been carrying out work on the butcher's water supply and paid the plumber's bill of £100. Another bill settled.

The plumber had had some legal work completed and still had a bill outstanding. A visit to the Solicitor cleared his account and both parties felt very much better for it. The Solicitor had been engaged with a PR project with a young lady artist and decided that it was time to settle her account which the Solicitor duly did.

The lady was quite pleased because she had hired rooms at the hotel for a promotional seminar and the account was well overdue to the proprietor of the hotel; £100 for the service rendered. She had a break in her engagements and promptly made her way to the hotel, saw the proprietor and gave him the £100.

No sooner had she gone out of the door when the gentleman who had originally come in, and had fortunately taken a little bit of time making his decision regarding the room hire, declared that he was not really interested in the room, could he have his deposit back. The landlord reluctantly gave him his £100 back and the man left to go elsewhere.

That is money in circulation.

A recession is when that circulation slows down or somebody in the circuit puts the money under their bed. A 'booming economy' is where more people join the circle and the money moves around faster and faster.

Now given the 'money go around' scenario (oh don't you hate that word), situation, it is perhaps easier to understand how the pace of money transfer can affect certain sectors that recycle the money constantly between themselves. The Construction Industry would certainly lend itself to that situation. I am sure you can think of others, transport and the like.

Let us return to the point of these observations. 1988 was a time of a reasonably booming economy. 1987 was an unfortunate 'blip'.

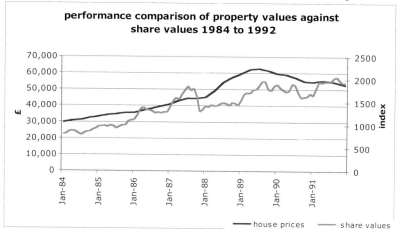

performance comparison of property values against share values 1984 to 1992

Fig 12.1 clearly shows that the stock market had collapsed in 1987 (October 19th.)

We, my business partner and I, were Fund Managers for 'broker funds' and the value of the money that we were responsible for investing on behalf of members of the clients went down by between 30% and 50% over a couple of days dependent upon which fund we were evaluating. **There was nothing we could do.**

I recalled in an earlier chapter that National Employers Life (NEL) in Dorking was one of the broker fund administrators that we used as fund managers. We were endeavouring to get in touch with their internal fund administrators in order to switch (move) out of equities into a safer less volatile environment.

A caretaker answered the phone:

"I would like to speak to a fund administrator please," I heard myself saying.

"Fund administrators mate – there ain't no fund administrators here, I'm the caretaker and there are ten trees down on the drive".

End of conversation. 'Hurricane Herbert' or whatever it was called, had hit the south east of England, tearing up trees in the most unexpected places bringing transportation to a halt. Fund administrators couldn't 'administrate' in the centre of activity, let alone for our team out in Lincolnshire. It was chaos. That was the Friday; 'Black Monday' followed in due time.

How did that situation in the stock market affect Julian?

Not at all.

Julian was not invested in the stock market; he was invested in trade stock: televisions, hi-fi equipment, stereos and electronic gadgetry. Julian's business was not affected at all and it did not affect most of his customers.

Julian just kept selling to people who wanted to 'view' and 'listen;' people with money available to use, to buy entertainment equipment and keep up with the latest in big telly's, and they *were* big, and expensive; as were stereo units and surround sound systems. Inflation was still high and many individuals preferred to buy things than save at a negative real rate of return.

The fact that the news media reports were informing the viewers and listeners that "the world had come to an end", may well have concerned people with regard to their pension schemes or savings plans but fortunately, at that point, most of them did not put their 'umbrella up' just because it was 'raining in Peterborough'. (I refer to the metaphor earlier in this Chapter).

In fact few people, even in 2010, actually associate the performance of BP (British Petroleum) (recently a news item regarding the Gulf of Mexico oil spill) or the problems regarding the banks (RBS is 87%

owned by the government and is not paying dividends) with their company or private pension fund savings, their Individual Savings Plan, or their Endowment Assurance or other similar contracts for saving.

For a lot of my clients however, who were reliant on income from capital invested, they were concerned, and rightly so.

In Julian's world the retail sector was working quite well. Sales were up, but the rent on his property was a sizeable element of his overhead and Julian felt he could probably utilise that money better. A property had 'come onto the market', for sale. It was quite sizeable.

The property would provide him with the retail frontage that he wanted and also provide for workshops to the rear, and it was located on a spacious, busy, main road site, just 'out of town', with plenty of roadside parking capacity.

Above the retail element on the ground floor were two first floor flats; which Julian could rent out (let). The rented property market was looking reasonably well priced, property prices were rising and Julian took the plunge. With the help of a substantial mortgage, provided by the local Building Society, he was able to execute his move: and then he watched his turnover drop and interest rates rise.

Life's predictability is the one thing that makes it, life, interesting.

Did I say predictable?

Well if Julian could have predicted the interest rates rises that were going to hit him, he would have perhaps had second thoughts about committing himself. But he didn't, and in conversation twenty years later, he admitted that the exercise was not only character building, it was very worrying, at the time.

I mean; what do you do when your 'fixed' overheads go up by 25% (the interest rate rose from 12% to 15%) and the turnover of the goods that you have for sale, slows down to a trickle? "You just keep going," Julian stated, with hindsight -

"The difference between 'survival and liquidation' may be a matter of weeks, and if you can get through those weeks, then you survive."

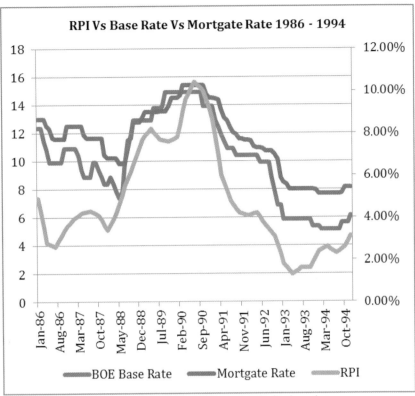

Fig 12.2 monthly figure for mortgage rates - inflation date

Fortunately Julian did survive. Tenants in his flat ensured that the mortgage was paid, the business contributed towards the overheads, by paying Julian rent and Julian using that to pay the interest due to the building society that provided the commercial mortgage.

In 1992, domestic and commercial property prices 'collapsed.' Well 'collapsed' is perhaps an overstatement, the property values certainly 'went down.' But, once again who did that affect?

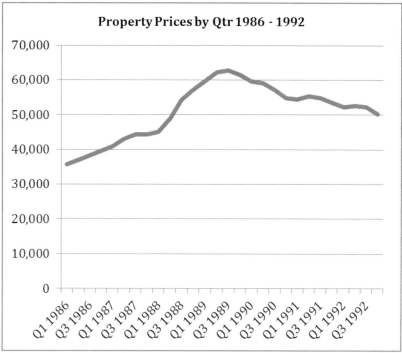

Fig 12.3   source Nationwide B.Soc. data

The reduction in property values affected, as it always does.

Those who '**had** to move' and therefore

Those that '**had** to sell'.

Those whose **income could not support the higher interest rate** and were forced to relinquish their property to repossession by the bank or the institutions providing their loan facility.

Those with **overdrafts** and

Those small **business proprietors** like Julian, who perhaps needed an overdraft to pay for stock to come into their establishments in the hope of sales that would then gradually whittle that overdraft down until they restocked again and the overdraft moved back up.

Julian was not affected by the stock market crash. However, he was now intimately involved in the property debacle.

Market movements perform in a cycle. The change in property values was broadly predictable. Julian's timing was okay. Although there were stresses and strains in 1992 and 1993, they were overcome as people started spending again.

Goods got cheaper, and profit margins were 'tight.' Whilst retail goods were getting cheaper, a substantial number of people stopped spending in anticipation of retail goods becoming cheaper still. That is one of the enduring features of a recession.

However, once the retail goods market prices had 'bottomed out,' once people felt that goods were as cheap as they were going to get, guess what? People started spending again, the recession ended and money started moving around the cycle once more. At an ever faster pace.

By 1997, everything was running in 'high gear' in the stock market. Money was permeating through to the banks where they were multiplying the money that was moving through their account, out into loans, gearing up an individual's ability to pay for goods they would otherwise not be able to afford, from companies that were able to finance their stocks - in short, Julian was on a roll.

Julian was typical of a huge number of small traders (SMEs). Many more SMEs had been added to his ranks because the larger companies, during the recession, had shed workers, managers, technicians, engineers: and many of those had decided to set up 'on their own' with bijou enterprises that paid the bills, and grew on the back of established expertise.

Fig 12.4 sets the whole investment cycle in context and hopefully shows how investors sheltered themselves. But what of the Fund Managers?

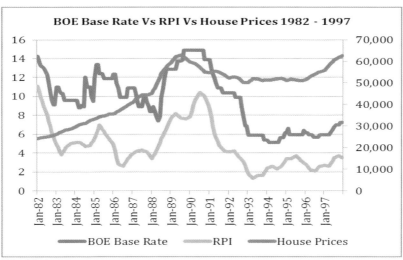

Fig 12.4

In 1987 a £2 million fund had become a little over £1 million – it had halved in value over a very short period of time. Investors became restless. Property was booming. Perhaps a large portion of the 'losses' could be recovered through a 'fund switch' (transfer within the investment fund portfolio) from equities into a property (commercial real estate) fund.

Just look at Illustration 12.4 and judge for yourself the affects of that, because in the short term it worked.

Without foresight (born of hindsight) and perhaps ignorant of the knowledge that whilst it is easy to trade shares and government gilts on a 'minute by minute' basis, it is downright impossible to liquidate property when you just can't sell the stuff, at any price, the mess that one can get into looms large indeed.

Commercial property tends to fall into 3 to 5 year value slumps and therefore the liquidity of property funds dries up very quickly as people endeavour to remove their money to avoid the collapse of property values and find it impossible to 'sell.' Of course the attempts of a large number of investors to withdraw from any commercial property based fund forces the value of the fund down, due to the enforced selling by the fund managers of the property stock that they have 'on the books' in order to meet the demand for a return of investors' money from the resultant reduced liquidity. There are, at that point, more sellers than buyers.

Prices, values, whatever one would like to call them, reduce, and leave the investor stranded, if, as is normally the case with property (illiquid funds), a 'transaction' moratorium is imposed. In plain English "NO DEALS ARE ALLOWED". That situation can, and usually does, last for anything up to a few years, most of which is evidenced in unit price decline.

Individual moratoria for dealing in property 'units' of anything from 6 to 12 months are not unheard of. Funds are just 'locked' up until the appropriate time imposition on the investor's transaction (the notice period) is expired.

The effective release of the fund and, therefore, the availability of switching on an instant basis centres on when sales and liquidity can be achieved, or more likely, when funds start to come in from new investors. The latter is an unlikely situation due to the adverse publicity and opinion that builds up. When you look ahead you really do have to LOOK AHEAD; **timing** (not time in) **is essential**. 'Time in' comes later.

Julian's timescale (time in) still (in 2010) has another 10 to 12 years (to 2020 -2022) to run during which time the value of his commercial retail shop and flats (above) will oscillate from good to bad and back to good again. Provided that Julian's exposure to loans does not exceed a reasonable percentage of his 'loan to value' and his ability to pay his mortgage, the lenders should be comfortable to let him continue with his mortgage subject only to his ability to pay the interest.

At some stage of course the capital outstanding on Julian's commercial mortgage may have to be repaid. An upward shift in the market will hopefully deal with the capital repayment coincidental with the time of Julian's retirement. He will not need the property to trade from after he retires.

Julian could, of course, renegotiate the existing mortgage at the time of his retirement, retain the property, ignore its capital value fluctuations and rely on the income from rents collected to provide him with an income stream rather like a pension plan; that is another possibility encompassing a different dynamic, and a different appraisal.

You may recall that Gerry and Linda purchased their office property in 1978 (page 92) at the bottom of the market. The property was transferred into a Self Invested Pension Scheme and was therefore subject to valuation every three years from 1988 onwards.

The valuations were like a yo-yo, up and down in value from £13,500 to £32,000 on the transfer into the pension and then back down to £26,000, up to £88,000 and then down to £36,000; and so on. Until in 2007 it sold for £230,000 at the top of the market.

The point is that the property was a utility property, therefore its underlying value did not matter other than at the two relevant points in its existence, the purchase date price and the sale date price. Everything that happened in between was inconsequential because the property itself was providing a service just as Edna's investment was providing her with an income.

Chapter 13

WHY THE BANKS COLLAPSED
(2008 – 1993 – 1978)

People ask me when do you stop it: the greed, the avarice, the mass marketing taking over and the answer is always: "When it becomes apparent that is it getting out of control." People bring markets under control, not governments.

Seriously, human nature being what it is, emotion is impossible to stop. It is what drives us to do what we do. Couple that with the fact that we are inclined to trust few and condemn many, and the stage is set for a drama.

That is what happened with 'endowments.'

Instead of implementing the Maximum Commission Agreement (MCA), in order to curb market place 'bias', the banks and mass market lobby prevailed (by default) in their quest for higher remuneration from the life assurance companies for volume override payments through higher commission payments. The MCA, which had been agreed industry wide and took three years of considered debate by those of us with expert knowledge to devise a workable solution, was 'dumped' by a government department, the Office of Fair Trading, through Gordon Borrie, who was knighted for his ineptitude, threw out the Maximum Commission Agreement on the basis that it was 'anti competitive.'

That single move allowed building societies and banks to demand, and get, 80% more than any other distributor on standard commission terms because they were supposedly "doing extra administration."

No! They, the banks and the building societies, were actually ripping the heart out of the contracts that they were selling, that's what they were doing. The payment of commission (a payment correctly due for the sales process) has to be at an acceptable level, because the money paid to intermediaries has to come from somewhere, and the only 'somewhere' that it could be produced was out of the contracts, the policies being sold and the premiums being paid on them. Is that situation any different from the banks 'over lending' when it is quite plain to see that the market had reached its zenith?

The timing for this diversion of funds (through enhanced commissions) to the banks? 1994. Nothing to do with refloating the banks (who were in trouble) then?

Is the problem a lack of foresight by people who are unqualified and inexperienced when making market changing decisions? Or is it a naïve attempt to reallocate money quickly?

Politicians pushed the endowment regime to its extreme and then undermined it, and it was politicians who pushed the banks to the extreme and then undermined them, for the public 'good' of course, in 2006. The fact that it cost the 'public' their savings was for the good of the cause to save the banks (2009).

One can almost detect a design in the decision making process, to refloat ailing banks and other financial institutions after the property collapse in the early 1990s out of savers funds. OK, I am a conspiracy theorist but, where is the theory defective?

It is almost a challenge:

a) The Office of Fair Trading under the control of a left wing barrister, Gordon Borrie conspired to encourage 'capitalism' to be left to its own devices, allowed to err, and then subsequently be 'reigned in'.

b) The new government came in and undermined the system through control and the imposition of punitive regulations.

If that attitude prevails, generations to come will suffer unnecessarily. If good rules, decided by the industry: and that means all parts of the industry and attendant professions: those that advise, those that sell, those that 'manufacture,' i.e. design products. They all need to be part and parcel of that decision-making process, for future generations to prosper. However, the people who certainly do not need to be in that process, is the government and its bureaucratic 'Muppets', or the 'pretenders to the throne' (the banks and supermarkets).

The Government committees and the new generation of so called 'think tanks' (political activist groups with posh titles) compile regulation that is always too lax when it should be tight and inevitably too tight when it should be relaxed; because of political considerations. Their reaction is always too heavy handed and seemingly contrived to score political brownie points, rather than provide solutions that fit the circumstances. The cost is inevitably borne by 80% of the population that we now call the 'middle class'. It is unnecessary and the author has firsthand experience of it, and so does the reader, most times unwittingly.

Supermarket methodology states that it can always sell things cheaper. No it can't.

What it can do, and does do, is hold manufacturers and providers to ransom for a bigger margin.

Eventually, the public pay and the public might just as well do that with honest pricing rather than deception coupled to £billion turnover accounts that end in collapse and anxiety to the consumer, when the business tide turns: Enron, Woolworths et al.

BUT what if the conspiracy theorists, of which I am one, are correct and the descent of the banks to the brink of oblivion in 2008 was contrived rather than an accident of incompetence?

Did anyone see, was anyone aware of the impending disaster, could anyone feel the unease, the dis-ease in the system? Here is the text of a letter that I wrote to the Daily Mail, Mail on Sunday and Daily Telegraph, financial editors on the 10th August, 2007.

> *Dear Jeff/Tony/Ian*
>
> *This is the season of liquidations and bankruptcy largely borne of overtrading in an expanding economy. Two areas of expansion have occurred; the construction industry which employs about a third of the British workforce, and the public sector which also employs a third of the British workforce. That leaves about a third of us wondering what to do with ourselves.*

The two sectors are related in financial effect terms.

For some three or more years I have been predicting a major downturn in the property market going forward, but that is not the centre of the story. The real story is that the banks are now in trouble (due to property devaluation).

One of my clients is in the construction industry. Eight months ago NatWest were happy to take his business from a rival bank and provide him with an overdraft of £200,000 secured by at least £430,000 of property assets, at 2% over base. He also had a significant barn conversion project which stood at about £130,000 and they promised him facility up to the £320,000 that he would need to complete the conversion prior to selling on.

About four months ago the whole process seemed to stall. NatWest did not answer calls and asked for more figures and, coincidentally, I was dealing with the client with a view to strategic financial planning.

A small limited company that was overtrading - they owed more than they were due to receive. They had fallen into the trap of having too thin a margin and poor control of the workforce, but all of that was getting under control.

However, NatWest, as is often the case at this stage in the market:

1. *Changed the bank manager looking after the account;*

2. *Withdrew support for the barn conversion;*

3. *Sent a new overdraft agreement letter outlining their new terms:*

   (a)   5% over base up to £200,000 overdraft facility;

*(b)   9.99% (they might as well have made it
10%) over base default rate of interest;*

*(c)   £1,850 per month administration fee for the
duration of the overdraft.*

*It was 3(c) that alerted me to the fact that the banks were
now in deep trouble. What do I mean?*

*As we know from experience with regard to life assurance
funds, all financial institutions have a solvency margin;
basically, and very simplistically, assets against liabilities.
Every £100 that we as consumers place with the institution
is a liability and they have to have a certain amount of
assets to back that liability off and continue trading.*

Assets		*Liabilities*
(£100)	*Life Assurance*	*(£100)*
£8	*Banks*	*£100*
Nil	*Unitised products*	*£100*

*Banks fall into the middle group. They need £8 of assets
against every £100 of liabilities. In other words, if everyone
went to the bank tomorrow and demanded their money only
1 in 11 would get that money back.*

*The banks' assets are primarily in property, but not their
property, it is in property that they have a charge over. In
other words their clients' property, and banks are
experiencing, as I did three years ago, those property values
slipping away. Houses are taking longer to sell. The buy-
to-let market is laden with naïve investors who have come
into the market in the last couple of years, hoping to make a
killing, now unable to meet their interest payments from the
rental income that they are receiving.*

With their £8 to £100 asset to liability ratio under threat, the banks only have one option open to them, and that is to get money in, 'quick': and the first manifestations of that are now happening in the marketplace.

What they have done to my construction client is not only penal, it is probably terminal. They are extracting the life blood out of his firm as quickly as they possibly can, and will get as much as they can from the outstanding creditors before everything goes against them and other creditors take priority or equal status with them. This is the worst face of the bank and I recognise it from 12 years ago, I also recognise it from the late 70s. I have written a number of articles over the years, the banks are a friend today and your deepest and most aggressive assailant tomorrow.

The reason for this letter is to alert you to what is happening and to point out that it is not only part of a regular cycle, but it is something that you as a financial journalist can help small businesses, in particular, to avoid.

SMEs must get the overdraft down because banks can withdraw that facility with 24 hours notice. If they have got finance out, try and get it on a fixed term loan. Get their money in from creditors. We are seeing companies like supermarkets extending their credit lines from 30 days to 90 days to 120 days, again, as they use small traders as their bankers. They too have solvency margins (I guess).

As a financial planner I know the signs only too well because this is the third classic market (my definition) that I have worked through and they all follow exactly the same predictable pattern.

This is a plea, really, to avoid too many small business owners falling foul of bankers who, quite simply, cannot be trusted to look after the customers' business before they look after their own.

Yours sincerely Terence P

Consider, if you will indulge me, a grand plan for undermining savings (perceived to remove money from the system when politicians require it to be spent on Government schemes and then nationalising the banks (for the public good).

Can an astute team of academics rely on the markets (equities and property) to perform in a pre-ordained fashion? Hopefully the previous chapters have proven that they could rely on the market cycle and so, therefore, could a team of academic politicians, and their researchers.

Following the collapse of the banks in 2008 several people asked me why the circumstances of the banks' collapse had not been foreseen.

My observation in response went along the lines that; it could either be a tragic mishap, a one-off occurrence that left the most astute of economists aghast with incredulity, or, it was part of an economic pattern and had those people in their position of responsibility acknowledged that a pattern existed and acted earlier, the major effects on the financial institutions could have been reduced considerably. The observation above acknowledges that what did happen would have happened, but to a lesser magnitude.

Now there was of course a third option and that it is the political option. If one knew what was going to happen and one wanted to accentuate it to create a crisis, then one could well have done so.

In an email to some colleagues I put that latter 'conspiracy theory' to them in very simplistic terms and they were surprised that anyone could even think such a thing. Politics is a dirty business. I repeat the email for your consideration.

The 'socialist philosophy' seems to demand expenditure.

It is not hard to find the money: the money in a thriving economy can be found in everyman's savings.

Over one thousand billion pounds was scheduled to be redirected, or spent, where could the money be found?

The UK has more money in pensions alone than the whole of the rest of the 27 EU nations put together.

Consider 1997 - £5.4 billion, (that is thousand million pounds sterling) extracted from pensions per year, every year which sets the scene for undermining public confidence in savings for pensions; magnified and hidden through the escallation of the pensions review set up in 1995. (Let's find some really bad people and practices to expose and pillory them).

Commercial protocols were brushed aside and begging letters were sent to consumers to generate complaints. Those letters were issued by every life assurance company to policyholders. This; when private pension benefit payments to the retired exceeded those of the state for the first time ever?

In a sentence: preach savings, but stop people doing 'savings' at all costs.

In the year 2000 technology stocks caused the collapse of stock market prices. At this point the government focus and 'spin' machine fell on to the savings market; and the undermining of long term regular savings – the endowment debacle. This was the second strand of attack and redistribution from the savings institutions to the government, but it was very subtle.

Consider the situation in March, 2003; at the bottom of the stock market the treasury and the FSA, acted in concert to dis-establish institutional long term savings (endowment and pension funds providing GUARANTEES) with funds invested in shares (too risky) and insist on a safer haven for those invested funds (your funds) in 'secure' Government Gilts.

Standard Life Assurance company encashed £7.4 billion (that is 7.4 thousand million pounds) of shares without disturbing the market: an incredible achievement, in order to transfer those funds, your money, into the safety of Government loans (gilts) and other fixed interest vehicles.

Interest rates fell, shares recovered half their losses and the capital value of Government bonds descended into the abyss, starting a downward cycle that took several years to recover. The net effect was for your savings to exit from profitable shares and move into unprofitable but "safe" Government stock in order to 'protect' the savings guarantees within Endowments and pension funds. (See Fig 13.1)

Fig 13.1 The sale of inordinate amounts of gilts persisted well into 2009

New issue Gilts were 3¼% - 4½% dated stock to 2035 and beyond. That is what you call a 'long term loan'. The **Government coffers were being filled** for further spending on relatively cheap interest rates well into the future. Some would call the move astute, but then so do the people who steal copper from power company supply line and railway signalling systems on the premise that a fail safe will stop consumers from being hurt.

When Gordon Brown sold gold (1998) at around $280 per ounce, having given 6 months notice to the world that he was going to do so, almost ensuring a low price, he bought back high coupon debt 13%,14%,15% coupon for 2011, 2012, 2015 and replaced it with 3¼% - 4½% debt to 2035 and beyond. The Government could now borrow three times as much money for the same public cost in interest paid on Gilts and 'lock people in;' well into two generations time. Astute? Possibly. The price of gold in 2010 is $1040 per ounce.

These were not opportunistic, poorly considered, actions. This has the hallmark of a plan that married precisely with the *'classic market.'* The timing was perfect and the outcome could be known. Socialism depends on dependency and Brown was using capitalism to destroy capitalism and create dependency.

As the stock market values fell property prices rose. They rose dramatically but the body that had been put into place to protect the public; the Financial Services Authority (FSA), failed to act in almost every regard to stop the ensuing crisis with the banks and related financial mortgage providing institutions from developing. The FSA served 'the plan' well.

In 2005, 2006, the race by the incumbent Labour (socialist) administration to get re-elected depended upon one thing and one thing only, the stability of property prices. Almost 70% of family units in the United Kingdom own their own home. Had property values dropped, coincident to a General Election the outcome would have been less assured for the Blair/Brown administration.

By encouraging profligate lending, and failing to pull back from 100%-125% LTV (loan to value) lending, to a more sensible 80% LTV to at least give some 'headroom' to the institutions if the property market retraced, the opposite was the case.

The FSA and the Treasury had to know that banks were 'bundling' mortgages (refer Chapter 6, shared equity plans – 1996) and selling them as financial instruments; in bulk. (Is the practice any different than Gordon Brown putting all his debts together and selling your pension fund a 3¼% or 4½% gilt dated to 2035)? The only promise is given is that the Government of the day (i.e. in 2035) will repay the face value of the loan and pay interest along the way.

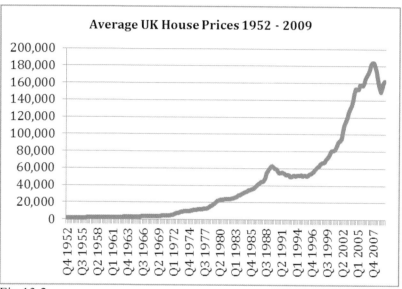

Fig 13.2

Mortgage 'bundling' is a commercial version of exactly the same thing. The only problem arises when there is a revaluation of the underlying assets, the property base; or in the case of gilts, Government assets.

NB 2010 Greek sovereign debt is in real trouble because assets against liabilities and the cost of servicing the debt just do not add up. So much for guaranteed government loans. There is, and always will be a finite boundary beyond which one should not go, or one accepts a 'haircut'.

Some are convinced that Northern Rock was a test piece, an experiment in modern day public panic. The experiment worked.

The Northern Rock mode of operation was well known. Borrow short; lend long. They were an easy target. The asset base was in a rarefied atmosphere, and the lack of wholesale money to fund the 'building society' cum bank lending had dried to a trickle as caution took over the international banking system.

In 2005 the Government changed the Bank of England rules ensuring that the Bank of England could not, independently of Government, mount a rescue if a bank got into trouble. Major reports have it that Alastair Darling was a 'White Knight' (more like a 'Black Widow') when in September, 2007 who but Robert Peston of the BBC created such a negative furore in his BBC financial news report that queues formed outside the institution and the share price collapsed. Capitalism could be defeated, purely by bad news. Peston had proved it.

Having proved the mechanism, all one needed to do was to set up the next phase.

In every *'classic market'*, property becomes overvalued - usually, residential first and then commercial property 12 to 18 months afterwards. The prices collapse by between 20% and 30% for residential property and 50% on commercial premises. That reduction in residential property values had been forecast since 2004/5 by many observers.

The banks' solvency margins rely on asset values. Property forms the bulk of the bank's asset values, other peoples' property, over which the banks hold a charge. By forcing the bank to revalue the assets within a bundled mortgage book it is then easy to establish what is now known as 'toxic debt'.

Repossessions then accelerate the process as forced sales drive the market values down further and the banks' solvency margins are put under further pressure.

Now all that was needed was another huge press announcement that the banks were in trouble and, having tested the system with Northern Rock, the outcome was inevitable.

Robert Peston, said to be the autobiographer to Gordon Brown and a friend of the Brown family, whose Uncle is apparently a Labour Lord, and who appears to have an extremely privileged position in gaining inside information, reported on the content of a 'secret' meeting, before 9.00am the next day, announcing to the world that "Lloyds Bank and RBS are having to be rescued by the Government." Game set and match!

The Government effectively acquired, 'bought into,' RBS and Lloyds Bank on the cheap, undermined shareholder funds and completed an action which they set out to achieve in 1983 when their manifesto declared that they would 'nationalise the banks'. Northern Rock, HBOS, Lloyds and RBS had all effectively gone into public ownership. The New Capitalism of Robert Peston (read his book) could well have been spawned.

Yes; the **banks** brought it on themselves, but they **were encouraged** to do so. Every step was part of a political game and was carefully constructed to achieve the end result. Using the human traits of greed and avarice to the full; could the outcome have been any different? RBS was encouraged to grow and Lloyds Bank was encouraged to 'buy' HBOS.

What is the end game? Well, try this for size.

The Post Office has now been denuded of nearly six and a half thousand entrepreneurial businesses, using public funds to pay compensation, (they do their accounts differently to commercial enterprises even though they are supposed to be a commercial enterprise). Controlling entrepreneurs is difficult. Union manpower is what is desired, perhaps. *The Fight For Our Post Office* will provide a deeper insight.

It was well known in 2007 that 5,000 sub-postmasters were at, or near retirement age. They would merely 'go' by normal wastage. Many sub-postmasters were running poor quality businesses.

Footnote: *The Fight For Our Post Office* is a book providing a resume of the campaign against Post Office closures and an analysis of the accounting and financial arguments incorporating that were put forward from all sides of the eleven month duration campaign.

In the grand closure plans of 2004/5 and 2007/8 it was the viable businesses that had to go to make room for the new order. A huge initiative is now underway. Lord Mandelson (he who spent nearly 3 years in Europe for what purpose (and is still, apparently, 'paid' over £100,000 per year according to press reports) was trying to create the Post Office Bank, which one can only assume would be part of a huge pan-European conglomerate.

The Dunfermline Building Society has gone the same way as Northern Rock. With that branch network, the post office Peoples' Bank and the creation of credit unions together with state run savings plans, the Government can enter the banking and savings arena and save the world with a new, 'trustworthy,' mechanism for the public to shower praise on Gordon Brown and his entourage for astute commercial common sense and returning responsible saving to the common man, having apparently misappropriated their savings in the first place.

The fact that they destroyed, or at least severely undermined pensions and savings in the late 1990s will be conveniently forgotten.

By 2009 the FSA had effectively made the banks solvency margins tighter still – if the banks were not in trouble before that (and they were): they would certainly be in trouble after it, (and they are).

Returning to the original two theories: could the events of 2008 actually be described as a one-off? And the answer is a most assured: 'No.'

The banks and financial institutions were in similar difficulties, circumstances, whatever you want to call it in the mid 1970s and again in the early 1990s. In fact the occurrences are roughly fourteen to fifteen years apart which fits in with the economic cycle that I have described as the *classic market* fairly comfortably.

If such a convenient cycle exists why has it not been picked up on by those who govern our banks and monitor statistical evidence? The answer is: 'I just don't know.'

All I do know is that my own research indicates that each of these situations was created from exactly the same source and that source is the reduction in value of underlying property used as security by the banks. Therefore one can fairly safely state that 2022, 2023 will herald another similar occurrence.

If we accept that there is a pattern and we can use it to good advantage then I believe this book will have completed its mission. I am not clairvoyant but then one does not have to be clairvoyant to know that the sun rises every morning and sets every evening and that the seasons follow each other in broadly the same succession over time. Financial markets, it appears, are no different.

The main point that I am seeking to make in contrasting these possibilities is that no matter what politicians do, no matter what the inflationary effect, no matter what the interest rates, the two basic market mechanisms of equities and property and the relationship of property with the banking system delineate the market driving force throughout a known fifteen year cycle, which I have called *'The Classic Market'*.

It seems that nothing external to those areas has any real effect on their direction of movement only on the quantum of that effect. If we can understand that, then we can accept the *classic market* and if we can accept the *classic market* then we can plan to benefit from its attributes.

In 2011 – What is the prognosis?

The stock market is about to rise, in fact that rise in value is already well underway.

House prices will stabilise at a low level for a good few years.

Interest rates will be on the up because of inflationary pressures (watch the spin for savers).

Gilts? Perhaps we should forget Gilts. The capital value of gilts can only decline as interest rates rise.

The arsonist became the fireman, the destroyer became the Architect. If you believe in conspiracy theories; the last 20 years has proved their worth.

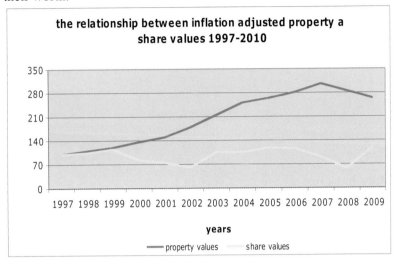

Fig 13.3

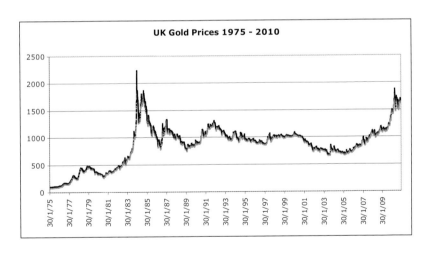

Fig 13.4 Graph of gold prices 1975 -2010. Source Deutsche Bank AG

CHAPTER 14

REGULATION BASED ON THEORY AND HOPE

Those that do the job of proffering financial advice have, in many ways, been 'academonised' by those who 'think' that they know how to do the job.

History has proven it to be a fact in a number of professions, that doers give way to thinkers. The content of this book is the work of a doer. We that do the job, engaging with the investing public, can and should find time to write and record what has genuinely been experienced. Surely it is in that experience that the truth exists for future generations to use?

Many of the commentators and regulators that I have come into contact with are poorly placed academically or experientially to have a valid opinion on how the financial markets' professionals should be governed or what constitutes real risk at any point in time. Hindsight has shown that to be so on many occasions.

The answer is 'this' they say, or the answer is 'that' they say, yet it is often, as we go through the financial history of the world, and the UK in particular, that gainsay, which harbours the vested interest that inevitably is using the theory to meet its own ends.

The manifestation of that is usually the condemnation, by governments or Quangos, of the trade associations run by volunteers plus a small select group of hired hands. Instead the authorities work in favour of seeking opinions from disconnected professionals and vested interest groups melded into a monolith of overpaid, politically inspired, commercially inept, academic, poorly-principled individuals called Quangos. Oh the Financial Services Authority, I hear you cry. Perhaps; is my guarded response. They are on an annual budget of over £600 million, and encourage letters of complaint from the buying public, actually asking them to complain!

The truth is that money does not buy the answer from academics, or anyone else. The vocational skills of those who actually do the job and willingly volunteer to enhance and promote their professional, or trade activities, invariably provide the best answers. Human frailty notwithstanding, volunteerism is a more honest endeavour.

The road to paradise and index linked pensions is littered with the likes of TECs, (Training and Enterprise Councils), which were supposed to replace Chambers of Commerce by being more efficient, and similar organisations with QUANGO (Quasi-Autonomous Non-Governmental Organisations) writ large above the doors of their superbly appointed palaces.

Of course the Financial Services Authority; which replaced LAUTRO, FIMBRA, IMRO and a raft of other trade regulators never got 'top side' of the Bank of England. Why? Well the FSA was, and is, run largely by bankers. And, yes it is 'cockney rhyming slang' but used here in its wider sense.

Proof, as they say, is in the eating. Let's have a look at the menu.

I think it all started with 'wannabes' who took charge of the financial services marketplace; they emerged from the emaciated rump of those who had been made redundant from the Bank of England when the change of authority was carried through parliament. Ex-employees of the Bank of England, through almost 'in house' recruitment agencies, simply recognised 'the main chance'.

'Miraculously,' the people that emerged as senior staff at the regulator were from a banking background, stockbroking, accounting; or, over time, where recruitment agencies swiftly moved to the lucrative yet time-saving model which led largely to employ the same group of people that they had worked with in 'The City' and who therefore had the so called 'knowledge' and high earning expectations (please do not mention the percentage 'commission' to the agency).

The end product was a failure to perform four defining duties, just four: improving consumer financial confidence, eradicating financial fraud, increasing financial protection and improving consumer financial understanding. (Financial Services Marketing Act 2000).

Theory abounded on theory and one of the main determining theories about investment became the lynchpin of failure, stochastic modelling. 'Asset allocation' became the by-word of the regulator and the New Model Adviser. The computer model would fix everything by ensuring that a high proportion of guaranteed gilt edged securities appeared in every portfolio, and by interrogating recent past performance a model portfolio for the future could be achieved.

It was only a lack of experience and real knowledge of the marketplace that stopped that group of individuals from getting the timing right, six years later, when then the banking system all but collapsed.

Now would be a good time to make amends for that short sighted but devastating mistake.

Just look at the facts. Case histories invariably prove the point; they are formed throughout the market cycle, and like the text, get analysed as theory turns to experience for guidance to create more theory for the whole process to start all over again.

The problem with busy people is they are too busy to be full time theorists. Just look at the evidence, but, at the same time consider 'the feast' that has been provided and who's money paid for it.

YOURS. Your money.

This book is about financial market cycles. Genuine observable mechanisms that can give real guidance to the investor.

Would it be prudent, indeed necessary, for a regulator of such stature as the Financial Services Authority (the FSA) to understand and react to the cyclic rhythms of the marketplace with some authority in order to meet their objectives of monitoring the market place, with all its diversity and the aspirations of the consumer to benefit more effectively by way of their savings and investments, in that same market place? And do so without external consultants.

The marriage of all of those independent organisations (run largely, in FIMBRA's case, by volunteer IFAs) that became the advisory body and the seat of governance by way of the FSA was made in a hell comprising the consumer's associations and Bankers' boardrooms. A toxic duo if ever there was one.

Understanding money is a trial for everybody. However if investors understand money and they can use that knowledge and understanding to advantage, then along with the psychology that goes with it, they - and you - can be a winners, whilst affording to ignore what others are stating. A prime example of that principle might be taken over a 10 year period from 1997 - 2007.

Let us suppose that you had authority over a large volume of money and in the thrusting, upward moving, equity market you could envision vast profits being made elsewhere, and therefore being denied to you whilst others thrived. In other words avarice had dulled the reality of your view and others benefited from that growth instead of you.

If that notion was to be combined with the same capital expansion of gilts, increasing in their capital value because interest rates had been decreasing steadily over time; added to the fact that inflation was also reducing, might you think that you could introduce an extra 'tax' to divert a significant part of that 'benefit' being enjoyed by others, if you had the power to do so?

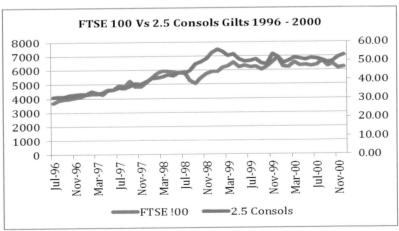

Fig 14.1

It might be that you could alter an existing taxation provision or principle, to cream off some of the excess profit that was being generated within, say, pension funds. This would be 'to the public good', of course, and without undue detriment to the pension funds which were 'trawling profits in' at an inordinate pace.

In short: no one would notice your action by way of detrimental effect. Their funds would still exhibit growth. If it were possible to top up the tax coffers without anybody noticing that would be classed as sharing in others' prosperity, surely?

As much as £5.4 thousand million could be extracted in this way, £5.4 billion a year, every year. Just by a simple sleight of hand. And so it came to pass in 1997 when the tax rules regarding dividend corporation tax relief was altered, I suspect that the move had been planned years beforehand.

The analogy is also applicable to you, in respect of your savings, particularly if you make use of what the Americans call Mutual Funds, or that we in the UK refer to as collective investments such as, Unit Trusts, Open Ended Investment Contracts (OEICs) or Investment Trusts, perhaps through ISA or pension savings arrangements.

If the underlying funds were invested in equities and gilts during 1993 through to 1997: noting that interest rates during that period were reducing; which boosted the value of shares and 'gilt' values within your fund portfolios, your fund would grow significantly. This is where temptation comes in and, like the government, you might think that you can take a little more out than you have been doing in order to provide those little extras.

It is a fallacy, of course, but a very attractive proposition.

This is the hallmark of the Achilles heel of the ISA savings regime (and one which governments love): the accessibility of funds. Unlike pensions or Endowment policies, ISAs are fluid contracts that can be accessed at any time. Investors and savers alike will, inevitably, 'dip into' their plan when the 'need' arises.

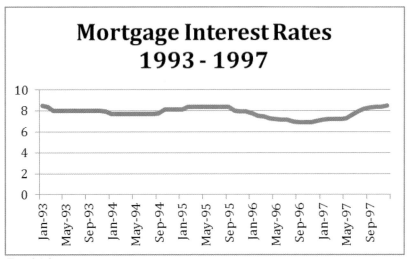

Fig 14.2

When growth rates for savings or investment plans are quoted, they are always averaged over a number of years and that is very much the way we have to deal with long term savings, by considering averages; over the longer term. The problem with 'upsides' is they always have 'downsides'.

In 1991 performance forecasts moved well into double digits. Returns of 14% per annum had been accumulated over the previous ten year period. Now inflation was under control and interest rates were reducing, surely it would not cause any upset just to redirect a little bit of the profit that had been accumulated? Legislation was brought in forcing pension fund managers to have a premium holiday because their pension funds were too big. Can you imagine it? Well, please do imagine it, because it happened.

1996/1997 was really the start of the most recent *'classic market'* phase. It was about that time that shares and the share markets took on a life of their own. Emotion took over from fact and the end result in 1999 was a levelling off of the market and the period of volatility that ran for almost two years largely created by technology shares, until it finally gave way to a long predicted, and savage, halving of the stock market's value.

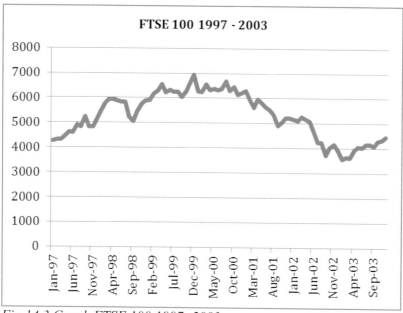

Fig 14.3 Graph FTSE 100 1997 -2003

Over that period of time however, just like the £5.4 thousand million per annum from pension fund taxation that the government came to rely on, you, quite possibly, as an individual came to 'live up to' the new level of return that had been created for you, or that imprudent providers (life assurance and unit trust companies) had forecast, albeit from a false premise. We all did it, we lost sight of reality. It was, after all, different this time around?

Two years of market 'levelling' (1999-2000) then descended into three years of market reversal, the stock market that is. The financial market place became a nightmare situation for pension fund managers who had been invested 70 to 85% in the stock market with trustees praying fervently for a reversal of the downward slide. But the government was still collecting the £5.4 billion every year (or thereabouts). The tax is related to dividends, NOT share values. It stayed relatively constant.

The collapse of share prices also put a strain on the companies themselves as capital dried up and the pension fund premium holiday took effect, born of 'over funding' and a government diktat. The situation for the companies providing pension facilities for their employees had now become 'the norm', contributions to the fund were originally shared by both parties, employer and employee. Post legislation only the employees continued to pay in.

Suddenly, pension contributions became a budget item for expenditure as the payments to the pension funds were forced to recommence in full measure, and for the first time pension fund deficits became a balance sheet item for accounting purposes.

Ouch! To echo ET's immortal words.

Because interest rates were still declining, gilts were steadily climbing in capital value terms. For the first time that I could remember 3.5% War Loan Stock had moved its price above 50p to eventually achieve 90p before falling back.

Fig 14.4 graph of 3.5% WAR LOAN STOCK 1998 - 2009

A further detrimental aspect of the market movements was also taking place however. Gilt yields were reducing therefore the pensions being purchased (annuities) which are linked to gilt yields were costing more to provide, for workers that were retiring, but few in authority felt the facts worthy of mention to the public in these terms. And still the government took their £5.4 billion from the pension scheme funds.

Someone's 'goose was being cooked' and the 'chickens were coming home to roost'.

These are, hopefully, self explanatory clichés.

If you, as a fund manager, or pension fund trustee were 85% invested in equities, the fact that 'gilt' capital values were rising had little balancing effect on your portfolio. Quite the opposite was the case in the circumstances pertaining to pension provision.

Once the share values started to reduce the reduction in yield from the gilt element of the pension portfolio, such as it was, exacerbated the problem rather than assisted in balancing the books. So much for asset allocation, as Equitable Life found to its policyholders' cost. The coincidence of interest rate reduction, the acceleration and follow-on collapse of the stock market, were only offset by the reduction in inflation which held the spending power of pensions in check coupled with the timing of a resurgent property market.

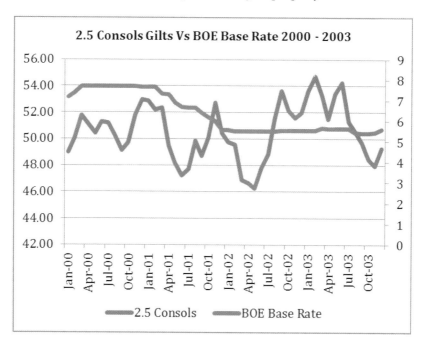

Fig 14.5

The only way for the majority of fund values was to go down and the government, was and still is, extracting that extra amount per month or per year to fund their new level of spending! All £5.4 billion of it (five and two fifths thousand million pounds out of pension funds – possibly your savings). £5,400,000,000,000 per year.

The lesson is hard learnt, yet often forgotten, and, even more frequently ignored.

The effect of just an extra 1% per annum tax charge, management charge, or additional withdrawal per year on a savings plan can be, and in the circumstances described here, was cataclysmic over time.

If dividends are not reinvested, the effect over a working life is absolutely astounding, just imagine what the effect of £5.4 thousand million (billions) being taken out of pension funds every year would have given the market profile that presented itself between 1945 and 2007. You wouldn't want to be there: but you probably were. These are probably your savings and investments possibly set aside for your retirement.

£100 invested in the share 'Equity index' in 1945 would have grown to a return of:

Dividend reinvested   £131,639,
OR
Excluding dividends   £8511.   (figures from Barclays Capital)

<u>Define one billion!!</u>

There is much to be said with regard to:

Understanding the meaning of a Billion

How many zeros in a billion? 1,000,000,000,000   TWELVE

The next time you hear a politician use the word 'billion' in a casual manner, think about whether you want that politician' spending YOUR tax money.

A billion is a difficult number to comprehend, however one

advertising agency did a good job of putting that figure into some perspective in one of its campaigns.

In 2010

A.

A billion seconds ago it was 1959.

B.

A billion minutes ago Jesus was alive.

C.

A billion hours ago our ancestors were living in the Stone Age.

D.

A billion days ago no-one walked on the earth on two feet.

E.

A billion Pounds ago was only
13 hours and 17 minutes,
At the rate our UK government Is spending it.

Building Permit Tax
Cigarette Tax
Corporation Tax
Income Tax
National Insurance (Tax)
Fishing License Tax
Fuel Tax
Inheritance Tax
Stamp Duty Tax
Value Added Tax
Alcohol Tax
Marriage License Tax
Local Rates(Tax)
Development Tax
Vehicle License Registration Tax
Vehicle Sales Tax
TV licence Tax

This is the reality.

Well no; it was never funny was it? What is astounding is that we allowed it to happen.

Not one of these taxes existed 100 years ago...
And our nation was one of the most prosperous in the world.

We had absolutely no national debt...
We had the largest middle class in the world...
And mothers stayed home to raise the children.

What happened?

Can you spell 'politicians?' or 'bureaucracy?'

What caused the banks to 'crash' is to a large degree academic. Emotions run high when markets are moving forward. The 'me too' syndrome takes over - much the same as it did in the later years where house purchase was rampant and commercial property popular.

It gets 'too good to be true', but hey! "I need to have some" and that's exactly what Georgina said (to herself) when she decided in 1998, that everyone else was making money. She was determined to throw caution to the wind. It was just a small investment of just £7,000 into a tax free savings plan, an ISA, what could go wrong?

Well, by 2003, that £7,000 had reduced to £1,237 and 16 pence. It still (in 2010) has not recovered its composure even today. It will, one day. £2236 as at Oct 2010!!

Place yourself in her position; if Georgina had been taking income out of that £7,000 investment (because in her case, dividends were actually being reinvested) what would have been the result? If the investment amount had been £70,000 or a £700,000 pension pot what would have been the effect on Georgina's lifestyle?

Many people use the expression, "it's not timing that's important, it's time in". Always the contrarian, I have to say: "that's a load of tosh."

(Tosh? – It is an actuarial expression. It means, basically, the statement has no foundation in fact).

Timing, in my book, this book, is everything.

If more attention had been paid to TIMING the banking crisis would have been a blip rather than a blot on the financial landscape. More importantly your savings would have been protected; unless, of course, the whole situation was politically conspired to achieve the current situation. Hindsight could well have provided the astute politician with the foresight to make it all happen, in just the way that it did.

Could something have been done to avoid the worst effects of the banking crisis in 2008? The answer is assuredly yes. Could it have been foreseen? Once again the answer is assuredly yes.

It is easy to say that things go wrong, but, of course 'wrong' is a very 'black and white' statement. The secret of success in the financial markets is recognising the grey areas and when 'white starts turning grey,' that is when you need to act at one end of the spectrum. Perhaps that is the investment end and as the situation gets darker then the application of a counter mechanism can do a tremendous amount of good.

Bearing in mind the fact that this book has been about the relationship between property and the stock market and not ignoring cash and fixed interest, but acknowledging that they too inter react with circumstance and the overriding connection in terms of circumstance with property and equity movements, there surely has to be a fiscal mechanism to avoid disaster; though still allowing the markets to function which of course, they must.

In life there have to be winners and there have to be losers and we are not required to feel bad every time somebody loses; because, hopefully they will learn and they will win next time.

Of course some of the stories here, (which are all true by the way, they are not contrived in any way they are all real figures, real people just the names have been changed to protect the innocent), some people just never learn. It is always 'different this time'. The great thing to learn from this book is that it is never different. It is the same, it just looks, sounds, feels, different; and that is the catch.

If I was to concentrate on one thing that would stop the markets moving as enthusiastically as they do, then it would be to concentrate on the property market and return to some of the 'practices' of the 1970s.

Just look at the graphics from the three 'Classic Markets' that have taken place since the late 60s. Examine the three, just look at them side by side and bear in mind the relationship of property to everything else.

We have already concluded that the reason that the initial collapse of the stock market is not a major catastrophe in commercial terms is purely and simply because there is a transfer of money from the stock market, or a transfer of emphasis away from the stock market to residential property initially and latterly the commercial property market. And we can understand why that happens.

As the stock market rises and companies become more confident and more ambitious they expand. Wages rise, people become more affluent and they invest in the stock market and the capital value of their savings goes up. Their household earnings rise, their well-being rises and then they look for the bigger house if they are already home owners. Those that are on the sidelines suddenly realise that they may well be able to buy a house at this juncture. Approximately 70% of households are owner occupied.

Surely that would be the time to offer 100% mortgages? At that point the property market would have been moribund for seven or eight years (following the last crash). Peoples' memories and hurt would have faded a little, the grief of either losing money from negative equity or being stranded in a house that you did not want to stay in but had been forced to, that all starts to recede into the background. Surely that is the time to encourage people, gently, to go into the market by making the market affordable?

The increase in property values is usually quite dramatic with the domestic residential market doubling in perhaps an eighteen month to two year period. That is when the grey starts getting darker.

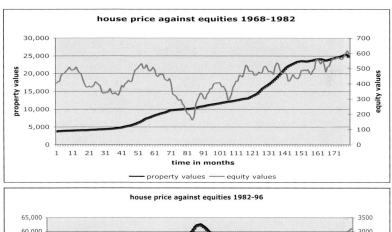

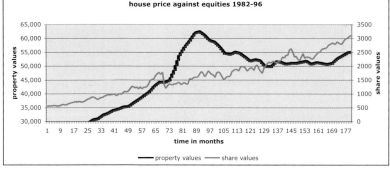

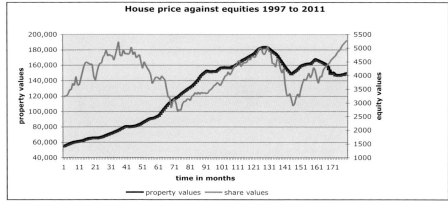

Fig 14.6 The three Classic Market periods:
1968-82,   1983-97, 1997-2011

As we have already discussed the decline in the stock market does not affect the banks too dramatically because the banks themselves, the lending banks, do not hold shares as security; they hold property.

183

The equity in property adds to their ability to lend because the banks' solvency margins can take account of the equity in the property that they hold on charge. This 'point in time' the market is where banks feel good, they have got plenty to lend and they can put money back into commerce which has lost share value but now has a staple asset value to borrow against and the banks have plentiful reserves above their solvency margins to be able to lend.

At the first doubling of the domestic market, the banks should revert to 95% then 90% then 85% then 80% 'loan to value' lending and that should be enforced across the board. If it was the only regulatory requirement it would be 100% more effective than what we had from the Financial Services Authority from 2003 onwards.

As the domestic housing market flows, the banks' confidence in lending turns, as it always does, to the commercial property market. There is encouragement there for company proprietor/owners to invest in their own properties or to expand their infrastructure loans set against the security of those properties. But again as the hue moves from 'white to grey,' in other words as commercial property values escalate, the banks need to move back from 75% or 80% 'loan to value' to 70%, 65% and 60% because they know they need their safety margin if the property market comes 'off the top' - and it will; every time.

In the background to all of this the Construction Industry which employs about a third of the people in the country apparently, will have been gearing up; to initially produce new houses, build estates, more high-rise flats but they will get the warning signals that money is not available for them to keep going into the world of 'make-believe'. Once we experience the introduction of free white goods and 'pay your legal fees' offers, or 'carpets are included' the usual prelude to a slowing market, then the banks would be alert to the fact that they need to drop their percentages of 'loan to value' back to realistic levels.

Similarly with commercial property, and there is a natural movement from residential to commercial property unless, as I believed happened in 2005, government intervention actually distorts the whole market and brings the two property markets, residential and commercial down together. It is when that occurs that you get the catastrophic problems that we had in 2008, because property was devaluing so quickly the banks just could not claw in enough cash to make up their solvency margins deficit.

So deep was their entrenchment in property related mortgage loans with a shrinking equity margin that the banks had a huge task on their hands particularly as a dive into oblivion with the stock market is usually accompanied by a movement down in interest rates which is necessary to increase bank margins so that more of what they take in interest goes to their balance sheet as mortgage rates stay high whilst base rates go low.

By using this mechanism to the full, (grading percentage 'loan to value' thresholds for mortgage loans) the drama is reduced, the housing market will level out earlier. There will always be a 'blip' upward in house prices because, there are always 'market enthusiasts', who believe the bottom has come therefore it is time to get back in, ignoring as they do, the fact that the banks have to rebuild their reserves and that process of rebuilding will take time. Therefore it will take time for lending to get back to anything like its previous volumes.

If more discipline was introduced into the market mechanism there would be no need for drama or State bail outs. Closures would happen because they always do; the economy would slow because it always does. It is the 'ebb and flow' of life. However, the catastrophic "fallout" like that of 2008 would, I believe, be avoided.

Reverting to first principles the stock market will start to recover again because it is basically the only place that people can generate the income that has been lost through low interest rates (which investors will stand for a twelve to eighteen months but not much longer).

Gilts as we know, are a 'no-no' because if interest rates rise from a relatively low point then the capital value of most fixed interest stock will almost assuredly go down. The capital market at the front end of the *'Classic Market'* turns into an income based secure underpin (well fancy calling shares secure) and the whole cycle starts all over again.

CHAPTER 15

FINANCING THE NATION'S STATE PENSION

International concern over the provision of income in retirement, whether justified or not, became a major topic in early 2002 due to the decline in stock market valuations.

Indeed, State Pension provision has been a major topic for a number of years and the gatherings of the wise to discuss the topic plus actuaries, economists and administrative providers to dissect the nuances that engage their thoughts from time to time, have brought together a general consensus that there are indeed three strategies, three pillars as described by the World Bank Organisation, for the adequate provision of income in retirement.

These three pillars should form the clearly defined mechanisms adopted by nations to ensure that their retirees and elderly live in reasonable comfort and that those people do not become a drain on state welfare.

Pillar One

Denotes a 'Pay-as-you-go' system of contribution through taxation, social contribution, National Insurance, whatever one would call it, to be redirected by government from taxpayers to retirees.

This can be described as a National Insurance Scheme, un-funded. In other words not invested, providing benefits that are only paid to those eligible in proportion to their contributions. (This should not be confused with Social Welfare which is paid to anyone in need of state support whether they have contributed to the coffers or not).

Future generations' contributions will pay the benefits of today's contributors, who are "paying" the pensions of past contributors.

Pillar Two

Incorporates compulsion and is effectively a partnership between state and commercial providers, whereby funds are collected and invested on behalf of a population of contributors. The funds derived therefrom are distributed as pensions to qualifying individuals at an appropriate time. This is an 'assurance' scheme where those who contribute are assured of benefits when they retire.

Those benefits, however, are dependent upon the performance of the underlying funds. The individual funds their own pension 'pot.'

Pillar Three

Provides wholly commercial pensions on either an employer/employee contributions paid basis, or a personal pension plan basis. Contributions are paid through employment with either a defined benefit or defined contribution driving the scheme or by individual arrangements, arranged privately by the individual or as a series of individual arrangements supported and administered by an employer.

The benefits in this element are on the face of things individual. They certainly are 'individual' where personal pensions (individual arrangements) are involved. Defined benefit arrangements, however, take on a 'group fund' dimension which can rely on new entrants cross subsidising mature members.

....

Some nations have facilities that bear a resemblance to all three but most just have one or two of the pillars in place. In common with a 3 legged stool the lack of that third element can prove catastrophic when circumstances dictate.

An overriding feature that emerges from examination of pensions on an international basis is that local customs, emotions, feelings, call them what you will, override pure economic accounting and fiscal considerations. Trust stems from the cohort acceptance that in return for contributions made, benefits will be paid. Certainly in the United Kingdom: security, certainty and guarantees are the primary requisite of any scheme provided by the government through the pay-as-you-go system.

There is an innate expectancy that benefits will be paid even though perhaps, there is an underlying knowledge that those contributions that are being paid today are being distributed, literally, tomorrow.

The least publicised, yet most common form of pay-as-you-go pension, is that installed for the United Kingdom Civil Service in 1834 under the Superannuation Act of that year and revised by the Superannuation Act 1859. It was via these two acts of Parliament that the criteria for 2/3rds final salary with an accrual rate of 1/60 of earnings per year, was established.

Changes have taken place since that date to create the current regime where there is an absence of commutation to cash within the pension accrual rate of 1/80 of final salary to a maximum of 40/80 (half final salary as defined). The tax-free cash sum available on the United Kingdom government employee system is separately calculated to avoid confusion at a rate of 3n/80 per year of service. Put more simply 1½ times final salary (as defined) can be taken as a tax-free cash sum after 40 years service and the accrued pension must be taken as income.

Civil Service pensions were non-contributory and are totally unfunded. They operate therefore, on a pay-as-you-go basis. An element of contribution exists in some areas of government employment as explained in Chapter 9, but it is largely cosmetic in reality. Since 1997 public sector pay has risen by 6% (against private sector 3%) in order to 'show' a contribution to pension benefits.

It was not until the 1947 National Insurance Act that a genuine State Pension scheme was put into place in the UK (1948), although in the Beveridge Report this too was on a pay-as-you-go system with benefits at a subsistence level.

In the meantime public sector pension schemes have expanded dramatically and by 1956, when the first individual pensions were allowed by act of Parliament to have full tax relief on contributions and the underlying funds to similarly be tax exempt, the public sector had grown to 3.7 million members.

It is perhaps worth noting that at this time (1956) there were 4.3 million employees in private pensions with just over half that number in insured schemes.

Fiscal incentives were making people less dependent on the State but it was recognised that an underlying, base level, state provided pension was essential; pre-funding of such a scheme was seen as politically untenable.   How could those who were paying contributions (effectively being drawn by pensioners immediately) be expected to put extra money away for their own pensions as well and how would the government deal with that money in any event? Public finances work on a 12-month income and expenditure cycle. Governments are not acknowledged to have expertise in fund management.

Underlying much of this state provision was the influence of the Trade Union Movement in order to establish a *'de minimus'* standard of living for citizens in retirement.

In the 1960's the desire to link retirement pensions provided by the State with earnings created a new awareness. Germany had moved into the provision of such a facility as had other European countries and Britain therefore, set out to improve pensions in two directions.

First of all the State wanted to divest itself of as much pension provision responsibility as it could and centralise private pensions but secondly, as already stated, it set out to enhance the income that it (the government) was providing.

However, this second, earnings related element (Graduated Pension), was once again to be provided on a pay-as-you-go basis and build up benefits for the future – which future generations would have to fund.

Fertility rates in those years were relatively high at 2.2 children per family. The post war baby boom had created a young workforce and by the mid 60's, politicians could perhaps feel that for the older generation to rely on the younger generation for its income in retirement was not an unreasonable assertion. But things do change.
By the late 1960's wage inflation was starting to come through and coincidently a new style or construction of savings media had come to the fore. The economy was propelling itself forward, property

prices were moving up in rapid leaps, commensurate with the new found wealth of individuals and the State was promoting home ownership at the same time as the savings media was entering a phase of equity investment. Promises could be made but could they be kept?

The 1970's heralded very mixed messages and the pay-as-you-go system of pension provision was to suffer dramatically during the passing of that decade. Stock market growth and property price inflation moved ahead rapidly in the early years of the 1970's. The stock market started to decline in 1972 and it lost 73% of its value over the ensuing 2 years. The FT30 Index rested at 146 before suddenly racing ahead to recover 2/3 of its loss by mid 1975, climbing in 1976 and forging ahead subsequently through the end of that decade. Progress continued ever upwards at an alarming rate until almost the end of the next decade.

Inflation had also taken hold in the 70's, rising through 1974 coinciding with the depths of the stock markets' misery, to 24.6%, and at points reaching almost 30%.

Many associate the 1980's with an increase in the number of self-employed. What observers often failed to connect is the huge numbers of failures, large stock companies that reduced their workforces dramatically in the wake of the stock market downturn and international recession, throwing those people onto State benefits. Those benefits had to be paid for from taxation.

They had created a situation where those retiring from local government and civil service positions gained the full benefits of the Pension (Increase) Acts of the early 1970's, which made their pension benefits inflation proof.

Those areas of government employment where the pensions were being paid on a pay-as-you-go basis were suddenly increasing at 25% per annum. This increase also had to be paid out of taxation. In a pay-as-you-go system there was absolutely no buffer to lighten the burden. What government needed was income; and they needed it quickly.

About that time (1973) the then Conservative government Social Security Minister (later Sir) Keith Joseph put forward a notion that the Graduated Pension Insurance fund (GPI) which was wholly inadequate and that there should be a funded second tier of State Pension.

In 1975 the government changed but an all party consensus agreed that a State Earnings Related Pension Scheme (SERPS) should be installed, but still PAYE based. This would be funded by an extra National Insurance contribution paid by employer and employee (in addition to the National Insurance contributions already being taken to provide the basic State Pension and certain other social benefits) and that this new contribution would build up over a 20 year period to provide 25% of average earnings over a rolling 20 year period.

As a pay-as-you-go system this meant that the government were taking in approximately 20 times more than they needed to pay out and the extra would be very useful in coping with the added expenses that have already been mentioned in other areas of the pay-as-you-go system that government were responsible for. There was no room for a funded scheme because there was no excess of income over expenditure to put away if one took the pot as a whole.

Of course the stock market collapse (it was said) was caused by oil prices increasing very rapidly over a short space of time. It does appear that if the State had been able to take advantage of the stock market recovery, the current situation may have been different.

By the mid 1980's the full effects of paying inflation-proof pensions to retired government employees, plus the realisation that in 1998 the SERPS as originally designed would be delivering a high level of supplementary pension benefit on top of the basic State Pension at a rate of 20/20 the government actuary decided that some 'horns should be drawn in.' Contributions remained the same, benefits were downgraded to 20% over a rolling 20-year basis and widow's pensions would also be discontinued. The latter from 1998 and the former would become effective in 2006. A promise is a promise – unless it stems from government.

This manipulation of the scheme and the later denial that SERPS was an 'insurance' scheme paved the way for yet more effort to be put into directing the public into pension arrangements that were not the responsibility of the State but rather funded schemes that were the responsibility of commerce.

The 1986 Finance Act withdrew the ability for an employer to compel an employee to join a pension scheme and a new breed of personal pension was brought in, in 1988, to allow those employees who wished to make their own provision in their own pension funds more able to do so. Employers had lost the ability to insist that their employees joined company pension schemes if they had one, individual choice prevailed.

The result of that initiative and the tax benefits that went with it, together with a very strong and determined commercial sales force working from the backdrop of a very successful and sturdy stock market was that 22 ½ million people out of 27 million employees and self-employed were either in occupational pension schemes operated by employers or personal pensions on a broadly 50/50 split basis. The ploy had seemingly worked and the pressure on the state to provide benefits in the longer term was reduced in line with the reduction already mentioned under the SERPS entitlements.

It is perhaps interesting to examine the tables that show the escalating cost of civil service and local authority pension scheme provisions during this time because of the burden in cost of pension benefits and the fact that the trade union movement had been contained during the late 70's, many local authority people were made redundant (as were many from the private sector). It was a slimming-down process that once again fell to be funded from pension schemes.

However, whereas private pension schemes had benefited immensely from the upsurge in equity growth in their funded arrangements, allowing them (rightly or wrongly), to enhance benefits by adding additional years to service for those who would 'leave quietly' under a redundancy package, the State had no such provision.

All the State had was the excess of SERPS money if people were making contributions that were over and above that required for benefits that needed to be paid out. Local Authority pension schemes were a mixture of funded and un-funded and we shall talk about those in a subsequent chapter. But here was the manifestation of the negative aspect of a pay-as-you-go arrangement. Cost escalation can clearly be seen from the table on the following pages, compiled by the author when working with the Federation for Small Businesses (FSB).

In the year 1998 SERPS had reached full maturity. By 2002 the Basic State Pension, which was decoupled over a decade ago from wage inflation and became linked to prices (which invariably rise at a slower rate and are open to interpretation) had fallen back from 25% of average national earnings to 17%. Once again the government actuary had reportedly taken a view of the future under a pay-as-you-go system, that SERPS was "untenable." It was in effect an escalating burden on future generations and fertility had now dropped to 1.7 average children per family whilst mortality had improved by an even greater rate.

There is still much disquiet about the mechanism of pay-as-you-go being a viable means of providing State Pension in the future. There are uncertainties which go with it. Fertility is an obvious problem as fewer and fewer babies are born to each family cohort. Individuals are settling down later. Morbidity is improving and personal saving is at an all time low.

The move by government to transfer the cost of providing pensions from the State 60% and the private sector 40% in the early 60's, to a new regime where the State provided 40% of pensions and the private sector 60% has not only not been achieved: such progress as was made is now in reverse.

Choice, in essence, has failed. The free market through commerce has been so badly undermined by rhetoric, innuendo and sensationalism, coupled with a good dose of ineptitude, that public confusion and that element of trust that is so essential to provide security, guarantees and certainty as outlined at the beginning of this analysis must lead to an alternative strategy and that alternative strategy may well lie in the second pillar.

Data	1979	1980	1981	1982	1983	1996	1997	1998	1999	2000
Employed Population 000s	22991	22991	21892	21414	21067	23220	22812	23699	23929	24000
Contracted Out Population 000s	8947	9040	8992	8841	8600	13769	13750	13750	13750	13750
Contracted In Population 000s	14044	13951	12900	12573	12467	9451	9062	9949	10179	10250
Average Earnings £pw	92.00	111.15	125.35	137.15	148.77	351.50	367.60	384.50	389.37	392.76
Basic State Pension £pw	23.20	27.15	29.60	32.85	34.05	61.15	62.45	64.70	66.75	67.50
Contracted Out Serps Recipients 000s										
Serps Recipient 000s	81	278	479	663	888	4962	5317	5655	5655	5865
Average Pension £pw	0.38	0.60	0.83	0.97	1.13	10.51	11.40	12.62	13.00	13.00

What can be seen from this table is the effect of the slowly growing population of serps recipients over time. The excess of contributions over benefits paid was not " put on deposit" to quote Baroness Hollis, it was spent!

What this table does not show is that if the excess SERPS contributions had been invested 25% in government gilts and 75% in the stock market for the full 20 years the surplus in the National insurance fund would not have been the notional (where is it, please) £31 billion, it would have been a clearly defined and accessible (to the contributors to that fund) of £332.36 billion. And they were told.

195

Chapter 16

STATE AND COMMERCE COMBINE TO FUND THE LONG TERM

The structure of the second pillar for pension provision has already been categorised by the World Banking Organisation (WBO) (notice that these major provisions for government workers always follow a major financial catastrophe).

Contribution levels and benefits were prescribed under the 1975 Act and only those local authorities that had created schemes under their own act of parliament prior to 1937 were exempt from operating under its rules. This is therefore, the United Kingdom's Second Pillar Pensions model. These local authority schemes were funded as an alternative to the pay as you go system.

Industry based (Printers, Construction Industry, etc) and affinity pension schemes have been created by large employers under actuarial guidance or the auspices of life assurance companies whereby if an individual was employed within a certain sector or by a certain employer then the terms and conditions of that employment were that they joined the pension scheme and that a proportion of the individual's income was deducted to be put to one side for their future benefits.

In the 1960's wage constraints became such that pension provision was one of the bargaining tools for encouraging deferred pay as a means of circumventing the restrictive wage conditions and high tax regime that prevailed. Many other European countries adopted a similar philosophy, Holland, Denmark and Germany being among them. Typical contributions would be between 3% and 6% of earnings for employees with the employer topping up at a contribution level that was necessary to maintain the financial integrity of the scheme and create sufficient reserves to service future benefit liabilities.

Following the Finance Act 1921 changes also occurred in the taxation of pension funds, which allowed such funds to be exempt from taxation on income accruing to the fund.

The fiscal changes, post 1921, were certainly helpful in creating an environment where occupational pension funds could grow and by 1930 more than 1,200 funds had been approved under the Act. By 1936 nearly 1,900 schemes were in operation, mainly provided by large employers.

All such schemes had to be set up under a reputable trust and there were costs involved in doing so which made such schemes less attractive to smaller employers. It was not until 1956 when the membership of such schemes had risen to 3.7 million in public sector schemes and 4.3 million in the private sector (2.3 million of them in insured schemes) that action was taken under the Finance Act of that year.

Life assurance companies were empowered to create a separate fund for pension investments, entirely separate from the life fund, which would not be subject to tax. This put insured schemes on exactly the same basis as company self administered schemes under trust, as already mentioned, and brought the cost of pension provision down as the fiscal advantage improved the overall level of investment returns. It was also at this time that a specific individual contract was made available under the Act for the self-employed and those in non-pensionable employment. (S226 Retirement Annuity.)

It is worth reiterating the point at this stage that those in pensionable employment were obliged to join the scheme.

Thus Second Tier Pensions gave way to Third Tier (wholly commercial pensions), which will be discussed later.

Holland and Denmark had very strong Trade Union representation (although not necessarily Trade Union membership) when negotiating with employers. Therefore, they continued to develop strong strategies that contained wages and maintained retirement benefits within all encompassing schemes, within the confines of either an industry or employer environment. In excess of 90% membership and coverage was achieved within these nations whereas within the United Kingdom the proportion of employees covered by first and second pillar pensions was said to be much lower.

Indeed, with the exception of Local Authorities, Police, Fire, Health Service and Teaching together with the Judiciary and other smaller elements of what could be described as public employees a strictly defined Second Pillar Pension has never been applied to the general workforce within the United Kingdom. Even the compulsion to join company pension arrangements was removed under the Finance Act 1986, as Trade Union power within the United Kingdom diminished through the late 70's and early 80's encompassing the recession and huge redundancy programmes of that era.

National Insurance as we have discussed had moved into the Graduated Pension (GPI), pay as you go, second tier addition to basic State Pension but funded National Insurance schemes were not really debated until 1973 and then only briefly prior to the SERPS being brought in under a strict 'pay as you go' system in 1978.

Local authority schemes do however, provide us with a very useful model to examine and comment upon. Local authority schemes are not assured schemes. They are managed internally and benefits are paid out from a central fund operated by the authority. Any shortfalls are made up through local rates and latterly community service contributions. Authorities have their own investment department and pensions administrators but often take advice from external investment consultants with regard to the balance of those funds.

In Denmark the situation was entirely the reverse. 94% of all employees were covered by the Second Tier Scheme and each scheme representing its own particular sector would be invested in a 'With Profits' style of fund which smoothed benefits over time and was underwritten by a life assurance company. That still pertains to date.

Stock market growth from the mid 70's right through to 1987/1988 was very high and so were the inflationary influences of, broadly, index linked pay and, certainly, index linked pension benefits.

When inflation reached just under 20% per annum in 1979 retired colleagues of working local authority employees were earning more in pension than their colleagues were in salary. The strain on pension funds was becoming intolerably high because local taxation could not catch up on the deficits that would arise if stock market returns were to fall. The government endeavoured to address the situation by depopulating local government and forcing external contractors to take over the work, and thereby the pension costs for their employees. It was a fool's errand.

Departments have still to carry the burden of over-enthusiastic over-optimistic promises - for upwards of forty years!

However, the Trade Union movement was and is still very strong in local government as well as national government areas and TUPE became the order of the day. This meant that any employee leaving local government service and entering a parallel private provider of employment had to have pension benefits which were broadly in line with those that he or she had left. A transfer was therefore affected from the public sector to the private sector for the future pension liability build up under the existing contracts of employment.

Concurrently to this process, many local government employees were urged to take early retirement. Early retirement was affected between aged 50 and 60 and under the terms of the local authority pensions provision regulations up to 12 years pension enhancement was available which meant that although a local authority employee would still have to wait until aged 62, say, for their pension to be paid, it would be paid as if they had continued in service until that age if they were now only aged 50.

The full economic impact of the practice can be established and the shortcomings of such a system analysed. The trimming down of major nationalised industries such as steel, mining and so on all adopted the same process with similar results. There was an obvious assumption that equity markets would continue to provide the very substantial returns that they had hitherto and the eternal hope was that that would make up for the cash deficits that would invariably arise on more modest assumptions.

The reality was that with inflation running ahead of investment returns the real returns were negative whilst the actual pension enhancements were very positive. When severe market reductions occurred, and if they were prolonged, then the adverse mathematics of the situation highlighted the disadvantages.

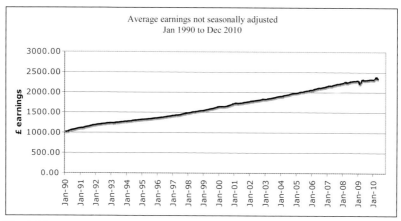

Fig 16.1

There is, despite the foregoing, a very good rationale for a true second pillar public private partnership for the general population.

As discussed previously SERPS had not failed in or of itself, it had failed because it was not a funded scheme. As the table in the previous chapter intimates, had SERPS contributions been invested (instead of being used for other social purposes including the makeup of deficits for local authority schemes and funding early retirements with pensions in immediate payment) a substantial surplus would have been built up by the year 2000 (£332 billion).

Therefore, historically one can justify that basic methodology but accept the need for an entirely different managed investment methodology. The problem associated with such a methodology was the commercial implications of such a mechanism and its political (capitalistic) implications.

The basis for a long term investment or savings strategy is rather akin to a ship on the ocean with the wind moving in one direction, the tide moving in another, the boat's thrust driving it in yet another and all the time moving up and down laterally and longitudinally, forever adjusting to attain a final destination. Financial markets are no different. It is the control and management of those conditions that are essential for second pillar partnerships to succeed.

From the foregoing it does appear that governance of schemes is all important and that whatever attributes one applies to contribution, internal costs and final benefits; there has to be a relationship between all three of those and the ability of those that provide the overarching decision making process concerning those elements to deliver on promises.

The years 1921 and 1956 are significant because at those two pivotal points governments recognised the need for a controlled environment either through a board of trustees or through a company limited by guarantee (the life assurance companies). Little appears to have changed. The only difficulties that manifest themselves and create shortfalls or misdirection of funds appear to be politically motivated therefore if that element can be removed such that the overriding focus of such schemes, within the second pillar regime, is wholly and solely on the eventual benefits delivered to contributors to that scheme then the problem can be resolved.

Is there any international model for that assertion? That answer appears to be yes. Denmark and Holland have both operated second pillar pension arrangements successfully over a long number of years. Therefore, the mechanics of those two national schemes bears investigation and analysis but, unfortunately, not here.

In the United Kingdom we have endeavoured to provide a second pillar function by what is termed contracting out. Mandatory contributions are made to a scheme which allows part of an occupational pension scheme or personal pension arrangement to be established as a separate entity from the main scheme, to be funded by rebates passed on directly by the employer to the institution under an occupational scheme environment and by government through the contributions/benefits agency to "protected rights" personal pensions on an individual basis.

In the United Kingdom such a system was introduced in the 1960's when graduated pensions were introduced and occupational schemes could 'contract out' of that government sponsored – earnings related – addition to N.I. In 1978 that system was enhanced and 'perpetuated' under the SERPS regime and in 1988 that was further extended so that those contracting out of SERPS by way of personal pensions could also have a fund which provided a measure of additional benefit that removed the burden of funding from the state to the public environment.

Contributions to the scheme, one way or another, were compulsory but of course there remained a commercial bias and a marketing and distribution cost that needed to be accounted for. It is the marketing and distribution costs of such schemes that have paved the way for the United Kingdom's £20 billion plus compensation marathon that has reduced public trust in the pensions provision mechanism and decimated huge swathes of the pension provision infrastructure.

To succeed therefore, in practical terms, marketing and distribution costs need to be removed from the equation, but is that practicable?

Marketing and distribution costs are essential for the long-term security of pension providers and thereby the security of those pensioners whose funds are entrusted to their safekeeping. But there is vested interest in the whole process which can be taken account of in a free market, as under a third pillar, but has no place under a compulsory second pillar arrangement. Indeed, it is counter-productive to use the Chilean example at this point to merely explain the commercial aspects of risk/return of market penetration and the effectiveness of the sales process.

Chile started from a green field site. There was no pension scheme therefore the strategy was that one should be established on a wholly commercial basis with sales people entering the market place to purvey products. It was probably a correct assessment and good value for money. Sales were achieved, those providing that sales mechanism were remunerated and the products with the long-term horizon were created for future pensioners to benefit from. It has been a success. It, in itself, regenerated commerce.

The Chilean model was compulsory, and by definition a hybrid Second Pillar arrangement, it provides an ideal mechanism for comparison. Analysis of the Chilean experience had been deferred to the area of this publication dealing with the third pillar because that is where it belonged. But what it does highlight is the changing nature of a marketplace and the changing risk/reward status of investments used within those marketplaces.

The advent of that regular contribution, investment orientated mechanism, in similar vein to equity investment through regular savings plans in the United Kingdom, America and other sophisticated economies drove the Chilean economy forward. As demand for equity investment, along with government stock grew, the whole mechanism grew in stature. As it grew contributors and potential contributors could see, feel and understand what that growth meant in regard to their contributions. They could see their funds growing and that generated more income to the funds, which further perpetuated the growth of those funds.

A problem only arose when the Chilean economy had indigestion and money had to find other markets to invest in (foreign money was now starting to come into Chile to take advantage of the growth potential there) and more importantly the sales people had run out of people to sell to. This was no longer a green field site; it was a semi mature market place, thus highlighting the changing nature of this type of venture.

In that environment the commercial influence could truly be felt as providers competed in a tighter, far more competitive market place by proclaiming the benefits of their fund over a competitor's. Transferring money away from one provider to another became the salesman's preoccupation. Does that sound familiar in the UK 2006 – 2010?

It is the only way the sales force can earn money and the only way that the underlying fund managed can continue to grow.

'New business strain' at this point would also become more of a feature because whereas the liabilities to pay pensions, which were now becoming due, would have been taken from new premium income, those who were economically seen as less efficient but in truth would only be guilty of less heavy capitalisation, would need to sell investments to pay benefits.

The number of providers fell rapidly from double-digit numbers to low single-digit. Competition became stultified and the whole system stagnated. New business became tempered by new entrants who in effect started to pay for exiting pensioners' maturity proceeds.

That pure commercial model takes on the mantle of a 'pay as you go' sandwich with a funded core to act as a buffer. Any major market movement would create a disaster. Such a disaster occurred in Argentina, which had adopted the Chilean mechanism. The result of this was the government in Argentina seizing on funds put aside for pensions to get them out of their national financial difficulties. There is a ring of familiarity there.

Compulsion must therefore be safe. All major surveys in the past 10 years have concluded that the British people require security, certainty and guarantees at all socio economic levels with regards to benefits provided from their National Insurance contributions.

As with France the workforce view National Insurance as a separate entity to tax, providing a long-term benefit to which there is an undoubted entitlement. Everyone accepts taxation provides for today's expenditure but few readily acknowledge that there is a chance that their benefits will fail to be paid at retirement from their National Insurance payments. People expect: 'security, certainty and guarantees'.

The model therefore, for a true second pillar pension has to be founded on governance that is entirely separate from government and its offices. Those providing that governance would be the major employer and employee representatives with some other general representation from trade bodies and consumer groups. The board would not be entrusted with fund management and should not have any influence over the distribution of funds. It would merely 'oversee fair play.'

'Contracting out' would cease to be an option because if this were a true partnership then the need to contract out and move away from government to commercial ordinance would be unnecessary.

The removal of marketing and distribution costs can only be achieved under a co-insured fund. As the 1921 Act and the 1956 Act clearly illustrate: the closely regulated, asset based, underpin of life assurance companies is the only mechanism that can provide security, certainty and guarantees without undue risk. Using the principals of 'With Profits' funding, such as that used in Denmark incorporating a broad portfolio where profits were held back to produce a smoothing of market fluctuation plus the application of a guarantee which would reflect earnings in every year of work from aged 16 to a chosen retirement age, would be extremely beneficial.

Phased retirement could also be a feature of such a scheme, which would allow an individual to take 1/5 of their income at an age of their choice and 2/5 in a subsequent year, eventually building up to 5/5 of complete pension as they enter total retirement. This would allow mentoring in the work place and a steady progression from full employment and the level of income that is attributed to that, to full retirement and the adjustment to the lower income from pension alone.

Such a system would also allow mentoring, as older experienced workers are financially able to devote time to the non-productive activity of teaching youngsters moving into the industry or profession the "tricks of the trade".

The self-employed would also benefit from this arrangement and feel that they were getting value for money for Class IV National Insurance contributions because these could similarly be invested on their behalf and as the surplus of contribution over benefits paid is invested on their behalf, a small incremental amount would be added to their basic pension. It should be noted that self-employment is not a lifelong status for the majority of people.

Self-employment is something entered into (as in the 1980's) as a necessity when redundancy or unemployment presents itself. Redundancy money can very often be invested in a notion of self-employment that in 80% of the cases sees a return to employment and a completely extinguished capital resource within 18 months to 3 years. The system therefore, can allocate a second pillar pension benefit in the same way that it does for employees.

Any move to higher risk or broad market speculation needs to be carried out in the full commercial market place of the third tier.

Chapter 17

SOCIO ECONOMIC STRATEGIES THAT WORK LONG TERM

The commercial structure of pensions takes many forms and has evolved over a long number of years in varying market conditions, some outlined in the previous chapters. Pillar III is a hugely varied landscape to examine.

What we need to consider separately is the whole long term planning market place under different headings. Most occupational pension schemes because they are large funds, controlled by a board of trustees, appoint external managers to create a balance to their investment portfolio. Perhaps a good place to start is to emphasise that the concentration on pension provision reflects the importance of long term planning and analysis in order to understand how one creates and maintains a balanced investment portfolio.

Defined benefit pension schemes have a target to reach, a goal to attain, a guarantee to be met. The nature of the schemes and the decisions made in the investment process are therefore extremely interesting. The performance of pooled funds, where the trustees create what I euphemistically call the tea urn principle of popping all of the investments in one pot, mixing them up and then as people desire an output, the tap is opened and whatever consistency has accrued inside is dispensed. It may change over time as the ingredients change. To continue the metaphor more water may be added, teabags, milk and so on.

The component parts vary in strength and proportion over time but they contribute to the whole rather than a composite of individual separately managed funds with individual separate constitutional parts. Regulations change over time to determine the acceptable and non-acceptable investments that can be used in these funds. They have increasingly become measured in the short-term with under-performing managers "taking an early bath" whilst thrusting, upwardly mobile, pretenders to the throne are brought in to replace them.

But is that a philosophy that works? I do not subscribe to it.

The trustees by and large have no specific knowledge of investment fundamentals. They are lay people with a responsibility to the beneficiaries and potential beneficiaries (members) of the pension scheme to obtain best value by avoiding fraudulent activity, misappropriation of funds and downright dishonesty. They can certainly question investment decisions but most are poorly placed to actually make them.

The trustees will convene several times a year to receive reports from internal and external accountants, to go through an assessment of the pension scheme's income and expenditure.

Actuaries will be brought in to assess the scheme's viability over the long-term in meeting its liabilities for benefits promised and the assumed investment returns that make those promises being realistically attainable or not. If the benefits are unachievable then the board of trustees will need to call on the host company to increase the funding rate. In the reverse situation however, contributions may be decreased in the short-term or as a permanent feature. Permanence lasts until the next review of course. A full review is legally required to be completed by an actuary every 3 years.

This is no different than you, as an individual, may do in your own private life.

Those delegated to look after the investment profile of the scheme would also report for the short, medium and long view in an endeavour to convince the trustees, the accountants and the actuaries that they could sleep at night. The investment managers' strategies vary tremendously and, arguably, so they should. Hiring individuals determines an individual view.

Whichever window one looks out of, one get a different view even of the same landscape if one moves up two or three floors. Investment management is anyone's view of the landscape from where they happen to be at that particular time. As we will see, there is no model portfolio that is valid over time. Like most things in life the scene is constantly changing.

In many ways one form of investment management predominates over the rest. Equity biased, stockbroker based advisers have an intense dislike for institutional investments incorporating guarantees. Very few schemes pay a fixed fee unless of course it is a fixed percentage of the fund, which is illusory as a fixed entity. Very few costs are transaction based, as there have always been concerns about commission bias. Which is the best? Only time ever tells. A growing platform of "expert" media appear to have an ever changing and profound effect upon the market place in one way or another.

But what do the results look like?

There are very few genuine **managed** funds. It is relatively easy to switch several hundred thousand pounds worth of stock from one place to another, without adversely affecting the market place. However, when one moves into multi-million pounds of funds changing direction from say equities to gilts, gilts to property, property to cash, whatever happens to be in favour, then major problems can occur. It is in that context that one can readily understand that managed funds become more and more restricted in their ability to 'manage' as they increase in size. They are more worthy of the title "mixed funds."

A fund manager therefore, such as Phillips and Drew Fund Managers (PDFM) in the late 90's, may start to divest investments in, say, equities, sooner rather than later where they have a view that that market is going to deliver inferior returns or maybe even go into reverse. Much is said about September 11th 2001 or as the euphemism now is '9/11'. But the truth is that the markets were already showing signs of over valuation and correction well before '9/11'. For many professionals '9/11' was just seen as an excuse to act rather more quickly than one would prudently have done under normal circumstances.

PDFM had identified that the stock market was fragile. They did reduce their equity holdings in anticipation of the market correction starting as early as 1999 and their short-term performance suffered as a consequence. Over time the trustees of a large number of pension schemes advised by their accountant, actuary and investment managers elected for a major shift in focus and changed their **fund manager,** rather than their fund's constituent parts.

Indeed, PDFM who specialised in advising local authorities were seemingly rewarded for their prudence by losing a reported amount in excess of 40% of their funds under management; a great disincentive to do what turned out to be the right thing to do. The funds are hugely significant and the fees attending them apparently worth the occasional stab in the back. There was no direct access however to real property in the move away from equities. REITs did not surface in the UK until 2006.

The pressure to change invariably comes from people with the least knowledge but the most to lose, or gain. It is rather like the driver of a motorcar stripping down the engine using a rudimentary mechanics guide to a highly sophisticated fuel injection system. The motoring analogy can continue with regard to hazardous conditions.

Adapting to the markets is somewhat akin to adapting to a skid. When we drive a motor vehicle, we wouldn't dream of making sharp corrections to our direction of travel even in dry conditions. We learn from an early age on a tricycle, bicycle, roller skates, ice skates, roller blades, even the humble scooter, that abrupt change in direction creates at worst, an immediate toppling of the vehicle into metaphoric oblivion and at best a swerving and swaying from side to side that only accelerates in magnitude the more we attempt to correct it.

On the skidpan (or perhaps on ice or hard packed snow) we learn very quickly that "every action causes an equal and opposite reaction" that can lead to disaster, without experienced control.

What on earth has that got to do with the stock market?

Everything.

If savers would only save and investors would only invest with the cohesive view as to where the destination is, and allow their vehicle to travel using the experience of professional guidance, then more would perhaps achieve the journey without incident. However in modern times they tend not to. Change is thrust at the investor constantly. Short term losses or gains are wedded to short term past performance graphs.

When the markets turn down (the beginning of a swerve) they immediately try to adjust. That is the beginning of the skid. Instead of buying in to it (as one steers into a skid) they do exactly the opposite. They withdraw their funds, which only serves to accentuate the problem and drive the markets further down.

Of course the situation looks worse in the short term.

When a car gets into a skid, and we steer into the skid, it appears as if we are steering towards the obstacle that we are endeavouring to avoid. However, as experienced drivers know, most times, if you are not quite sure what to do or which way to steer, then, take your hands off the steering wheel and the car will right itself.

Fortunately most people invested in Managed Funds do not bother to steer at all. They leave the contracts to roll until they need the money. But of course a vehicle cannot get to its destination without some change in direction. Even in the worst conditions we do know that gentle adjustments, correctly timed, can get us round the worst obstacles if we just apply the pressure appropriately.

As with motoring in good clear dry conditions, changes in direction can be made without endangering the progress of the journey or those making it.

The metaphor works in exactly the same way in the stock markets. During less turbulent and troubled times adjustments can be made to a portfolio. But in more volatile and hazardous times any correction, and certainly drastic corrections, made at an inappropriate moment can merely exacerbate the situation making the outcome even worse.

In times past (2004-2005) we have heard a number of commentators urging people to leave equities and get in to property. Properties are a great investment. Property funds have been doing well. Well of course they "have been doing well" but does that mean that in 2010 they are going to continue to do so?

The time to move into property was surely when it was still in the doldrums; when equities were heading for their peak. A controlled approach in 1998-2000 by gently moving funds out of shares and into real property would have reaped generous rewards.

I don't know about you but; when I see a traffic jam coming, perhaps where I know there is a point on my journey which is always a place of congestion, I will look at my map. Is there an alternative route? Let's take it. On a motorway that point of anticipation can be miles ahead of the exit and missing the turn can place us in distressing circumstance for a considerable period of time.

The headline in the business section of *The Daily Telegraph* in late March 2010 said it all. Simon Halabi (a property tycoon who had been worth £3 billion in 2007) had been declared bankrupt. The significance of Mr Halabi's bankruptcy is central to this book and the collapse of the banks. It was foreseeable.

This Syrian born entrepreneur had a portfolio of commercial offices that provided the Headquarters of J P Morgan Accountants, AVIVA and other major life assurance companies. Another of his tenants was the 'In and Out Club' the 'in' place in Piccadilly and meant more towers at the former home of Baron Mayer Amschel de Rothschild.

Why is this bankruptcy so significant? It is significant because it exemplifies the foresight that I had and others should have had in 2006 when Mr Halabi's London office portfolio was worth £1.8 billion as against the £929 million, a 50% drop, in June 2009. Much of that drop in value would have occurred long before June 2009.

Many will say that property is worth what someone else would pay for it. That is not the truth because very often in the market place nobody will pay anything for a property. It stands on the market for three, and four and five years.

It was Abbey Life's property fund that purchased the first £1 million property in London in, I believe, the late 1970s. It was a 'landmark purchase' at a 'landmark price' by what Abbey Life wanted to be 'a landmark property fund.' It stood empty for fourteen years. The property is Centre Point. For my purposes it will be central to my argument in making a specific point.

Most commentators seem to miss the link between property and equity values. There needs to be a more informed understanding of the link between property and the rest of the financial market place.

There are millions of published words describing the stock market and the eccentricities of that market and the possible links with the fixed interest market and how the two work closely together along with the capital market where interest rates and the movement thereof, determines a profit or a loss over time.

The one adage, and falsehood, that is often proclaimed is that you can never lose money in property. That is certainly true if you hold on to it for long enough but then virtually the same can be said for the stock market which gets a lot more press and a lot more attention in the media because shares are tradable on a 'minute by minute' basis in the stock market and it seems that there are always 'buyers' and always 'sellers.'

The same can be said of the fixed interest market where government stock (gilts) and corporate bonds (loans to the large corporations) can also be dealt with, with a huge degree of immediacy.

Not so property. An investor can be stuck with property for a very long time before it finally 'comes good' and it is that trait that possibly, no probably, creates the link that I have set out to describe.

How does the link benefit you the reader? Well let us have a conspiracy theory and supposition thrown into one and imagine one particular guardian of the Nation's investments who might understand what I am about to describe, not quite in the way that I describe it and probably not for the same reasons as I present my experience, however the foresight works very much to their ends.

Performance tables are that map to an alternative route and by consulting that "map" and acknowledging that the high possibility of interest rates going down, the capital value of Gilts might well rise and property values increase, action can be taken. Further analysis might lead to the view that a severe movement of Equities in a downward direction will create a higher risk element for corporate bonds which might well come under strain as far as capital value is concerned.

If rental incomes are rising and becoming stronger in the market place then we know that there is a move towards the purchase of property and therefore a rise in capital values. It is pretty well inevitable.

But if you are no good at orienteering, if you can't read maps for love nor money, if you don't understand the fundamentals of what happens in the marketplace, give the money to a manager in a Managed Fund (which is a balanced portfolio) or a With Profit Fund and let them look after the detail for you.

Boots Pharmaceutical Group pension trustees reportedly transferred £2.3 billion of their pension funds from equities to corporate bonds circa 2003/2004. It is for you to judge whether that is an appropriate manoeuvre in the circumstances.

Some ask if tracker funds would provide a return consistent with the relevant indices?

The art of letting the market reflect itself is perhaps the most recent phenomenon to take on gargantuan proportions on the back of a myth. The ebb and flow of market capitalisation for any company should reflect the investors' confidence in the underlying share value.

In our modern society we have become obsessed with 'short termism' to the point of myopic incompetence. The generic term 'tracker' probably alludes to the following of a known path. Certainty security, but hopefully not the thought of underlying guarantees, accompanies the perception that this is a trodden path and therefore, can be relied upon.

If you tread a path too regularly it becomes rutted, unsafe, dangerous and eventually collapses. In physics every action has an equal and opposite reaction; examine then, the historical phenomenon known as tracker funds.

The whole precept relies on the fact that certain shares consistently perform at a level that delivers value to those that hold them and the measure would be a particular index. In the United Kingdom the predominant tracker index became the FTSE 100, the index of the top 100 companies by value.

By investing in the index, which you could do via derivatives, you could perhaps square the circle if you were inclined to clichés. However, if you invested in the index, in other words bought shares in the underlying portfolio of companies that formed the index, then the results could be so much better. What transpired over a 10-year period was laughably predictable and ingeniously profitable but unfortunately, it seems, for the wrong people.

Pensions fund management, returning to the obligations of the trustees, has a responsibility to provide best value for the members. In the short-term that was certainly achieved. The short-term view prevailed as a cascade of new funds entered into the spirit of the tracker theory and the pure weight of money drove the index upwards. What was not appreciated, seemingly, is that gluttony begets a bilious attack.

The companies that formed the FT 100 index became bloated in capital terms such that their underlying ability to transact business in the market place reflected badly in the accounts. Improving performance therefore, became a priority, consuming smaller companies through takeovers and mergers became a necessity and pole positions started to change. Very large companies' boards of directors were suddenly feeling very uncomfortable.

Just to add spice to the mix, in the late 1990s technology companies came on the scene in the wake of the enlargement of the World Wide Web and e-commerce. Firms with no bottom line profit entered the realms of the top 100 companies in the United Kingdom, displacing the established entities that had fallen foul of their own marketing abilities.

Consider the scene in very simple terms. The way to make money is to buy something cheaply and sell it at a higher price. The difference between the buy and sell amount is known as a profit. Buying an item at a high price and selling it cheaply is known as a loss. These two fundamentals appeared to be lost on many commentators.

What transpired within the tracker fund market was that too much money was chasing too little stock, forcing prices up and there was a profit. Your imagination does not need to go into overdrive however, to understand that once a stock has been declared inferior in the

FT 100 hierarchy and therefore had to be displaced, the stock would no longer be as desirable. The need to sell was very high, this was no longer a stock that could be held in a true tracker fund.

At the same time those stocks nominated as new entrants to the FT 100 would be the subject of much attention, as the stock was required to fill the void. The transaction could be carried out by computers. It didn't take half a brain but of course the price is not set by computers, it is set by confidence and desirability. Desirability meant that the incoming stock was perhaps overpriced on entry only to become under-priced on exit. The spiral now becomes self-feeding in a downward direction.

The medium to long-term view therefore, has to be at best mediocrity, at worst catastrophe. Tracker fund managers invented many ingenious mechanisms to maintain the "true tracker" status of their fund but soon degraded the whole philosophy by adopting a "look alike" strategy that purchased telecom shares that looked like telecom shares that were in the FT 100, or banking shares that looked like banking shares in the FT 100 and so on. Post "9/11" tracker funds had lost most of their 'street cred', for the time being at least.

What tracker funds proved more than anything else is that the idea of a stable model portfolio is completely false. Confidence and convention are of the moment but if you disturb the basis of the convention by creating a replica of the natural order then the creation overtakes the natural order and destroys the very basics of its underlying properties. That is what happened with the FTSE 100 and the tracker fund phenomenon.

Much is said and written regarding taxation and tax relief, particularly about pensions in recent times. I found the following offering on the Internet and I felt that I could not better express the naivety of some commentators any better.

"A friend sent this to me, it is interesting and true..."

Our Tax System Explained: Bar Stool Economics

216

Suppose that every day, ten men go out for beer and the bill for all ten comes to £100. If they paid their bill the way we pay our taxes, it would go something like this:

The first four men (the poorest) would pay nothing.
The fifth would pay £1.
The sixth would pay £3.
The seventh would pay £7.
The eighth would pay £12.
The ninth would pay £18.
The tenth man (the richest) would pay £59.

So, that's what they decided to do.

The ten men drank in the bar every day and seemed quite happy with the arrangement, until one day, the owner threw them a curve. Since you are all such good customers; he said, I'm going to reduce the cost of your daily beer by £20; Drinks for the ten now cost just £80.

The group still wanted to pay their bill the way we pay our taxes so the first four men were unaffected. They would still drink for free.

But what about the other six men - the paying customers?

How could they divide the £20 windfall so that everyone would get his fair share?

They realized that £20 divided by six is £3.33. But if they subtracted that from everybody's share, then the fifth man and the sixth man would each end up being paid to drink his beer.

So, the bar owner suggested that it would be fair to reduce each man's bill by roughly the same amount, and he proceeded to work out the amounts each should pay.

And so:

The fifth man, like the first four, now paid nothing (100% savings).
The sixth now paid £2 instead of £3 (33%savings).
The seventh now pay £5 instead of £7 (28%savings).
The eighth now paid £9 instead of £12 (25% savings).
The ninth now paid £14 instead of £18 (22% savings).
The tenth now paid £50 instead of £59 (15% savings).

Each of the six was better off than before. And the first four
continued to drink for free. But once outside the restaurant, the
men began to compare their savings.
I only got £1 out of the £20 declared the sixth man. He pointed to
the tenth man, but he got £9!
Yeah, that's right, exclaimed the fifth man. I only saved £1, too. It's
unfair that he got ten times more than I got.
That's true!! shouted the seventh man. Why should he get £9 back
when I got only two? The wealthy get all the breaks!

Wait a minute, yelled the first four men in unison. We didn't get
anything at all. The system exploits the poor!
The nine men surrounded the tenth and beat him up.
The next night the tenth man didn't show up for drinks so the nine
sat down and had beers without him. But when it came time to pay
the bill, they discovered something important. They didn't have
enough money between all of them for even half of the bill!

And that, ladies and gentlemen, journalists and college professors,
is how our tax system works. The people who pay the highest
taxes get the most benefit from a tax reduction. Tax them too
much, attack them for being wealthy, and they just may not show
up anymore. In fact, they might start drinking overseas where the
atmosphere is somewhat friendlier.

David R. Kamerschen, Ph.D. Professor of Economics
University of Georgia
For those who understand, no explanation is needed.
For those who do not understand, no explanation is possible.

CHAPTER 18

STORING CAPITAL TO PRODUCE PREDICTABLE RETURNS

Pensions epitomise long term saving. Many pension scheme investments require guarantees and in a nutshell the guarantees are at the centre of the problems facing those that value pension funds.

Much of this book has discussed property and equity values in an endeavour to show the relationship that subsists between those entities, but, what of cash and gilts, the other two major component parts of the financial markets' make-up? Surely they also have a part to play in financial planning and in the assessment process when considering long-term investment strategies? Pensions are a prime example, as I have stated.

Interest rates, by and large, follow a pattern set by other parts of the market. Interest rates tend to be reactionary although the Bank of England would probably argue that they are a 'driving force' to achieve certain ends, which is certainly said to be true where inflation is concerned. My contention would be that the advent of inflation at increasingly high levels elicits upward interest rate movements, and reductions in inflationary trends give rise to bank, and thereby interest rate, reductions - not the other way round.

In other words, in practice, for most of the time, inflation drives the bank rate or some other force or consideration does.

If I can start at October 2010 and tell the story backwards, it may hopefully clarify the position that I am trying to expose. Picture if you will a Bank of England official presenting a quarterly review at a University in the Midlands.

The bank base rate was at 0.5% and the Bank of England official presents the premise that; - a year ago his colleague Amos had shown a graph illustrating that by November next year (the point at which we are now viewing the situation) the bank base rate would be

219

4% in order to stem inflation. Our speaker goes on to point out that Amos's forecast had failed to materialise, but had it?

Cuts in interest rates

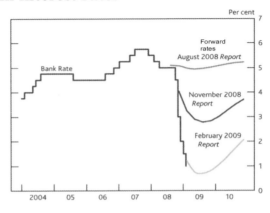

Fig 18.1 Bank of England sequential interest rate forecasts 2010

This is where viewing the marketplace becomes all the more difficult because if we roll the clock back five years and refer to that letter in Chapter 13 written in August 2007 to the Daily Mail, The Mail on Sunday and Daily Telegraph it was quite clearly pointed out that interest rates on overdrafts (not the base rate) were effectively escalating, and escalating very rapidly, as banks endeavoured to fend off the effects of a reducing solvency margin caused by a slump in property prices and started to impose fresh, almost punitive interest rate rises on their overdraft facilities for 'selected' clients.

The bank's reasoning was twofold:

1) The banks required the overdraft facilities to be reduced because any overdraft 'facility' is a liability to the bank whether it is used or not, therefore the overdraft facility's presence weakens the solvency margin of the bank as a liability and,

2) The banks needed more margin to get cash 'in' to bolster their balance sheets (the solvency margin.)

NatWest Bank overdraft facility – alteration 24 hours notice - 2007

Loan on overdraft £200,000

The monthly cost of servicing the overdraft went from

		Per
Basis 1	£833	Per
Basis 2	£3,542	Month

					month	Year	% equivalent	Total Int Rate	%
Basis 1	0.03	% Over 1	0.02	Fee 1	0	0		0.05	5.00%
Basis 2	0.05	% Over 2	0.05	Fee 2	1875	22500	0.1125	0.2125	21.25%

Fig 18.1

Overdrafts can be altered, or called in, at 24 hours notice.

You will recall from the letter in Chapter 13 that a 2% over base rate overdraft facility was raised with immediate effect to 5% over base and a monthly fee was imposed which made the effective interest rate even higher.

It could be said therefore that the raising of the base rate by the Bank of England, which had started off in 2003, became a selective imposition on businesses in trouble in 2006 developing into the situation in 2008 where the random imposition became a more generally acknowledged cause for concern. 'Commercial risk' became a high priority consideration which brought about the need for the fundamental assessment of a bank's lending procedure.

As a direct result of those assessments and the shrinkage in the property market valuations and thereby the banks' solvency ratios the lending margins had to increase dramatically; therefore interest rates overall were stabilised at a fairly high level compared to the base rate as published by the Bank of England. That excess margin remains in order to enable the flow of capital back into the retail banking system to restore the solvency ratios.

It is true that banks were having to pay more for their money internally (in the wholesale money markets) to support their own needs than was previously the case but nevertheless their margins, in other words their ability to restock their own shelves with the commodity that they deal in, money, and thereby strengthen their balance sheet and their solvency margins against a continuing decline in property values was achieved without too much duress.

The public perception was that borrowing rates were not too bad even though they were eight or ten or even twelve times the banks base rate as a multiple. Those individuals borrowing money through from the year 2000 would have noted little change in the cost of borrowing for mortgages and fixed term loans. I believe that means most borrowers would not get too upset about the cost of their borrowing.

The LIBOR rate (that is the inter bank rate, in other words the rate that the banks borrow at between themselves) had certainly increased and I don't doubt that good banks and bad banks have to match the risk that that particular bank poses to the lender in order to attract the same percentage increase over LIBOR, but that is not really the point of this discussion.

This reactive phenomenon is why I state that the bank base rate is reactionary. If commerce is failing because the banks are withdrawing financial support or making that financial support so expensive that it is draining the resources from commerce, then the Bank of England is more or less obliged to bring interest rates down (or at least the bank base rate, which they control).

That is exactly what happened following September 2008 when the stock market started to slide and property values were already in the descendent. The underlying asset support for overdrafts was shrinking, banks were imposing penal interest rates at 4% or 5% over base rate for smaller firms (see fig 18.2) plus the banks were imposing a monthly fee for having an overdraft facility per se - yet the Bank of England base rate dropped from 5% to 0.5% over a six month period.

The **commercial rate of interest** actually being charged in the situation illustrated (inclusive of the fee) was **21.25%**

We talked about a recession earlier in the book and related the story of the £100 "doing the rounds" of various trades and professions only to end up back up in the hands of the original 'owner' (for want of a better word) of the £100 that started the process.

A recession therefore is just a slowing down of money circulating in the marketplace. There were talks (Oct 2010) of deflation, in other words things were getting cheaper (I wish). What sorts of things were getting cheaper? Second-hand cars, new cars, computers, white goods - but certainly not food, fuel and to a large degree, mortgage repayments, although those on 'tracker' mortgages were 'coining it', as the saying used to go, at 'tracker' mortgage interest rates of anything from 0.5% to 1.46%. The 'normal' variable mortgage interest repayment rate was nearer 4.7%.

Was it Lord Young that said that many "had never had it so good"?

Moving back to the Bank of England presentation in October 2010 - the inflationary charts that were presented certainly showed an upward trend in inflation at 3½% and that despite the fact that a loaf of bread had moved in price (tempted to say risen) from 75 pence to £1.40 a loaf, the price of milk had doubled and diesel fuel was now £1.30 a litre, pretty well £6 a gallon. But I digress.

The forecast, he said, was that inflation would reduce.

We use the term 'inflation' in a very perfunctory manner and it wants a little bit of explanation, if I can do it justice, because it is, apparently, 'of the moment'.

In January 2011 VAT rose by 2½% of the value of the goods purchased (a rise of 8.75% in the VAT taken) and that will increase inflation but only for the next year even though that 2½% will be a permanent feature. VAT has moved from 17½% on purchased goods and services to 20%.

I hope I haven't lost you yet because we are only beginning to get to grips with the fact that even though that increase in price will move on into the future, the inflationary effect is only at the point that prices rise. Twelve months later that price rise drops out of calculation therefore if there are no further price rises in the following twelve months there is no inflation. It is actually simple and logical when you think about it, but the cost of goods has still gone up therefore the effect of inflation is residual, it stays with us.

Now of course if prices come down and let's say commodity prices, like fuel, or probably more importantly wheat, rice and milk reduce; then that becomes a deflationary effect which economists would have us worry about. However, should we worry?

If inflation (prices) went up by 3½% this year (you might wish it was only 3½%) and came down by 1½% next year then surely the net effect is that we have had a rise in prices of 2% over that two year period. Of course it is simplistic, but it does mean that we can be lured into being concerned about things that really should not raise our concern at all.

Many analysts use a rolling 5 year average in order to 'even the lumps' out of the figures in order to make more sense of the situation. What we should be concerned about is that when inflation moves ahead too fast the Bank of England raises interest rates in order to restrain that inflationary pressure.

If I can ask you to visualise three layers in a small firm that is trading, the bottom layer is the staff, they support everything else. They are the people that do the work but they also need to spend their own money and the amount that they are spending on what I would call 'staple goods'- food, clothing and fuel is rising at 3½% in October 2010 (even though we think that the rate of increase is far higher than that). They need more money to live and therefore they will undoubtedly ask for more money from their employer.

The top band is commodities. These are the things that the employer uses to produce whatever they produce and if they are in engineering or food processing, then those costs are rising also. The middle band is the cost of borrowing. All of these are known as fixed overheads, your domestic environment is no different. The problem is that the middle one at the moment, the banks, are creating a problem that is affecting the other two and it is that effect that we believe is undeniably inflationary; in other words costs will rise and they will continue to rise.

For the record the county's economy runs in just the same way, just bigger numbers.

How does this information help you in making your decisions regarding investment?

There is a rule of thumb that says if inflation is going to rise, buy the goods that you want now while they are cheap. Many individuals have been waiting to spend their money, thus creating a recession by slowing the flow of money around the system.

Other individuals have, quite sensibly, been reducing their debt in anticipation of even higher interest rates that are almost bound to come. However that could be less of a problem in the short to medium term than they actually feel is the case and that is because as the bank base rate rises the lending institutions, in the knowledge that there is already a lot of pressure in the marketplace, and wishing to avoid repossessions or debt defaults, will maintain the market lending rate and allow their margins to be squeezed and that situation could well be maintained for some little while.

There is a vulnerability curve. What some would call a 'feel good factor' turns into a 'feel vulnerable factor' and again it follows a cycle which runs right the way through the *classic market.* When people feel good 'the brakes are off' and that is when we get those surges in investment and a reduction in the observation of risk. The reverse is true when vulnerability clicks in. We have an innate urge to protect ourselves which manifests itself in a reduction of exposure to risk, we reduce our debt, we increase our savings and if we increase our savings we take money out of circulation at the consumer level.

It is a point in the market cycle where we start to take note of what our savings are returning to us.

The other side of interest rates on loans being repaid is, of course, the rate of interest that is paid to depositors. It is at this point that fixed interest investments enter the storyline in the shape of government bonds, which we have already discussed, and corporate bonds which we haven't. The name gives the character of the entity away in that Public Corporations such as ITV or Vodaphone issue Commercial loan Bonds in the same way that Gilts, government bonds, are loans raised for government purposes through the Treasury or the Exchequer or special purpose 'undated' loans such as War Loan stock and Consols.

Commerce raises money in the marketplace in much the same way as the government and may well ask the public to contribute to a corporate loan rather than buying shares. The lure, of course, is stability, a regular fixed interest rate, which is prescribed, and a maturity date which is defined at outset which gives rise to the fact that a corporate bond is of course perceived to be safe: secured by the assets of the company. The key word is secured. Like banks secure their lending with real property.

When a large entity like Enron in the United States collapses, that is when the security of such commercial loans is tested. Therefore, looking back to 2008 or perhaps even running the clock back to 2005 is there a reasonably secure mechanism that can be relied upon in a *classic market* to deliver a return despite the fact that there is an expectation of the stock market and property markets falling into decline? Of course there is.

The answer, of course, is to enter the domain of fixed interest investments; the reason being that if interest rates have risen, as they did from 2% in 2003 to 5% in 2005, there is future scope for capital growth in the Fixed Interest sector. The base rate had almost doubled between 2002 and 2005.

The value of the housing and property market in general had flattened out at that stage in the *classic market* and we know, from what has gone before that this point in the *classic market* heralds a reduction in capital value of both the stock market and housing market. Therefore from what has just been discussed, the reaction of the Bank of England to that will be to lower Bank of England base rates. If interest rates go down the capital value of fixed interest stock goes up. Therefore the choice remains: should we choose government fixed interest stock or corporate bonds (corporate fixed interest, fixed term, loan stock)?

Consider, and see, how we feel about corporate bonds first. Those that are imbued in the nature of fixed interest stock have a very closed mind about their utility. For Edna, as we discussed earlier, the capital value of her fixed interest stock really did not bother her. She was ninety-two and she wanted the income and that was all she was concerned about. She was not going to move the money. The capital value was irrelevant.

If you are in your mid forties, as Colin is, and you decide to go into corporate bonds just as the stock market is falling apart you could be in for a rough ride.

I well remember talking to a corporate bond fund manager who had two years prior to the conversation produced a brochure that promised 8.6% per annum return and sure enough here we were two years later in 2002 and the bond was returning income at 8.6%. However, the capital value of the bond had reduced over the twelve months prior to this conversation by 8.2%.

The fund manager really could not see that it was detrimental to my client who, had he withdrawn his money on that particular day (and these were daily tradable investments), he would have actually made 0.4% over the year (8.6% income less 8.2% capital loss) and little or nothing was going to help him out. Twenty minutes further on in the conversation there was little movement from the other side, 8.6% was correct, as far as the fund manager was concerned, because that was the income produced.

Did the value ever come back? The answer is undoubtedly 'yes'; six years later when interest rates went down!

The point that is being made is that corporate bonds act in exactly the same way as government bonds. Interest rates go down, capital values go up, interest rates go up and capital values go down, but there is an additional dimension which one needs to consider in the disaster area that is the second phase of the *classic market* and that is that as the banks collapse concerns are raised about the ability of the companies the banks support to survive. A risk factor in respect of the failure of the corporate bond's underwriting company has to be considered.

Remember that in the first phase of the *classic market* bank borrowing supports the slide in the stock market. The banks are flush with money because property prices are rising and the banks' ability to lend to commerce is unimpaired; indeed, the banks have more financial capacity than they know what to do with.

In the second phase of the *classic market* the reverse is the case, not only is the stock value going down and with it the capital value of the company, but also, the company's ability to refinance its operations is under strain, as its asset values reduce as loan security. The banks simply cannot support industry in this instance and therefore closures, bankruptcies and liquidations become the order of the day.

In corporate bond terms the risk premium on the stock increases reducing the capital value at an equally rapid rate to the decline in the stock market as investors attempt to off load the precarious debt that they own on an unwilling, unreceptive, market place.

228

Where there is sound government, and one always uses the term advisedly, and interest rates fall (which we know they invariably will because the Bank of England needs to reduce interest rates to support industry and stimulate property purchase), gilt capital values will rise and therefore we have our third and final element for good financial housekeeping as we move into the last phase of our observation and use of the *classic market* to make positive returns on our financial investments.

CHAPTER 19

A THROW OF THE DICE OR A CALCULATED DECISION

The final throw of the dice is, we have said, a move towards **income** rather than capital **growth** accompanied by the final consolidation and levelling off of the property market values. Invariably there is ultimately distress in the political arena, financial turmoil and a rising stock market. As we approach the spring of 2011, is there any evidence that, that might be the case?

It was mid April, 2010 when I was at a meeting in Durham discussing property prices with a colleague there. He had recently acquired two newly built properties: three bedroom, semi-detached houses on an estate. The builder was in distress, the bank needed to reduce the builders exposure to debt (a polite way of stating that the bank needed their overdraft repaid or reduced dramatically) therefore properties that had been on the market, built by a developer, for £149,000 in April 2009 were purchased by my colleague one year later at £64,000 for one and £65,000 for a second property; and there was still some more down-side in the marketplace.

In May 2010 a £400,000 property in Skegness, Lincolnshire sold for £94,000.

For me that evidence represents the early part of the period that will confirm a final consolidation of property prices, a flattening of the market and a pronounced reduction in confidence in property as an investment, for six, or seven or more years. It marks the end time of the *'classic market'* and heralds the beginning of a new era, a fresh *'classic market'* capital orientated cycle due to commence in 2013/2014.

The political trauma that was all so very evident during the same period of time (2009-2010) was again very classic in its form; 'headless' politicians running from one crisis to another, a hung parliament in the UK (didn't we have one of those in the mid 70s) and bankers became, and to an extent still are, the butt of all bad jokes and public vilification (but still earning a crust on taxpayers money and contributing some 48% of the total tax revenue of the UK.)

The bankers are unpopular because they will not lend money to support ailing businesses post 2008. Banks are still closing businesses down through the withdrawal of financial support even now in 2011, replicating what they did in 1979 through 1981and also through the period 1992 to 94.

Pontin's holiday camp business went into administration in mid November 2010. Throughout 2010 many banks were reportedly still holding a stock of repossessed properties, some rented out – to get what can be retrieved from the debacle back into the coffers.

Other properties are left empty, for fear that if the banks that now own them by default, sold them at auction at distress prices, they would crystallise the losses that are almost certain to be made. That crystallisation of lost value will damage the banks' balance sheets once again, which will restrict lending, and therefore the financial support to business further.

Can the money, cash, coming in, stay ahead of any further property value oozing out through property devaluation? 2011 will probably be a watershed as property prices deteriorate further, eventually levelling out and the banks' ability to lend will be impeded without a strong asset value to secure their 'loan book', therefore the problem becomes more acute.

The banks have to pace the rebuilding of their cash reserves and, with those strengthened reserves, restore their solvency margins whilst judging the further decline of property values that currently support existing loans. This has to be achieved before the financial institutions can lend to the 'risk' end of the commercial market again.

The problem is that everything seems to fall into the category of high, unacceptable, risk if the offered security does not have a 50% or better loan to value property base to secure any loan request.

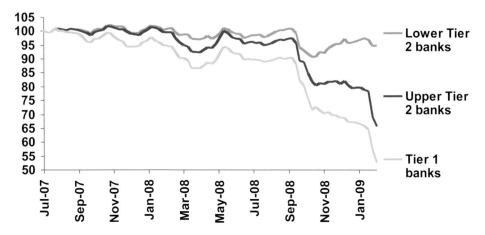

Fig 19.1 Assets to liabilities – the solvency positions of banks. Tier 1 is high street banks. See how the margin has collapsed and note the correlation with the property market. Source: Bank of England

We have already discussed how solvency margins are crucial to the banking sector, because those margins are kept under close scrutiny by the banking regulator. We can remind ourselves that part of the equation for those solvency margins vests in the underlying value of properties that the banking institutions hold mortgages on. There has to be equity, value above the mortgage amount, to allow the bank to use that asset to further permit that bank to apply its multiplier in order to make further loans to new customers, or restore support for established customers, particularly where 'risk' is perceived.

With asset values, in the shape of recent property valuations, still dropping, and expected to continue to do so through 2011, the amount of money for fresh lending, or even renewing or supporting existing debt (like Pontin's) on new agreements, becomes increasingly difficult for the banks to undertake. The cost of the banks' own borrowing in the wholesale market, LIBOR, is also high; though not as high as in late 2008, at the height of the financial meltdown.

The failure to understand, or perhaps disclose, that fact by the media, and politicians, leads to a general feeling in the population as a whole that the banks are merely being vexatious in recalling loans and closing businesses down (which sometimes they are) and

233

inconsiderate in not supporting business in their (the businesses') hour of need.

In this situation, and that means the circumstances of mid to late 2010, the banks' needs could be said to be greater than that of the public and the businesses they provide finance for. I will leave that for you to debate.

The situation is merely a repeat performance of previous times.

Consider the last three *classic markets,* 1968-82, 1983-96 and 1997-2010. Examine the historical evidence of those times. The conclusions are self evident. Little about those times is challenging in the process of understanding the inevitability of the cycles repeating themselves. Many will state: "But it is different this time, look at interest rates, or consider inflation," or some other, so called contributory factor. They seek to miss the point. That is all that can be said.

One thing is for sure, letting the banking system genuinely collapse would be 'Folly.'

In our modern world survival without the facility of multiple gearing on loans (leveraging) would be precarious to say the least, and the maintenance of our standard of living, whatever that might mean, would be almost impossible. This is not a time for ideological political posturing (unless it is ignored, or treated as the side show that it is.)

So: why would the stock market in 2010 be accumulating value rather than losing it, when times are so hard?

It is a matter of dynamics. The stock market, by and large, reflects 'what is to be' as well as what is now. What is now for those with financial resources (pension funds, savings programmes etcetera) is the need for a return on capital invested income. What is to be? Primarily, at this stage in *The Classic Market*, the need is for relative security coupled with a mechanism that will sustain or deliver income.

Of course we see 'peaks and troughs' in the stock market performance and short term volatility which reflects the happenings of the day. However for the most part those troughs, and indeed peaks, are short lived. The market trend in this part of *the classic market'* cycle is for equity income shares in particular and, subsequently, shares in general, to move forward because of the expectation of better things to come.

More relevantly, the income orientated part of the stock market is the only place that people, large professional investors, can find a return by way of income (dividends) and accessibility to capital on short to medium term money, with a low expectation of capital risk. Emotionally, it is worth taking the risk that is inherent in stock market dealing from a relatively low base.

Consider what the market looks like, analyse the factors that prevail; how would you feel about the relative risk factors:-

a) Commercial Property is depressed; land values, asset values do not represent good value for money in the foreseeable future. Rental incomes are down, tenant covenants have become difficult to assess and therefore tenant leases are viewed as precarious. In other words rental income is uncertain to the extent that a tenant may well go into liquidation, or declares themselves bankrupt, and the return on capital diminished as the rental stream (income) disappears altogether, for what can be extended periods of time whilst a fresh tenant is found.

b) Residential property, with minor exception, is the same as commercial property – and has the same tenant uncertainty through job losses or a pay freeze or reductions. Some tenants just leave and take what they can carry with them.

c) Interest rates have been reduced in order to stimulate the economy. Anyone with substantial amounts of money to invest may "suffer" a 0.5% interest rate regime for twelve months, but after that they get pretty wary about continuing the practice for very much longer. Where can they go for income and relative security? That is the nagging question that emotional pressure answers.

Inflation can also cause disenchantment with deposit based investments particularly if inflation is higher than interest rates as it was in the late 70s early 80s - then the real returns are negative. In 2010 inflation is 3.5% and bank deposits are delivering 0.1 to 2.7%.

d) Gilts and fixed interest investments certainly produce the income that individuals and businesses seek, albeit fairly restricted at say 2.5% to 5% (2010 rates) but what of fixed interest stocks' capital security?

e) Short dated gilts are fairly secure but producing poor income. (see the tables on the following pages.) Medium to long dated gilts are regarded as being 'insecure' because the only way that interest rates can travel from this point (2011) is up and therefore the capital value of the underlying fixed interest stock, be it gilts or corporate bonds, must be on a downward trend. (see the tables.) By this time the distress and capital values of corporate bonds are washed out to an extent therefore even a recovery from a distressed position presents something of a question mark.

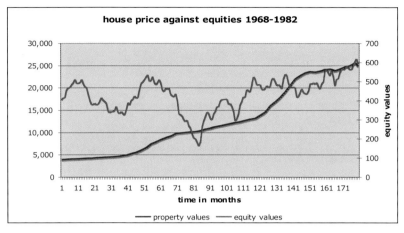

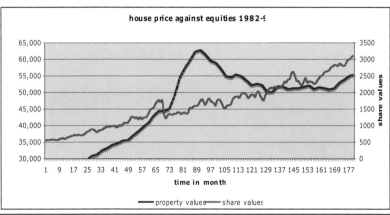

Fig 19.2   Visual representation of all three *classic markets*

Feb-03		Issue	Mature	Price	Yield Redemption
Short	10%	1/1/86	8/9/03	£103.84	3.57%
	6.75%	1/9/93	26/11/04	£105.30	3.72%
Medium	5.75%	1/7/98	7/12/09	£109.07	4.21%
Long	**8%**	**1/2/96**	**7/6/21**	**£144.83**	**4.41%**
	5%	1/11/01	7/3/25	£108.26	4.41%
	4.25%	1/6/00	7/6/32	£97.86	4.38%
					Real Returns @
					3%
Index linked	4.375%		21/10/04	£137.20	1.14%
	2.50%		23/8/11	£245.70	2.11%
	2.50%		**17/7/24**	**£194.33**	**2.12%**
Source: UBS Warburg					

Feb-06		Issue	Mature	Price	Yield Redemption
Short	5.75%	1/7/98	7/12/09	£104.99	4.33%
Medium	8%	1/4/93	27/9/13	£124.56	4.21%
Long	**8%**	**1/2/96**	**7/6/21**	**£143.47**	**4.14%**
	5%	1/11/01	7/3/25	£112.83	4.03%
					Real Returns @
					3%
Index linked	2.50%	28/1/82	23/8/11	£268.15	1.60%
	2.50%	**30/12/86**	**17/7/24**	**£240.41**	**1.12%**
Source: UBS					

Jul-10			Issue	Mature	Price	Yield Redemption
Short	**8%**	**2013**	**1/4/93**	**27/9/13**	**£120.82**	**1.44%**
Medium	8%	2021	29/2/96	7/6/21	£141.02	3.47%
	5%	2025	27/9/01	7/3/25	£111.54	3.96%
Long	4.50%	2034	17/6/09	7/9/34	£104.13	4.23%
	4.25%	2055	27/5/05	7/12/55	£101.04	4.20%
						Real Returns @
						3%
Index linked	2.50%	2011	28/1/82	23/8/11	£309.21	-1.64%
	2.50%	**2024**	**30/12/86**	**17/7/24**	**£272.59**	**0.90%**
Source:DMO						

Table 19.3a, b, & c. The tables show Gilt prices over three time frames indicating price variance. Source: Money Facts & Bank of England

The above tables illustrate quite clearly, how, in 2003 when interest rates were just starting to rise, the capital value for medium and long dates gilts was high compared with the 2006 levels. Index linked gilts (assuming 3% inflation to maturity) illustrate a real strengthening of capital value as interest rates dropped and real inflation rates grew to 4%.

Progress the comparison to the third table for July 2010. Once again the comparisons, which do pose difficulties for people, are there to compare. The 8% 2021 stock has moved from long to medium and the price is moving lower as an expected interest rate rise moves to meet reality.

The long dated stocks all show a significant increase in capital values and a reduction in the yield, confirming the gilt market reaction to interest rate reductions. Any rise in interest rates will have the opposite effect.

f) The investment medium that attracted depositor's interest in 2010 was equity income shares with people taking a view that in the year 2000 the index was 6900; in 2006 the index was pretty much the same. There have been two major falls to 3,250 in 2003 and again in 2008. By late 2010 the index on the FTSE was at between 5,700 and 5,900 and the market was still perceived to be 'cheap' and dividends still relatively healthy, if not improving.

g) If interest rates did start to rise would that affect the stock market very much? Indeed; if interest rates rose would dividends be forced up to deliver a 'hold' on investors' capital by more aggressive returns to share holders? If inflation continues to rise, it reinforces the stock markets determination to deliver. As industry, both service and manufacturing, becomes leaner the ability to earn profits and pay dividends improves.

Any move into the stock market would not be because the future for business looks particularly good, but because the income stream looks relatively safe compared to everything else that is available and the capital is viewed as redeemable at short notice. Therefore that capital, perceptively at least, secures income that the banks cannot provide from cash deposits.

It remains for you, and I, to witness how the third *classic market* of my own personal experience plays itself out. Of course for my own ego I can only hope that it 'pans out' as I have professed it will.

I am not clairvoyant; I don't have angels' wings. However, I do have forty years experience and I hope that by outlining the observation and research that I have 'logged' in the pages of this book it helps those who follow me, as financial planners or private investors, to gain an insight into, perhaps, a different view of the dynamics of the Financial Services market in terms of the interaction between the Property and Equity markets in particular.

There is I believe, an inextricable link between property and equities which has not been exposed hitherto to the extent that it should be. You have read it here and I hope you have enjoyed and been enlightened by the process.

What we have established at this juncture is that investing in the financial markets need not be a 'throw of the dice' and a 'trust to luck.' It has been shown fairly conclusively that if we take the three graphs previously shown (p.237) just the property and equity graphs against each other but placing them one above another, there is a broad pattern that has emerged.

In order to get the best out of the observations of this book the investor obviously needs to exercise some monitoring techniques and bring those to bear on their investment decisions and the obvious question is: 'How do we do that?'

Fig 19.4

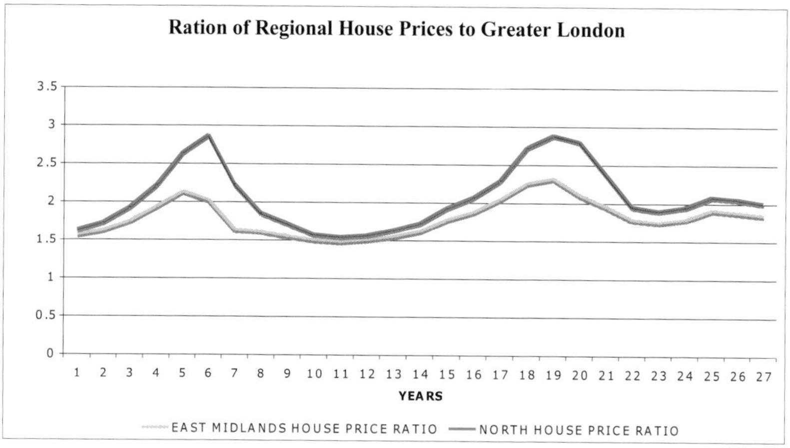

Ration of Regional House Prices to Greater London

EAST MIDLANDS HOUSE PRICE RATIO — NORTH HOUSE PRICE RATIO

The newspapers and the web provide a huge amount of basic data; however the signal for change is usually in the headline and the commentary: the emotion.

When everyone is saying 'get in' that is usually the time to depart for pastures new. We have said that the timescale is rough and it is, but if it is roughly inaccurate then it is roughly accurate as well which, in my view, means that when you see the climb of equities accelerating fast and you detect that house prices are starting to go up having been broadly flat in the marketplace and knowing that there is a twelve to fifteen year cycle that we are observing then you should be able to pick the first point at which you move out of equity income shares and into a real property fund.

A 'real property fund' is where you need to be invested; a fund dealing in bricks and mortar, real property, rather than property shares. Yes property shares can follow, and to an extent do follow, property prices but not with the same profile. Property has a more subdued, less volatile graphic profile, changing direction smoothly. This whole *classic market* strategy is about optimising the end product, your gain.

At this juncture you have to turn your view to house prices in the North; moving through the Midlands upwards, against those property prices relating to Greater London.

At the optimum point of entry into the property market there should be quite a big disparity between the prices of property in the South of England compared to the North of England and that data you can pick up from a website like 'Zoopla'. If you choose a three bedroom semi-detached house in different areas of the country and just plot them month by month you will discover that the prices start to move apart, or conversely drift back together.

When it is felt that the market is getting 'over the top' and that is usually when builders are offering white goods, carpets free, legal fees, in other words the kitchen sink, and the North/South divide on your database is narrowing considerably, then that is the time to switch out of property and into cash, or a deposit biased unitised fund.

Again, all you are looking for is a unitised fund that specialises in cash deposits preferably not government stock, unless you are fleet of foot and monitoring interest rates carefully and regularly. For the novice or inexperienced investor, at this point in the *classic market* cycle certainly do <u>not</u> choose corporate bonds.

The point that I must make is that when you switch out you can either do it in one big lump, or move 20% or 30% of your portfolio at a time within say an investment bond or an ISA portfolio; then you will on occasions feel as if you are losing out. In the first tranche the stock market may well suddenly surge forward and you may think, "I have missed it, I have jumped too soon." Well; don't worry, better too soon than too late. The same applies to property prices, "better too soon than too late."

Finally, when interest rates are at their very low ebb and gilt yields are high that is when you move out, back into shares again and that may be before the share markets bottom out. Your move out of cash (or more adventurous gilts) can be in stages just to ease you into the new environment; all you need is a switching form or, for the really sophisticated, an instruction for your professional adviser.

Keep this book handy, refer to it often and don't be afraid of being wrong, because, if the signs are right then you will generally be right in the longer term.

All we need to do is bring all the signs and signals together and the rest is relatively easy.

NB In order to create the graph at 19.2 merely use 'ratio' arithmetic. Divide the Greater London (GL) value by the East Midland (EM) and separately the northern (N) price for a similar property and the result is a table with two columns which depicts 'the ratio'. Then monitor and tabulate 'the ratio' values and then create the graph as per fig 19.2.

The graph below may look similar to the Invesco graph on page 110.
It makes my point beautifully.

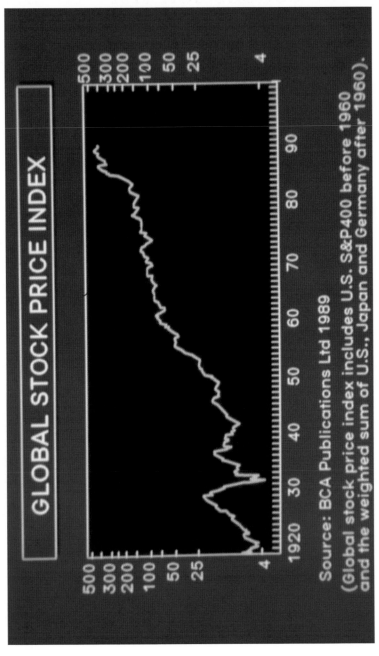

CHAPTER 20
THE CONCLUSION OF A VOYAGE OF DISCOVERY

People act in the financial marketplace in a manner that reflects their experience; which is why a lot of people do the wrong thing at the wrong time. I know, because, as you will have read, I did it. The wrong thing that is: in 1987.

If you have read the *classic market* cycles incorrectly in the past then just have a look at Figure 19.2 again. If you are in that part of the cycle that witnesses the potential collapse of the stock market, what do you do, where do you take shelter?

At the top of the property curve the line tends to flatten out. In 2004 to 2008 it flattened out to give an almost plateau effect much the same as the moribund lower value market which property prices exhibited at the bottom of the curve in 1993 to 1997 would have displayed.

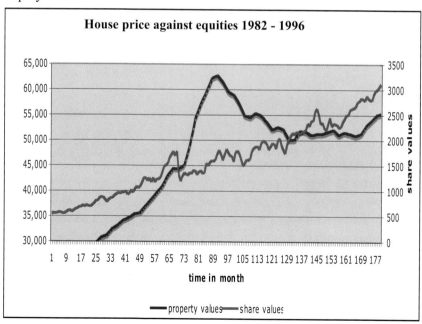

245

Fig 20.1 The relationship between property values and equity values.
Note mid 1987, between month 65 & 73.

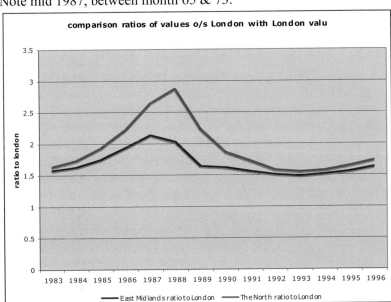

Fig 20.2 A graphic representation of the regional value ratios.
Source: Valuations Office

You could well 'read' that as simply a level property market;
ignoring the circumstances (i.e. whether the financial 'level of the
market,' was at a high or low point in the 'value,' or 'property price'
cycle).

If you had experience of the collapse of the stock market from 2000
to 2003; or in any other corresponding point in any *classic market* in
the past in its initial "capital" orientated stage, you may well, due to
that particular experience, expect property values to rise because that
is "what they do" during that phase in the market (i.e. when share
prices tumble out of control).

You may well react to the stock market collapse by perceiving that
the defence mechanism, to continue the growth of your investments,
or at least secure that value for the future, is to move your investment
funds into property and thereby to 'safety.' Subconsciously the
relationship in very simple terms would be: if the stock market is in
retreat then safety and an increase in capital value will be attained in
the property sector.

In actual fact, the situation encountered with regard to the collapse of the stock market in 2008 meant that there was to be an emphatic move from a 'capital' phase to an 'income' driven phase in the *classic market* where property is the agent driving the stock market down due to the undermining of the banking sector solvency margins which results in property being **the last place** anyone would want to be investing for security of capital value, let alone short term gains. Can you see how people would get it wrong? (See Fig 20.3)

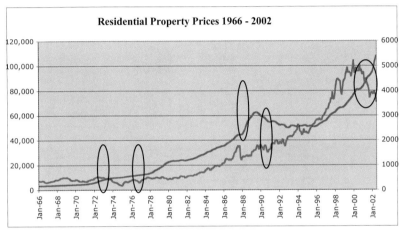

Fig 20.3   property values against share values 1966 to 2002
Source: Nationwide B.Soc. and The Bank of England

Very often experienced commentators confuse the two phases of the classic market and, as we have seen in the newspapers and magazines from 2009 through 2010 there is a constant, false, and I have to say worrying 'campaign,' almost, to drive property prices up, indeed to talk them up. It is all to no avail, because the market will do what it has to do – adjust to reality. Some areas appear immune. London had a property price renaissance due to the £ (pound) losing 25% of its value to the € (Euro). Europeans flocked to buy up The Capital (but not all of it).

What my forty years of experience has taught me through my study of what I now term the *classic market,* incorporating and evidencing the relationship between property and equity prices, is that individuals collectively can subdue the effects of the *classic market*; they can reduce the impact of the *classic market* by ironing out the extremes, but they can never eliminate it.

We have, hopefully, provided a convincing argument that emotion is what drives the market and; emotion will continue to drive the market as long as men and women exhibit an even polite form of greed. The quest for betterment through personal endeavour, to achieve personal satisfaction, or even plain financial elevation, whatever that is, every one of them is an overriding emotional force to a "feel good – secure – factor."

What each individual can do for themselves is: accurately gauge where the market is in the *Classic market* phasing. Individuals, and arguably financial institutions, need to establish what the counterpart values are of property in relation to equity, in order to establish what phase of the market is in evidence and **that** will give them an unobstructed view of where they should be invested to improve their personal circumstances.   It will also indicate quite firmly and categorically where they, as an investor, should not be – what to 'sell' or avoid.

If we move to Figure 20.4 and you can see some lines have been introduced to add clarity to your understanding. For those that really want an easy life and a simple generator of upward value in their investment ISA or Bond then a simple schematic may help. All one needs to know is where one is on the schematic. Months from January 2011 are shown as are the corresponding years underneath the time line as a double check.

The graphic is simple in its application and in no way implies anything other than an observed pattern, which, if followed could well prove to be profitable over a ten to fifteen or forty year time span.

Please do not rely on the count regarding the months or years precisely because the markets really do not work quite like that. This is not a clockwork, 'to the minute' style of relationship.

However they are fairly good approximations that will take you from say, a property crash (2008-10), which is where the relationship with equities starts to manifest itself as that equity element moves into a genuine stock market boom which will then peak in 5-6 years from the 'bottom;' 2010 to 2015 by which time property will have started

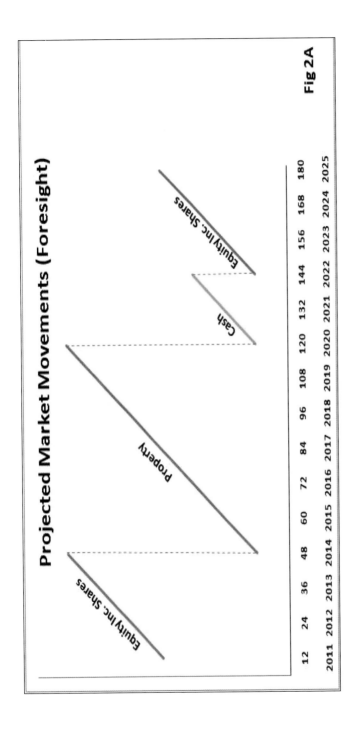

Fig 20.4 This is Fig 2A from my standard report

its inexorable rise as confidence, gingerly at first, as returns through the rental market growth and property yields attain rich double digit returns for the professional landlords.

2015-2020 The 'buy to let' period of over enthusiastic amateurs is still a long way off. Caution and bad memories still control the property purchase world at this point.

As the property market values rise they will take equities back up with them and in a sense at that point you can invest in either/or, but you might stay with property and probably invest through institutionalised funds in order to provide a spread of risk.

This becomes a personal choice and, certainly, direct investment in residential property (carefully chosen) can, or has in the past, result in an exceptional return on capital, which can be 'geared.' The problem in the developing property market period is that bank solvency margins are still 'tight'. The financial restrictions are inherent in the mortgage criteria. It is that relationship between property values and the banks' solvency margins that hold the market back. (2010-2015) but it does eventually improve.

To repeat what was stated in Chapter 19: the tell tale signs of an impending property adjustment is the divergence of values North to South. Fig 20.5. In other words, as the price variation between the North of England (NE) and Greater London (GL) becomes wider the time to invest is at hand. At the point of convergence comes the point to divest from property to gilts.

The introduction of the data from the East Midlands (EM) is to provide more clarity to the graphic portrayal of the correct positions as the two run parallel when the market is poor, because prices outside of the GL region have caught up with that regions.

The ratio is calculated taking:
GL divided by NE and creating a table. Then
GL divided by EM and creating a table, which will then enable a simple graph to be produced (if you want to go to that trouble).

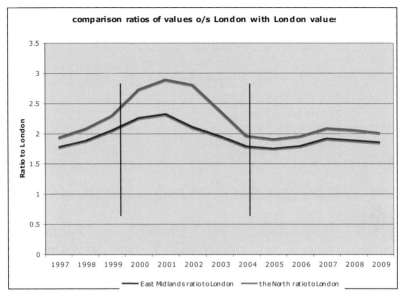

comparison ratios of values o/s London with London value

East Midlands ratio to London — the North ratio to London

Fig 20.5 ratio of property prices between greater London/the south and the North of England 1993 - 2010

The twin influence of constrained mortgage availability and the memory (for potential purchasers) of negative equity, plus the associated horror headlines, keeps the property market in check for several years.

For those with the willpower, and the time on their hands this will be the opportunity to get into 'buy-to-let' for anything up to six or seven years in advance of the next rise in property values as mortgage money becomes more freely available (2013-2020). But then; get out, and get into cash deposits (2020-2021) unless, of course you wish to take the really long view and use the property to personal advantage.

As we can see from the graphs, government stock values in capital terms alter with interest rates. The last thing that medium to long dated 'gilts' are in the short term is a 'safety net' or a 'guaranteed' environment.

If you can 'flip' over into gilts, but not other fixed interest media such as Corporate Bonds, while interest rates are high then a declining stock market and a collapsing property asset value will inevitably force the authorities to reduce interest rates (to stimulate the market) in a vain endeavour to promote borrowing to make up the deficit (a feature that actually works during the capital phase of a *'classic market'*) and also acts to prompt people to take up mortgages: to buy houses in particular, in order to stimulate the Construction Industry. As interest rates go down the capital value of fixed interest stock rises, and you profit. See 20.6. But, be careful.

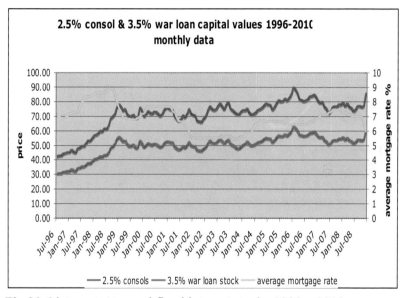

Fig 20.6 interest rates and fixed interest stocks 1990 – 2010

It is also interesting to note that corporate bonds, company loans, come under extreme capital value pressure during this period because of the possibility of loan defaults. Do you remember Woolworths and Kingfisher that went into liquidation (2008); their loans would have probably 'failed by default' and that is exactly what a corporate bond is, a fixed term loan, secured by the assets of the company (in this example Woolworths).

However, for the real stock picker acting decisively at this point in the *classic market* and establishing investments over a one or two year period, the fixed interest market can really do very well in capital terms until news headlines such as "gilt yields at their lowest ever" adorn the front pages of the financial sections of the popular press and mark the point in the capital value proposition for fixed interest stock where one 'cashes in one's chips' and switches allegiance and fund choice back to the Equity Income share funds.

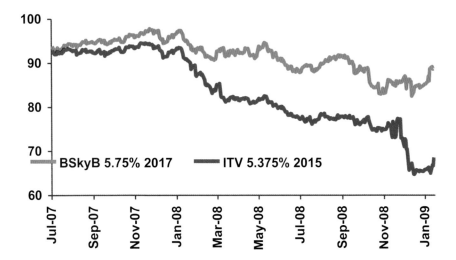

Fig 20.7. corporate bonds compared. Source Bank of England

Just compare the fortunes of a corporate bond investor in BSkyB as opposed to an ITV supporter and maybe the vagaries of that market place, with interest rates fairly low, can be appreciated. BSkyB outperformed ITV by 20% and yet the coupon, the interest rate and relative term of the Corporate Bonds (loans) are very similar. The difference is the 'risk of default' factor.

The stock market should retrace to about 50% of its original growth, but don't bank on it. In 2008 the stock market dropped in excess of 40% before finally turning the corner and starting an upward drive. The drop in value was far greater than expected; however, the pattern (the *classic market* cycle) remained "the same" in directional terms which is the criteria that needs to hold your attention if it is going to be of any practical use to you.

Prudence tells us to avoid corporate bonds during this phase of *The Classic Market* when interest rates are high and particularly as the stock market collapses. However a good assessment of risk and a judicious switch into a corporate bond fund where professional managers are perhaps more in command of the facts than you might be, could reap stellar rewards. It is not only the impact of fallen interest rates picks up on the capital value of the underlying corporate bonds but also the reassurance that the underlying confidence in the assets of the company that the Corporate Bonds, within a fund, are invested in are no longer at risk. Prices start to re-engage with reality and exceptional capital growth ensues over the short term.

Vodafone 5.9% 2032 breakeven analysis   Fig 20.8
Source : Bank of England

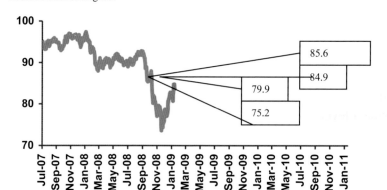

The story goes that the Vodaphone 5.9% Corporate Bond price in March 2009 was 84.9. The Bond value had to reduce by 11% over the next two years for the bond return to be as low as cash (3% over 2 years = 1.35% compound).

In order to match a gilt yield over that two years the price could drop to 79.9 (an 8.2% return over 2 years). If the price remained constant a 14.5% return was the forecast return and if the value rose to 85.5 the return rose to 15.3% over the two year period.

The reason for this illustration is to enable a realistic appraisal of the importance of the current price of both Corporate Bonds and gilts in respect of even short term gains on longer term stocks. At the end of January 2011 the stock price was 104.3.

The trick here is not to get caught up in the euphoria of historic corporate bond magic carpet rides. Once the party is over it really is well and truly 'over' and the time has come, just as with long dated gilts, to switch out and move into equity income shares for the last part of the *classic market* to play itself out.

Question:
Was it low interest rates that turned the stock market round, or, was it the fact that property prices had "bottomed out" and the banks could then 'restock' themselves with capital, re-establish their solvency margins and start lending again?

In other words, the 'market', whatever your definition of that might be, could breathe again.

Unfortunately the banks were still unable to breathe life into the small firms that needed their help. Things had not recovered to that extent in early 2011. Nor would they, until property prices (values) stabilise and the banks' solvency margins are refreshed to a compliant level.

Is property the 'gold' reserve of yesteryear? Almost.

In Western financial markets especially, but globally, gradually, the role of real property is of fundamental importance to the economic welfare of the populace because of the banking fraternity's reliance upon property for security. You may find it useful to read. *'The Ascent of Money'* by Niall Ferguson, regarding early banking and the securities required for loans.

The true situation is a bit of a mixture actually.

Low interest rates certainly stimulate a move away from deposit accounts, where the returns are paltry, and to some extent drive larger investors (reliant on a steady return) to equity income shares where the dividends are still reasonable even though the share prices are in some cases disastrously low. It is actually a bargain basement that takes 'guts' and 'confidence' for investors to enter into as an investment. The dilemma facing investors is contained in the 'risk to capital' assessment and the return on capital requirement. As share values bottom out the argument to move into equity income shares proves compelling. The *income* phase of the *classic market* beds in at this point.

For 'my money' an Equity Income share fund or portfolio is certainly the place to be in this 'income' oriented phase of the market. This is confirmed in respect of the North American market in *'Stocks for the Long Run'* by Jeremy Siegel, however there is no mention of property values in any genuine connective sense in this excellent book.

You can now have little doubt about the relationship between equities and house prices in particular and the effect of property valuations, both commercial and residential, in general, on the bank solvency margins, but, how do we use that relationship in order to get a good 'handle' on when we should move from one market to another?

Well perhaps Fig 19.4 'the ratio of regional house prices to Greater London from 1983 to 2009' will give the clue that you need.

Put simply, it appears to be an indisputable fact that house prices in Greater London in particular (and the south and the south-west in general, because of their tourist attraction) if used as a measure of value, will grow a lot faster than the provincial areas and particularly the north.

There is an attraction for people to move from the south to the north in order to discharge their mortgages and live their retirement mortgage free having purchased their house outright and perhaps put some money into the bank. The migration is not constant.

It appears from the previous graphs that house price decline and therefore property price decline (because there is certainly a correlation between residential and commercial property values) occurs when the ratio of house prices in 'the regions' is at its narrowest compared to Greater London. From the graph it is quite easy to establish that 1992, 1993 was when the housing market collapsed and that was when the ratio for the East Midlands and the north was around 1.6. The next market slump was 2006 and 2007; that is pretty accurate timing if the ratio is used.

This is, perhaps, an imprecise science, but, it would be true to say that if you were to divest property as that curve starts to fall you would probably not go far wrong. The safe haven at that point has to be cash, or for the fleet of foot, in tune with the market, perhaps, gilts (government stock).   By heeding the very clear signals you will have saved yourself from financial embarrassment.

Unfortunately the data was not readily available to us to check out the 1970s but anecdotally and from the experience of Gerry and Linda, there is no doubt in my mind that the 'picture' would repeat itself once again.

If it is that simple why haven't people used it before?

Well I imagine that people have used this before in some way but one has to perhaps get a perspective on the fact that widespread property ownership is relatively new.   It is only in the last 50 years that property ownership by individuals, for their own use as their own home, has become commonplace.   In 2011 70% of British homes are owned by the homemaker that lives there, that is an awesome statistic that separates the UK economy from our European counterparts, particularly in Germany and France where renting accompanied by tight mortgage finance hold sway.

Stockbrokers do not deal in property.   Property is not easily tradeable.

Property prices certainly do 'edge up,' immediately after 'the collapse' but, it is a 'blip' and it is a consistent feature of the graphic representation of the property market values. What we usually witness in the early part of the *income phase* of the *classic market* is a move upwards of 20% or 30% in the stock market price accompanied, in some primary areas (London and the South East) by a move upwards by some 10% in property valuations, or more precisely in selling prices from the low of the market slide.

That is followed (see the graphs) by a retracement of 10% to 20% in the stock market and that is followed by property values moving downwards at that point (2011/12), as the stock market recovers its composure and property values fall away once again to form that moribund valley on the property graph. See 20.9.

A strong upward movement on the stock market graph heralds the transition once again into a fresh 'classic market' with a 'capital' orientation that very soon becomes an irresistible force once again

(2015). In the meantime the emphasis in the stock market and the initial transition to the property market is the pursuit of security of return by way of income.

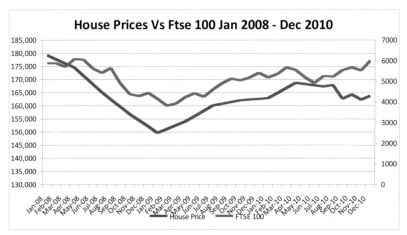

Fig 20.9 the relationship between shares and property 2008 2010

What 'market' is there that will carry the stock market forward? 'Climate change' and 'Global Warming' industries will probably power the stock market growth by virtue of the promise of long term income initiatives incorporated in grant supported capital expenditure on 'green' ventures, bringing the FTSE 250 and 350 midcap indices plus the Venture Capital funds along with them for the usual burst of overpowering enthusiasm before the next crash in 2016/2017 (a guess) brought about by the same wane in emotional power that has forever been the market adjuster. The 'bubble' will burst once again.

In late September 2010 the headlines read: "Investors flood to Gilts and Gold" and "the gloss returns to corporate bonds."

One of the great problems of 'asset allocation' and the process of investment analysis is that they rely on short term historical data for their onward divination. Hopefully the reader can detect from what has been written in these pages that this is a completely outmoded strategy; i.e. short term hindsight is 'fool's gold.' I do not use, and will not use, so called analysis tools because they lead to the headlines such as those that are described above.

Have gilts and corporate bonds performed very well in the last two years? (2008-10)?

Yes they have; exceptionally well. Does that mean that they are a good investment now, today? Absolutely and unequivocally no! is there a regular pattern to their performance? No there is not.

Why not?

The answer to the "why not?" is quite simply: "Please read the book again. *"Hindsight – The Foresight Saga"* is about long-sighted, not short-sighted, investment strategies.

Short-sightedness invariably results in the same thing: chaos and loss.

It is said that 95% of investors invest at the top of the market. 95% of investors, allegedly, bail out at the bottom of the market. Those investors are just like the bankers of 2003 and 2004 and onwards, in failing to recognise that there is a summit beyond which simple economics tell us that, in the bankers' case, property prices cannot go.

The bankers proceeded, caught up in their own enthusiasm (and lack of experience for the most part) to offer higher and higher multiples of both 'loan to value' and 'earnings' in respect of mortgage loans, under the misapprehension that the market could be 'force fed' to continue its climb ever higher. The delusion was that a low interest, low inflation economy could defy the laws of simple arithmetic. They were wrong.

What we know they should have been doing (and if you don't, please go back and read the book again) is tightening 'loan to value' margins down to 80% at the summit and restricting multiples of earnings back down to three and half times the lead applicant and one times further earners; not only to protect the banks themselves but to protect the depositors, the shareholders plus the people that were taking the mortgage loans out. Across the whole spectrum people inevitably get caught up in emotional euphoria, which belies common sense and logic. Any situation can be controlled in the future by common sense, logic and basic arithmetic; through observation.

Let the emotion of impending loss, financial and physical pain now be the institutor and the logical response that:

a)   In respect of gilts and fixed interest instruments:-
     When interest rates are low and have been kept low at 0.5% for 18 months there is only one logical way that they can go: UP. The result of interest rates going "UP" is that the capital value of fixed interest media and that means gilts and corporate bonds is "DOWN." Therefore:

b)   Although fixed interest short term historical data tells us they (gilts and corporate bonds) have had an exceptional time, over the last short period of time, with fantastic returns on capital growth please remember that the underlying reason for that is that interest rates had fallen from 5.0% to 0.5% very rapidly and the bounce back up will happen at some stage if inflation is present.

The equity and property markets were falling apart. Both of those criteria (in fact all three, if gilts are included) are now changed. Share prices are now rising. Interest rates will rise and property prices will stagnate. If you had fixed interest investments in October 2010 that was, arguably, the time to sell.

The world is a crazy place and it is going to get even crazier. When we consider that in 2010, looking back over the years to the early 1970s which is really what this book is using as its foundation, house prices have gone up by a multiple of between thirty two and thirty eight times what they were in 1970.

Average earnings (wages) have gone up by seventeen to twenty four times. The span of multiples reflects the variation in regional earnings. (NSO)

A draftsman working in 1972 was earning £2,860 per year. Per year. A draftsman in 2010 would be earning approximately £30,000 per year. (Personal records)

From that it is easy to see that the average earnings of what government refers to the 'lower paid' have risen far more steeply over the last forty years than what one would euphemistically call the 'middle class.' Indeed, centred on earnings alone, the middle class now represents in excess of 95% of the population.

Based on Institute of Fiscal Studies data, approximately 1% of the working population of 27 million people, give or take, are what we could call 'rich' earning over £100,000 a year, and 1% are 'poor', earning under £10,000. What one has to remember of course is that neither of those two extreme classes contain the same people from 'birth to death.' It is a revolving population (with some people going around for a very long time).

What I pull out of the data is the fact that this is a very good time in financial history to set the scene for a more stable financial environment and a more common sense approach to property prices which should, if my theories are correct, enable reasonable returns to be achieved in savings and investments whilst ironing out the huge fluctuations that occur in the stock market and of course the rise in property values which is extreme if the figures that I have mentioned are anything to go by.

However, whatever this book has uncovered by way of truths or cycles, the one thing that I have learnt is that no amount of logic will change the pattern of human behaviour. Emotion will continue to drive the markets this way and that, and all we can do is acknowledge the fact that if there is a cycle, and I believe there is, then the application of a little common sense in locking into those trends that have been uncovered can reap rewards that are worthy of the effort.

In fairness, who could not make just three switches every twelve to fifteen years in their life assurance, investment ISA, pensions and savings environment to ensure their future security? The answer remains to be seen.

The value of *"Hindsight – The Foresight Saga"* is now revealed. The insights that have been gathered and put together and the identification of the *classic market* now make it easier for investors and savers to get their investment and savings timing right.

For investors considering things such as Venture Capital Trusts (VCTs) which have a five to seven year time cycle (five years minimum) reference can now be made to the timelines leading up to major share price collapses.

That information will allow people to rethink their possible strategy, offsetting the benefits of immediate tax relief with the possibility of a substantial loss of capital in their investment at some later date. Investors can now invest within time frames, to increase their chances of success with more confidence.

The same principle would apply of course to Enterprise Investment Schemes (EIS), Employee Share Ownership Plans (ESOPs), Share Saver Schemes and Share Option Schemes (particularly pertinent these days to Bankers) with a time lock on the release of value from share options granted to employees and perhaps a window in time that is open in the future for encashment of such share options.

Timing will be important and the knowledge gained from identifying *the classic market,* its traits and its timescales will perhaps give more certainty and assurance to those who wish to get their timing correct and either remove themselves from the marketplace before a collapse, or stay in the marketplace to gain the benefits of that expected upward surge.

Those investing in structured products where a five or six year timescale may be set or a three-year option is available. These are fixed term contracts with perhaps a 'kick out' option where one can take advantage of the *classic market's* identification of a rising stock market or property value will force a 'kick out' and thereby deliver an exceptionally profitable return in the short term from what appeared to be a medium term contract in danger of overshooting a possible market peak leading to default losses.

For the saver and the investor who wants to keep things simple, the *classic market* gives a rolling time frame which allows unitised investment to be switched into the equity, property, cash or gilt markets at the appropriate time and similarly make an exit in order to consolidate gains and put safety first.

The saver; whether it be through a Maximum Investment Plan or an Endowment or ISA, will be able to enter the market in anticipation of a future rise or drop and with the *classic market* methodology push into the rising market to wash out the initial costs, switch into the collapsing market to gather up cheap units and even adjust their capital by simple switching as it builds up within the savings regime so that the investment is in one part of the market whilst the savings account is buying cheap units is in another. All that is made possible from the strategies, observations and timescales illustrated and discussed in this book.

"Hindsight – The Foresight Saga" should provide you with information that will run for the next twenty, thirty or forty years.

There is a sub cycle, or at least it appears so. You may well chuckle at this assertion but I believe it to be true.

I have alluded to the fact that much of the volatility in the marketplace has been caused by 'young buck' managers 'yuppies' being brought in to change the world whilst established mature managers have been put out to grass. Well bear that in mind when considering the possibility of an overall thirty year cycle. Two *classic markets* joined together.

We have just lived through the equivalent of the 1970s and the pattern certainly for the stock market is identifiably similar. It was in the 1930s. The 1987 stock market adjustment was swift, painful and amounted to over a 30% loss of capital value.

However, you may recall that using annual statistics, the 1987 crash all but disappeared from view. The housing cycle however stayed very much true to form. Could that smooth first phase of the *classic market* and, if we analyse it a very much more sedate stock market adjustment and property price collapse in the second phase have happened due to the fact that the thirty year old to forty year old managers looking after the banks and financial institutions and their middle management responsibilities had matured by some fifteen years?

Could they (the now 40 to 50 year olds) mature into the new generation of fifty to sixty year old senior managers with experience who at least have the gumption to exercise authority and draw back from inappropriate lending in 2016 to 2020. Will they carry through financial practices which are more appropriate for stimulating an economy that is at the bottom of the trough, avoiding over zealous lending as the markets are topping out?

One thing is for sure, we will only know the answer to that when we reach 2025 and look towards the start of the next *classic market* and what may be the start of the next 'thirty year cycle'.

The thing to remember about investment and savings planning is that you don't have to follow what I have prescribed. Treat it as a general observation if you will, but consider the facts.

If you had followed the 'Foresight' methodology for the last 40 years would it have been detrimental to you or beneficial? Well judge for yourself but again remember that these are figures born of an annualised return regime January to December each year therefore, as I have pointed out many times throughout this book, the data gives you a manifestly different end product than if we use monthly data, but, I suspect for this purpose, not a lot different.

If you had invested £10,000 in 1968 in a reasonable property portfolio somewhere in the South of England then you would have achieved £338,563 by close of play in 2010.

The stock market 'BLUE-CHIP' companies would have returned, say, £206,573 dividends reinvested.

If on the other hand you had put your £10,000 into gilts and left that investment to grow then you would have achieved £42,372 income reinvested.

As far as cash is concerned many think that we need not bother going there but, your capital, by and large, unless it was an Icelandic bank, was safe. Cash returned similar to gilts.

Bear in mind that the property values have just dropped and the stock market is moving ahead quite strongly.

As I think you will have gathered from the previous pages life at a particular point in time is not necessarily a stable reality because everything can change quite quickly. However, such is the human psyche that we tend to work on the 'now' and if we do, then we just happen to be on the cusp of the *classic market.*

In the next twelve to twenty four months the market will move from its current income driven phase to a capital driven phase and that is where I have chosen to end and begin the *classic market* however it is important to realise that it runs over any fourteen to fifteen year period and you can start it where you like and finish it where you like because it is the principle that is the *classic market*, not the timing of its start or its finish that is important.

If you had invested £10,000 using the broad based simplistic timescale that I have allotted in my example at Figure 20.4 (p.251)

> Over the first phase of 1968 to 1982 you would have achieved £48,054.
> Over the second phase 1982 to 1996 you would have achieved £44,660.
> From 1996 to the end of 2010 you would have achieved £46,343.

You may be interested to learn that the grand total of an investment £10,000 over the full duration of that forty four year period would have produced:

In equities £206,573

In property £338,553

And from *the Classic Market:*

£994,630 in return for nine (9) switches. I wish I had known.

What does it prove? Hopefully it proves that a little bit of interest, diligence and observation can improve the way your investments work and also of course your return on savings.

Please remember that your savings require an entirely different outlook to your investments. You look to invest in a rising market and you look to save into a falling market that is going to rise at some later time when your accumulated savings are needed.

Remember also utility, particularly with regard to property, because utility often comes before value. Value is only important if you need to release that value to either make life better or to move on to further investment potential.

I hope you have enjoyed reading this book and get value from it.

Terence P.

GLOSSARY

ARBITRAGE

This is a phrase used when referring to the difference between an interest rate that you can do a deal at and the increased rate that you can pass that deal onto someone else at. You create 'arbitrage'. Let's say the Japanese yen currency market is operating at a base rate of 0.5%. You may be able to borrow money at 2% above that base rate. If you know that you can trade that 'yen' investment into say a 'sterling' investment and obtain 4% over base, then you have created 'arbitrage' between the two. Very often in the market place a level of arbitrage can be extremely small percentage points but very significant amounts of money.

ASSET ALLOCATION

The art of utilising recent performance of differing investment sectors to then create a portfolio with a percentage mix of each of the constituent parts of that portfolio in order to meet the risk reward nature of the investor with a perceived optimum outcome linked to their risk profile.

BANK BASE RATE

This is a base rate set by a bank as a marker for its normal lending rate. The expression 2% above base rate would intimate a 2% addition to the banks normal base rate for the loan being engaged in. The bank rate may vary from bank to bank.

BOND MARKET

A North American term for the gilt market but also referred to in the United Kingdom as the market that deals in bond or fixed interest securities.

BUNDLED MORTGAGES

In simple terms a fund, perhaps a pension fund, seeks to secure an income over a period of time, or capital growth from say an equity release scheme, over a period of time in order to fund future pension and it lends that £25 million to a broad base qualifying individuals creating a portfolio of mortgages. This merely means bringing together a portfolio of mortgages or loans as an entity that has a capital value but would ordinarily be held to bring in a steady return through interest only or capital and interest repayments.

CLASSIC MARKET

A classic market represents a 12-15 year cycle of ebbs and flows in the marketplace primarily focused on the interaction between equities and property.

CLOSED FUND

It usually refers to a unitised fund that has, for one reason or another, closed its doors to new investment but remains open in as much as it continues to operate the current crop of investment assets for the benefit of the remaining investors.

COMMERCIAL PROPERTY	Ordinarily property that does not include private residential accommodation although it may include a Guest House or a Hotel. It is property used for commercial gain, individually owned or subject to a unitised fund. It can be portfolio based.
CONSOLS (Consolidated Debt)	Consols are undated loan stock which provide investors with a fixed interest return, as a government investment, in return for capital investment. They are openly tradable and the capital value varies on a daily basis dependant on market conditions but primarily interest rates in the open market.
CORPORATE BONDS	Corporate bonds are usually term loans issued by a Corporation (name any large company) to provide underlying finance as an alternative to bank finance through individual investors or through unitised funds investing in a portfolio of corporate bonds. Bonds are issued at fixed interest over a fixed period of time and are therefore classified as fixed interest investments.
CORRELATION	The relationship between price movements in one financial marketplace, or data set, compared to the price movements in another marketplace (i.e. share prices compared to property values).
CPI	The Consumer Price Index. The CPI measures consumer goods and service cost over time .CPI is an international standard measure of consumer goods inflation.
EQUITIES	Commonly used to refer to shares in Limited Companies (in the American market it would commonly be called stock).
EQUITY	There are two definitions used in the financial markets: a) A Company's 'equity' is the value of its liquidity with reference to the issued share capital of that company. Equity is therefore synonymous with shares. Purchasing 'equity' in a company is buying shares in that company. The balance between an asset's value and the value of the loans or mortgage secured against the property. This is usually denoted in a positive sense. Negative equity being where equity is a minus figure. b) The term 'equity' is also commonly used with reference to the difference between the amount of mortgage secured against real property (a house of commercial property) or other secured asset, and the market value of that property or asset.
EQUITY RELEASE	Equity release is achieved when the capital value of a property is such that part of the equity in that property can be extracted as a loan usually without repayment but with interest or an interest equivalent accumulating for the sum advanced and the accumulated value to be repaid on the death of the

person or persons exercising the equity release. There are a number of forms which I discuss within this book.

FIDUCIARY — Pertaining to one who has a delegated responsibility for assets held in escrow or under 'trust', hence 'fiduciary management' is the management by an individual or body, of property held in trust on behalf of a third party.

FINANCIAL MARKETS — A general description of the markets that individuals and corporations would invest in common under the headings of equity, gilts, property or cash and their respective sub divisions.

FIXED INTEREST — A non variable form of interest paid in respect of a sum of money lent or borrowed, invested or deposited.

This is a term applied to any investment vehicle that has a fixed interest profile primarily gilts and corporate bonds but preference shares and other forms of loan or shares that have a fixed interest rate applied would come under this heading.

GILT YIELD — Although gilts usually have a fixed interest and mature at a certain date they are tradable on a daily basis and as interest rates vary, therefore the yield from the gilt edge stock will also vary. In the 1970s and 1980s the only way that government could attract money on loan from the public, was to pay substantial interest rates in line with the then market conditions.

If you could buy the promise of 8% per annum for the next 3 years and the underlying interest rate in the market place is say 2%, then you might well be willing to pay more than £100 face value of a gilt certificate to do that. Even though the interest rate was almost four times the coupon, you would not pay four times the capital value for the bond because you are going to receive that extra income for a mere 3 years, so there is a formula. To define 'gilt yield' then is to get the balance between that higher price that you pay and the coupon that you get and that may well give you a yield to maturity of 2%.

If the roles were reversed and you had a 3¼% coupon bond to say 2034 and interest rates went up to 8%, then whilst you might like a fixed interest rate going forward, you would pay a lot less than the face value for that income going forward. It is fixed, you know what you are going to get and again, there is a formula to calculate the current price.

GILTS – GILT EDGE SECURITIES.	Like everything else in the English Language the Gilt edge bit is historic but these are normally fixed term (but not always) government loans with either a fixed interest rate or a fixed rate plus inflation repayable at full face value (normally £100) at a set date in the future. Gilts are 'open ended' ie have no fixed maturity date and are fixed interest bearing. NB (in the North American market these would commonly be called bonds)
HAIRCUT	This is rather like a market value adjuster and is there to protect the market particularly in times when it is in danger of collapse. The term 'haircut' may be used in the context of restricting the capital or market price of (in the context of 2010) sovereign debt where there is a danger that the sovereign state would default on repayment of its loans. In the extreme case 20%, 30% or more percent could be shaved off the normal market value calculation for a government stock or security, such that only those desperate to re-capitalise their investment by selling their stock in the market place, might be tempted to do so. Very similar to an MVA on 'with profit' contracts.
HOLDING A CHARGE/TAKING A CHARGE	A bank would normally hold a charge over say a property or a loan often referred to as 'taking a charge' but one can also take a charge on an investment portfolio, unitised or otherwise in order to advance money on an overdraft or a fixed term loan facility.
INDEX LINKED	An investment relationship that has its returns , or charges, linked to a particular inflation index or market index, in order to determine the underlying rate of return.
INTEREST RATE	Percentage of a capital sum paid to an investor in return for the loan of their money or paid by a borrower in respect of money lent to them.
INVERSE CORRELATION	Is encountered where the movement of one data value is directly inverse, or the reverse, of the other data value when being compared.
INVEST	To invest is t to place a capital sum into an investment facility in return for a return, e.g. to buy stocks or shares with a view to making a profit to provide income or grow that capital in the future.
INVESTMENT TRUST	Investment Trust is an investment company that buys assets, the value of which is reflected in the shares of the Limited Company and trades in the marketplace. Very often the shares in the Investment Trust will trade at a premium or a discount to the underlying share values of the assets held. The investor buys shares in the Investment Trust Company not in units representing the value of the underlying investments.

INVESTOR/INVESTING	Investing is normally associated with a capital sum being placed on deposit or under management to provide either income or capital growth or a mixture of both over a specified or unspecified timeframe, (ie an investment in a Building Society, a formal investment vehicle or a private Limited Company or partnership).
LEASE OR LEASEHOLD	When one rents a property or a facility (e.g. a car) the rental agreement is termed a lease and will usually grant use of the property for a fixed period of time at a fixed rental and can be renewed or reviewed at the end of that fixed period.
LEASEHOLD PROPERTY	The property is subject to a lease which could be for 25 years, 3 years or 999 years which will be termed medium, short and long term leases respectively.
LIBOR RATE	This is the internal rate of interest charged between banks where one bank is lending another money. It is not something the public would generally come into contact with but has been a feature of the news in recent years as it escalated well out of synchronisation with the Bank of England base rate due to the increase in risk of banks defaulting on their internal borrowing.
LIQUIDITY	The cash value subsisting in an asset based fund, acting as a buffer to accommodate cash withdrawals from that investment fund, which comprises its liquid resource.
LTV (LOAN TO VALUE)	It is commonly referred to in terms of mortgages or loans secured by property where the ratio of the loan being granted to the market value of the property acting as security is assessed (e.g. LTV on domestic residence 80%; LTV on commercial property 60% - the bank will lend 60% of the current value of the property).
MATURITY BONUS (Otherwise known as a Terminal Bonus)	Exactly the same definition as Terminal Bonus. This is the additional bonus paid at maturity of a with profit contract and is usually a percentage of the original sum assured plus any reversionary bonus that has been added over the term of the policy and is paid as a percentage usually on a sliding scale increasing with the duration of the policy term.
MONEY SUPPLY	The amount of money in circulation is controlled by two major factors: a) How much money the Bank of England prints or allows to go out into the marketplace. b) The percentage of tier one reserves that Banks have to keep to maintain their solvency margins.

MORATORIUM	A time lag that is imposed between instructions being given to liquidate a stock, unitised investment or savings plan and the time that the proceeds from the encashment or sale of that stock can be delivered. It is usually imposed in a difficult market where liquidity poses a problem and a moratorium is imposed in order to give the managers time to market the underlying assets and create sufficient liquidity to meet an encashment request.
MORTGAGE	A mortgage is the term used where a loan of money is made against the security of property secured by a deed transferring ownership of that property to the extent of the debt until the debt is repaid.
MORTGAGE RATE	Mortgage rate refers to the interest payable by a borrower to a lender in return for capital used to purchase a mortgaged property. The mortgage rate will vary from lender to lender and in this publication an average rate across the market has generally been used for comparison purposes.
MORTGAGEE	The recipient of a mortgage. The person purchasing a house, or other asset, by way of a loan secured by way of a legal charge secured against the property and incorporating a method of repayment of the capital and payment of interest to the mortgagor.
MORTGAGOR	The Institution or individual lending money to a mortgagee to enable that individual or corporation to purchase a property or other asset, over which the mortgagor has a legal charge, a mortgage.
MVA - Market Value Adjuster	The original term used in with profit funds for what the Americans euphemistically call a haircut. The Market Value Adjuster was imposed by with profit fund managers to dissuade investors from exiting the fund and leaving not only the fund vulnerable, but those left invested in the fund vulnerable to loss.
MVR – Market Value Reduction	A term brought in to replace MVA as it was felt that the market value adjustment would always take the form of a reduction in the pay out on the surrender of a with profit contract.
NEGATIVE EQUITY	The minus value when a property is valued at less than the mortgage outstanding on that property.
NON CORRELATED (INVESTMENT)	A non correlated investment is an investment that has a performance profile that does not rely on or reflect the main constituents of the investment market. An example might be ground rent funds which ordinarily would have a "life" of their own and a performance profile that does not reflect the property market in general (nor any other of the major markets, equities, gilts or cash).

OEIC (OPEN ENDED INVESTMENT COMPANY)	OEICs have in recent years taken the place of Unit Trusts as a major savings and investment mechanism replacing Unit Trusts primarily because of their fiscal advantage regarding internal taxation. The underlying company holds investments on behalf of investors through a wide range of shares, gilts and property and other assets and will be classed as a unitised investment. The value of the units vary with the value of the underlying assets.
PENSION: DEFINED BENEFIT	Defined Benefit Pension Scheme (otherwise known as an Occupational Pension Scheme and under the heading Occupational Pension Scheme otherwise known as A Company Pension Scheme).
PENSION: PERSONAL	An individual pension arrangement, which accumulates a capital sum in return for regular or ad hoc contributions over time in order to create a fund to facilitate an income in retirement.
PENSION: PERSONAL - GROUP	Normally a collection of individual personal pension arrangements combined under one banner by an employer on behalf of their employees (see Personal Pension).
POOLED FUNDS	This is a term used to describe any mechanism that comprises invested contributions from more than one individual and places them together with contributions from other individuals within a given financial strategy, in order to provide benefits at a future date.
POSITIVE CORRELATION	Is where both sets of data move in the same direction, one reflecting the movement of the other.
POUND COST AVERAGING	The effect of the fluctuations in the rolling values of a financial market that results in an overall enhancement of unit purchases in a savings plan over time which creates an average return being achieved as against the linear returns to a capital investment in the same market.
PREFERENCE SHARES	Preference shares can be dated or undated and reflect a shareholding in the company under a special category that delivers interest, usually at a fixed rate, and is a preferred class of shareholding to an ordinary shareholder in the event of a liquidation of the company.
PROPERTY BOND	An investment bond (single premium life assurance) that invests specifically in commercial property as a unitised investment vehicle for the general public. It is usually underwritten by specialist underwriters within life assurance companies. Similar in operation to a REIT.

REAL ESTATE INVESTMENT TRUST (REITS)	This is a form of investment trust where investors buy shares in a limited company an investment trust company and the money within that company is used to purchase 'real property' by way of a collective investment portfolio. It allows investors to get involved in larger real estate development projects.
REAL ESTATE	Where it is used in the book real estate will always mean 'real property' in other words it is a domestic residence or a commercial premise from which business is transacted or it is used for business storage purposes, ie a warehouse. It is bricks and mortar in the broadest sense and excludes shares in property.
REAL RATES OF RETURN	The rate of return achieved after the affects of inflation have been taken into account. A negative real rate of return would mean that the underlying investment had not kept pace with inflation. A positive real rate of return would mean that the investment had beaten inflation and was therefore producing an investment return above what is required to maintain the spending power of the capital invested.
REIT	A form of Collective Investment Trust, investing only in real estate (not shares). The purpose of a REIT is to allow a number of individual investors to group together to purchase commercial property on a larger scale than would normally be available to the individuals themselves as a unitised fund. PENSION
RESIDENTIAL PROPERTY	Ordinarily referred to within this publication as property used as a domestic residence and that would include 'buy to let.'
RETRACE OR RETRACEMENT	The propensity of the market to "retrace its footsteps," move back to say 50% of a downward movement in an upward move often before falling again. It is often seen as a saw tooth motion and Figure 10.4 is a good example of May and November in 2001.
REVERSIONARY BONUS	A mechanism used with particularly traditional with profits contracts which reflects past profits that are then allocated as a guaranteed uplift on the original guarantee incorporated within a with profit savings or investment plan.
RPI	The Retail Prices index. A general purpose measure of inflation in the United Kingdom. The RPI measures the rate of change in household costs on a month by month basis

SAVE	It is a verb and 'to save' means to take amounts on a regular or irregular basis out of income in order to build up a capital sum for the future.
SAVER/SAVING	Saving is usually accomplished out of income using money on a regular basis say monthly or quarterly or annually to create a capital sum for the future with the expectation of growth through accrual or enhancement of the underlying assets in the savings medium.
SAVINGS	Savings, the practice of putting away regular amounts from usually income to build up capital for the future has a different dynamic to investment. Investment is the placing of capital in an environment for reward.
SECURITIES	The securities market is usually referred to anything that resembles a gilt or bond, a share or perhaps property but primarily the fixed interest market traded through the securities exchange.
SECURITIES EXCHANGE	Like the stock market but deals in securities, ie fixed loan stock.
SHARES	This refers to certified financial shares in a limited company or corporation and may be private shares but more often, in the context of this book, shares in large corporations held individually or within some form of unitised investment.
SOLVENCY MARGIN	In the context of this book used primarily with regard to the banks it is the difference between assets and liabilities allowed by the Regulator. With the banks the assets should be greater than 11% of the liabilities that the banks carry, in other words the amount that the bank has lent out. If a business's solvency margin falls below an acceptable level then they have to cease trading or make arrangements to restore their solvency margin. Often colloquially referred to as strengthening the balance sheet.
STOCHASTIC MODELLING	The art of assessing an individual's risk profile and assembling a balanced asset allocated investment model to reflect the risk reward profile of that individual and carry it forward in time to optimise their returns. Assessing probability outcomes from random variations.

STOCK	In the UK stock usually refers to government or other fixed interest , or floating interest , loan stock. In the North American financial markets stock refers to what the UK term as company shares; i.e. company stock.
STOCK MARKET	Could also be called the 'equity market' and this is the market that deals in shares in Limited Companies. In the UK we tend to deal with gilt edge stock, in North America stock is the share value or equity value of a company or rather the shares that certify ownership in that value. In the UK the stock market deals in the share values of Limited Companies.
STRUCTURED PRODUCT	Usually an amalgam of a fixed interest or fixed term, element and a more speculative 'geared' element that may well be linked to certain criteria being achieved or providing a default under which the investment will either present a return or not to the investor. Structured products usually have a fixed term but can include random exit clauses if certain targets are achieved.
TERMINAL BONUS (otherwise known as a Maturity Bonus)	This is an additional bonus paid at the termination of a savings or investment plan incorporating with profits attributes and reflects any anomalous rise in the markets that should be passed on to maturing policy holders.
TOXIC DEBT	A portfolio of debt with problems that may be real or perceived. In recent years toxic debt has referred to the potential for a bundled debt portfolio to be liable to suffer high rates of non payment or default through a weakening market. (ie mortgage default with a housing market decline).
UNDATED GILT STOCK	2.5% consols or 3½% war loan stock are prime examples of undated loans to the government. You can redeem them at any time, however once again the gilt yield determines what the price of the bond is at any particular time. The price will be set not only with the coupon at 2½% or 3½% that will be paid every year, but also to the expectation of whether interest rates in the future are going to go 'up' or 'down' because at no time in the future is there a guarantee on what you are going to get back when you eventually sell the loan stock to redeem your capital.
UNFUNDED INVESTMENTS	A typical example of an unfunded investment would be the State Pension Scheme, or the fire service or Police schemes. These are provided from general

revenue without any investment element being present to create the funds.

UNIT TRUST — A form of unitised fund which investors can purchase units comprising a wide variety of invested collective assets. Unit trusts are accessed by direct purchase or indirectly purchased through an investment bond or a portfolio run by professional managers.

UNITISED INVESTMENT — In many ways similar to a shareholding. Units are allocated at a given price for investments in a portfolio of say shares or gilts or property or a combination of all under the auspices of a Trust (Unit Trust) or a Limited Company Investment Trust OEIC known in America as a mutual fund. The unit value is susceptible to fluctuation dependant upon the underlying value of the assets of the fund and/or income paid from those assets to the fund.

WAR LOAN STOCK — Government gilts which were initially brought in during the First World War to raise funds for the War effort as an 'open ended' stock and provides a fixed rate of interest in return for capital investment and is undated, in other words has no termination date.

YIELD — This is the rate of return achieved on capital invested, taking into account fluctuations in the capital value by reference to underpinning assets or market conditions, in conjunction with and in addition to, any interest accrued or accrueable to the capital over time by virtue of a fixed or floating interest rate.

The resources for data are:

Historical stock data
http://www.nma.org/pdf/gold/his_gold_prices.pdf
http://www.bankofengland.co.uk/statistics/rates/baserate.pdf
http://www.statistics.gov.uk/downloads/theme_economy/RP04.pdf
National Statistics Online - Finding RPI Data
Historical gold prices
Daily Gold Prices - London Gold Fix Price History
Bank of England | Statistics | Bankstats (Monetary & Financial Statistics) | Latest Tables
Yahoo! Finance - Indices Overview
National Statistics Online - Time Series Data
Economic Data freely available online | The Economics Network
Bank of England|Statistics|Statistical Interactive Database|Show Summary
RBS Databank
Debt and gilts: some history - Investors Chronicle
www.lifepublications.co.uk
www.ohalloran.org.uk